A HISTORY OF BLACKS IN KENTUCKY

A HISTORY OF BLACKS IN KENTUCKY

Volume 2
In Pursuit of Equality, 1890-1980

By
George C. Wright

The Kentucky Historical Society

Copyright © 1992 by the Kentucky Historical Society

Library of Congress Cataloging-in-Publication Data

Lucas, Marion Brunson, 1935–
   A history of Blacks in Kentucky.
   p. cm.
   Includes bibliographical references and index.
   Contents: v. 1. From slavery to segregation, 1760–1891/
by Marion B. Lucas — v. 2. In pursuit of equality, 1890–1980/
by George C. Wright.
   1. Afro-Americans—Kentucky—History. 2. Kentucky History.
3. Kentucky—Race relations. I. Wright, George C. II. Title.
E185.93.K3L83   1992   92-24574
976.9'00496073-dc20   CIP

v. 1   ISBN 978-0-916968-20-5 (hard cover)
        ISBN 978-0-916968-32-8 (paper)
v. 2.   ISBN 978-0-916968-21-2 (hard cover)
        ISBN 978-0-916968-37-3 (paper)
set   ISBN 978-0-916968-23-6 (hard cover)

The Kentucky Historical Society dedicates these volumes to Senator Georgia Davis Powers and Dr. Henry E. Cheaney. In 1978, Powers, the first black woman to serve in the Kentucky State Senate, sponsored the resolution funding this project. Cheaney, a pioneer in the study of Kentucky blacks and for many years chairman of the Afro-American studies program at Kentucky State University, helped lay the groundwork which made this project possible.

To my good friend, Terry Lynn Birdwhistell

—George C. Wright

Contents

Acknowledgments

Chapter 1. Black Life from the 1890s to the Great Depression 1

Chapter 2. Race Relations 43

Chapter 3. An Education: Providing the "Proper Kind of Training" for Blacks 103

Chapter 4. The NAACP and the Quest for Equality............................... 152

Chapter 5. The 1950s to the Present: Change and Continuity 193

Notes 227

Bibliography............................ 255

Index 268

Acknowledgments

THE completion of this book was made possible because of the financial support of several institutions and the scholarly assistance I received from librarians and historians. I owe a debt of gratitude to the reference librarians at Perry-Castañeda Library at the University of Texas, the Widener Library at Harvard University, James M. Prichard of the Kentucky Department for Libraries and Archives, and the staff of the Department of Special Collections at the University of Kentucky. Dedicating this book to Terry Birdwhistell, university archivist at the University of Kentucky, does not fully do justice to his support and encouragement. On my numerous travels to Kentucky, Terry provided an office and library facilities, photocopied any number of documents, and actively took part in helping acquire research materials by accompanying me on my searches for documentation throughout the Commonwealth. James C. Klotter, executive director of the Kentucky Historical Society, state historian and leading scholar of Kentucky history, shared his notes and made a number of helpful suggestions on the manuscript. My good friend, Professor Albert S. Broussard of Texas A&M University, read the manuscript and made his usual insightful remarks. Travel funds were provided by the University of Texas Research Institute, the Dora Bonham Memorial Fund of the Department of History, the African and Afro-American Studies and Research Center at the University of Texas, and the Kentucky Historical Society. Finally, I appreciate the patience, support, and encouragement that I received throughout this project from my wife, Valerie Ellison Wright, and my daughter, Rebecca Ellison Wright.

One

Black Life from the 1890s to the Great Depression

BY 1890, of Kentucky's 1,590,462 citizens, 268,071 or 16.9 percent were black. When compared with 1860, the actual number of blacks had increased, but always at an uneven pace from decade to decade. For instance, from 1860 to 1870 the black population decreased by almost 14,000, as many ex-slaves left the state for the North; yet from 1870 to 1880 the black population experienced its largest increase ever when it grew by 22.2 percent to 271,451. The next decade, 1880-90, saw a decline of 3,000 in the black population. But in a complete demographic shift from the previous ten years, the black population grew by almost 14,000 (a rate of 6.2 percent) from 1890-1900, reaching 284,706. By contrast, the state's total population increased consistently, growing from 1,155,684 in 1860 to 2,147,174 in 1900. Its smallest period of growth was from 1880-90, when it increased by only 12.7 percent. Throughout this period, and indeed down to the present, both the percentage and number of blacks in the total population of Kentucky remained by comparison much smaller than in any of the states in the South.[1]

Furthermore, by 1890 and most surely the start of the new century, the black percentage of the total population had decreased, and Afro-Americans were becoming concentrated in several areas and almost nonexistent in other regions of the state. In 1860 blacks comprised 20.4 percent of the total population. Thirty years later this had dropped to 16.8 percent; the percentage of blacks within Kentucky continued to decline so that by 1930 less than nine of every one hundred Kentuckians were Afro-Americans. By 1900 some of the counties in the eastern Kentucky mountains had less than twenty blacks, with Johnson and Elliott counties combining for a grand total of three black residents. At the opposite end of the scale was Jefferson County (comprising the city of Louisville), the central Kentucky area around Lexington, and an area in southwest Kentucky. Louisville had the largest number of blacks, around 44,000. The greatest concentration of Afro-Americans, however, lived in twenty counties surrounding Lexington. For instance, Fayette had 15,409, while Boyle, Clark, and Franklin each had around 5,000 and Madison had 6,690 blacks. In these counties blacks comprised anywhere from a fourth to a third of the population. A substantial number of blacks also resided in Christian, Henderson, Daviess, and Hopkins, all in southwest Kentucky. For instance, in Christian County blacks comprised 43.7 percent of the population in 1900.[2]

Like their counterparts farther south, black Kentuckians were migrating from rural areas to cities both large and small within the state. Of the state's total population in 1890, three out of four Kentuckians lived in rural areas; however, one in three blacks, roughly 100,145 of the state's 284,706 Negroes, lived in cities. Clearly, they made up a large percentage of city dwellers. They comprised 52.4 percent of the residents in Winchester, 46.7 percent in Shelbyville, 44.9 percent in Richmond, 44.6 percent in Danville, and 44.5 percent in Hopkinsville. After Louisville, the largest numbers of blacks were found in Lexington (10,130), Paducah (5,814), Frankfort (3,316), and Hopkinsville (3,243). According to the 1910 census, Afro-Americans made up almost 20 percent of all the people living in Kentucky's urban areas; by 1940 55 percent of the state's black citizens lived in urban areas.[3]

Undoubtedly, countless numbers of Afro-Americans migrated from rural Kentucky, and ultimately from the state, because of the difficulties they experienced in acquiring or holding on to farm lands. Despite the state's reputation for having very fertile land and being a place where industrious, hardworking farmers could prosper, most white and black farmers experienced hardships that were all too common to farmers throughout the South. To be sure, the state had a sizable number of self-sufficient farmers who produced livestock and food products to sustain themselves and to sell at the marketplace, but far more farmers relied solely on a cash crop, usually tobacco, and the success or failure of their crop determined whether or not they survived, were in debt, or faced foreclosure.

To be successful, farmers need equipment and animals,

capital, and access to credit. Not surprisingly, because they lacked these essentials, the vast majority of Kentucky blacks did not own the farm lands on which they toiled. The 1900 census listed 11,238 black farmers, but only 38.5 percent (4,322) of them owned their land. By comparison, of the 223,429 white farmers, fully 61.3 percent of them—137,015—had purchased their farms. Each census thereafter revealed a decline in the number of black farm owners, falling to an all-time low in 1940 during the Great Depression, when only 2,702 blacks were listed as owning their farms.[4] Regardless of race, all farm laborers received extremely low wages, with blacks being paid far less than whites doing similar jobs. Without a doubt, much of the racial violence that occurred in rural Kentucky centered around disputes between white farm owners and black farm laborers over pay and working conditions. Violence often erupted when black workers attempted to quit their jobs to protest the repeated abuses of white farmers.

Logan County, an area where white farmers relied heavily on black labor, was often the scene of violent confrontations. Though the white establishment claimed that murders and rapes by blacks were the reasons for the thirteen lynchings that occurred in the county between 1880 and 1910, in reality, labor unrest had often played a leading role in racial outbreaks. In July 1908, Rufus Browder, a black sharecropper, argued with James Cunningham over working conditions. Several days later as Browder and his family attempted to leave the farm, Cunningham cursed them and struck the black man with a whip. The white farmer next drew a pistol and shot Browder in the chest, whereupon Browder, though wounded, reached for a gun and shot Cunningham to death. Even though Browder had been shot and had clearly defended himself, he was arrested and sentenced to death for Cunningham's murder. After having his case reviewed by the Kentucky Court of Appeals, he was given a second trial and again found guilty; but this time, the all-white jury, aware that the court might intervene again, sentenced him to life in prison instead of death. Convinced that Browder was not guilty of first-degree murder, Republican Governor Augustus E. Willson commuted the sentence to ten years, but tragically the young black man, who was twenty years old when the incident occurred, died in prison.[5]

Several days after Cunningham's death, Logan County authorities raided a meeting being conducted by four sharecroppers, all friends and fellow lodge brothers of Browder. According to the outrageous rumor circulating in the white community, the four young men—Virgil, Robert, and Thomas Jones, and Joseph Riley—had expressed approval of the killing of Cunningham and had targeted other prominent white landowners for assassination. The authorities arrested them for "disturbing the peace," even though their meeting was being conducted in a private home. On the night of August 1, a mob entered the Russellville jail, took the four men, and hanged them from a cedar tree. The note pinned to one of the bodies contained a message for Logan County's other black sharecroppers: "Let this be a warning to you niggers to let white people alone or you will go the same way." Despite whatever official statements were given for the hangings, the four young men were lynched because they, like Browder, were sharecroppers who had expressed dissatisfaction with their working conditions. The white farmers of Logan County well knew what could happen if all their poorly paid, overworked laborers left the area. Fulton County, another rural area in western Kentucky, had an even greater number of lynchings than Logan County.[6]

Perhaps more threatening to white farmers than the "militant" sharecroppers were the few successful black landowners in their midst, who by their very presence exhibited the wrong type of "role model" for other blacks. From the end of the Civil War through the 1930s, black farmers were the special targets of whites as countless attempts were made to run them off their lands. (These attempts were called "whitecapping" in the Deep South.) This form of racial violence first occurred in Lebanon shortly after the war when a white mob destroyed the homes and crops of blacks and forced all of them to leave the area at once. In Daviess County several months later another white mob posted signs in an area where a number of black farmers lived, warning all of them to leave by the next day. They also informed several white farmers who had rented or leased lands to the ex-slaves that their property would be burned unless the blacks left. Several white gangs in northern Kentucky also attempted to force successful black farmers to move elsewhere. In the small community of Warsaw, whites began systematically attacking blacks, whipping them, stealing their property, and forcing them to leave the area under threats of death. According to the Freedmen's Bureau, these tactics proved to be effective as more than two hundred left the area, moving to Ohio for protection and a new start. A decade later in Henry County at least a dozen black farmers and their families were forced to leave the county. A group of whites openly acknowledged removing them, saying that they had been offended by a black's making lewd comments to a white woman. The charge of offending a white woman, a doubtful one at best, involved only one black; nevertheless, it became the occasion to remove from this northern Kentucky community well over thirty Afro-Americans who were innocent of any wrongdoing.[7]

Though the exact number is impossible to determine, additional black landowners fled the state because of the "tobacco wars" of the early 1900s. A group of western Kentucky farmers, many of whom were prominent citizens, formed the Planter's Protective Association and agreed to withhold their crop from market to obtain a higher price from the tobacco trust. These farmers became outraged when some of their neighbors refused to join the association. In response, a group calling themselves the Night Riders started destroying crops, burning tobacco barns, whipping reluctant farmers, and ultimately murdering several outspoken foes. Once the violence started, it was only a short time before the Night Riders began running blacks out of several counties, even though black farmers as a group had not expressed opposition to the association. While occurring all over the region, these attacks became especially pronounced in Lyon and Trigg counties. By 1908 no blacks remained in Lyon. The white mob next targeted the blacks living in the Birmingham area of Trigg. In March a large group of whites rode into the community and fired off hundreds of shots, wounding seven blacks. Signs were posted warning the blacks that they had ten days to leave the area. Most of them left Birmingham by the designated time. In their rush, they left behind household goods and farm equipment. The Louisville *Courier-Journal* made a telling point in describing the racial hostility: Birmingham had some of the best farming land in Kentucky, and practically the entire Negro population of Trigg County was concentrated in that area. Unfortunately for black farmers and landowners, what happened in western Kentucky occurred on a number of occasions during the next twenty years. Indeed, by the 1930s whites in some counties across the state had "cleansed" themselves of all black residents, while in other rural areas the only black residents were common laborers, not landowners.[8]

In addition to working as farm laborers, many of the Afro-Americans living in the state's rural areas and small towns worked as common laborers and personal servants. As laborers, blacks worked on road and bridge construction and on numerous jobs relating to shipping goods on the Kentucky and Ohio rivers. In small cities blacks were the garbage men, street cleaners, and stablehands. A number of small towns had manufacturing concerns that employed anywhere from twenty to fifty workers. Blacks, however, were excluded from these industrial jobs except, of course, as janitors. Indeed, what blacks experienced in the small town of Carrollton mirrored conditions elsewhere. According to a black newspaper reporter in 1890, "Carrollton has made much progress. The city has several manufacturing concerns: a woolen mill, a furniture factory, two saw and planning mills." But, the reporter concluded, "no colored hands work at any" of the jobs in these industries.[9]

The work career of Hugh D. Palmer illustrates what some Afro-Americans experienced in Kentucky until well into the twentieth century. Palmer's family had been slaves in Trigg County, and after emancipation they remained in the small community of Cerulean as employees of their former master. Born in the 1890s, Palmer began working when he was eight years old at a wide assortment of tasks ranging from running errands, to house cleaning, to serving as a driver for this prominent white family. Upon orders from his "master," Palmer was denied permission to attend school, a decision that resulted in his never learning to read and write. Palmer left Trigg County for the only extended period in his life when he enlisted in the army during World War I. He returned to Trigg County after the war and resumed working for the same white family. When well into his eighties, Palmer continued to perform the same chores he had been assigned as a youth.[10]

Indeed, all over Kentucky—in rural areas, small towns, and even the larger cities where Afro-Americans had migrated with the hope of finding new opportunities—blacks were hired to perform services for whites. Practically every white family that could afford the cost employed blacks in some capacity, from nursing their children, to doing their laundry, to completely running their homes. Arthur Krock's autobiography, which highlights his childhood in Glasgow, contains an excellent discussion of the role of black house servants. (Krock left rural Kentucky and became one of the best-known journalists of the early twentieth century.) Black servants, he pointed out, not only performed household chores but were a status symbol, one of the trappings of the ruling race. "In relating that all servants in a community such as ours were Negroes, I merely state a social fact of the time and place. But I recall one aspect of their service that gave me, young as I was, a strong sense of discomfort." Krock then explained that "Negro boys, equipped with small tree branches, were stationed at either end of the table where we took our meals, their task being to ward off the flies. I knew that in India these attendants were known to the British as punkacoolies; and Mr. Kipling having assured me that this was a fitting convenience to the master race in its pursuit of benevolent improvement of the 'lesser breeds' without the law, I took some comfort in the imperialist precedent." After detailing the chores blacks were required to perform, Krock, as did so many other whites, attempted to show that this working arrangement maintained good relationships between the races. "The Negroes served, yes, but also they were called into conference on equal terms on matters affecting the household, agriculture, and the security of the community from racial violence. For at least in our community, the responsible Negroes possessed in exceptional measure the instinct for wise solutions of such problems." On returning to Kentucky many years later, Krock was elated over a chance encounter with a black man who had worked in his home. The white journalist, whose writings on most subjects showed keen insight, failed to understand the human dynamics involved in the relationship between white employers and their black servants. Krock departed from Glasgow with a feeling that genuine affection existed between him and his (unnamed) former servant, convinced from his experience that black servants enjoyed and profited from the jobs they performed for whites.[11]

Krock also failed to mention the long and demanding hours for very little pay his "Negro friend" and other servants were required to work in the homes of whites. The experience of Arlene S. Martin of Shelbyville was typical. In the 1930s she started working in the home of a white family. Laboring ten hours a day, seven days a week, Martin returned to her own house in the middle of the day for several hours to prepare meals for her own family. Even though the pay was low and the working hours extremely restrictive, Martin worked forty years for the same family. A state commission investigating black life in the 1940s noted that salary and working conditions for household workers were major concerns of Kentucky's black population. "This field is marked by the least security of tenure, the greatest lack of standards as to hours and conditions of work, the smallest prospect of independence after long years of labor, the least dignity and the most exploitation. The principal if not the only incentive to entering this field is elemental need; not, as is the case of most callings, the hope of advancement, occasional leisure and more than a bare living wage." Despite the harsh realities of service work addressed in this report, a great majority of black men and women spent some or all of their working careers performing service jobs for whites. Indeed, in the Bluegrass State, just as in the Deep South, service jobs seem to have been a "rite of passage" for Afro-Americans who reached adulthood up to the 1960s.[12]

Many service jobs took place outside of the home. Owners of hotels and boarding houses employed blacks as maids, cooks, and waiters. In Louisville and Lexington waiters, especially the head waiters, on occasion made decent wages, and not surprisingly, blacks were often challenged by whites for such jobs in the best hotels. On the other hand, in smaller communities, because the wage paid all waiters was so low, the job was held exclusively by Afro-Americans. And, consistent with other service jobs dominated by blacks, in addition to the low pay the work was very demanding and often demeaning, with waiters working twelve-hour shifts six days a week. Clearly, other servants fared no better. Many blacks working as servants in restaurants and hotels undoubtedly had similar experiences to that of C.H. Wade, an employee of the S.S. Kresge's store in Louisville for several years in the 1930s. Wade, along with five other black men and one woman, worked as a kitchen helper in the store. They were required to labor fifty-eight hours a week for twenty-five cents an hour; wages, according to Wade, that were "the lowest paid by the company." Adding to an already deplorable situation, the company gave white helpers holidays off from work with pay while compelling Afro-Americans to work on holidays at an hourly sum less than their

Black Life from the 1890s / 9

William Henry Steward (left), "Louisville's leading black citizen for decades," resided at 621 S. Eighth Street in Louisville.

University of Louisville Archives and Records Center

normal pay rate. In a letter to the National Association for the Advancement of Colored People (NAACP), Wade explained that all of the blacks were raising families and were reluctant to agitate for a salary increase or better working conditions. After he finally spoke out, Wade was promptly fired from his job.[13]

There did exist a few service positions that were eagerly sought by blacks and filled, therefore, only by those individuals who were well known in both the white and black communities. In cities all over the state, highly respected blacks worked as messengers for banks and other businesses. William Henry Steward, Louisville's leading black citizen for decades, secured employment as a messenger early in his life and used his contacts with whites to acquire other more lucrative jobs. In Maysville, black leader L.D. Henderson was employed as a messenger at the State National Bank for three decades. Also, in several small towns black entrepreneurs were actually servants working exclusively for whites. Many black caterers, for example, made decent incomes by preparing food for parties and other social occasions.[14]

Barbering paid best of all the service jobs performed by Afro-Americans. Beginning in the antebellum period, a number of highly respected and, in a few instances, well-to-do blacks operated barber shops in Lexington and Louisville. In both cities they were able to retain their white customers until the Great Depression, despite numerous complaints by white barbers. Keenly aware that their white customers would find it very offensive if the same equipment were used on black patrons, the leading barbers in both Lexington and Louisville drew the color line, refusing services to members of their own race. In the smaller towns black barbers also dominated this potentially lucrative service enterprise. "All of the barbershops were run by colored men and were for many years afterward," noted the historian of Christian County. But, just like in the larger cities, black barbers in these smaller towns provided services to a white clientele only. As the reporter in Carrollton explained, the city had only "One barbershop run by a colored man but receives no colored customers."[15]

Though not considered a service occupation, the position of postman did in fact serve the public. Jobs at the United States Post Office provided stability in employment and decent wages, and the work was not overly strenuous. Given these factors, whites as well as blacks eagerly sought such employment. Local postmasters had considerable discretion in hiring, even though a written examination was required to obtain a job as a letter carrier. In Louisville, Lexington, and Frankfort, blacks were hired as postmen regularly though there were periods when whites called for the prohibiting of blacks from these jobs.[16] The postmasters in several smaller communities also hired blacks. For example, in Bowling Green in 1891 four new letter carriers were hired, two of whom were black. During the same time period, however, a young black man tried repeatedly to get a job as a postman in Covington. The postmaster refused to hire him, agreeing with white letter carriers who complained that it would be disgraceful for them if a Negro joined their ranks. Protest by Covington blacks over their exclusion from positions at the post office was ignored. They even pointed out that on one occasion two black high school graduates were turned down for employment while whites with lesser qualifications were hired.[17]

The discrimination that blacks faced when seeking jobs at the post office increased in intensity in the new century, especially in cities other than Louisville or Lexington. A 1928 report on black employment in Bowling Green documented that a ban on hiring blacks as letter carriers had existed at that city's post office for more than a decade. "There were several colored letter carriers, but none have been appointed since the last one was retired. Wilson's administration seems to have put a ban on Negro letter carriers throughout the South, and Negroes apparently are not qualifying for government jobs in a number of southern cities," the report concluded.[18]

When considering the almost universal exclusion of Afro-Americans from jobs having contact with the public, it is surprising to discover that in Lexington at the turn of the century several white businesses employed black clerks. When this practice started, how long it lasted, and the general reaction of the white public remains a mystery. What little is known comes from a national black journal, which reported the following in 1900: "The white business stores of Lexington are employing colored clerks. Graves, Cox and Co. set the example by employing Sam L. Tolley, who has held the post a number of years. The Kaufman Clothing Co. was next, who have in their charge Noah Wooldridge. Also, Mr. Louis Adler, the shoe manager, has recently added to his force J.B. Caulder."[19] Given the extent of racial prejudice in the nation, both North and South, it is highly likely that no other city in the country had black clerks working in white stores at the turn of the century. Without question, in Louisville, which has always been considered far more "progressive" on racial matters than its smaller rival Lexington, no blacks found jobs as clerks or in any capacity dealing with the public above the menial level.[20] At some point, these Lexington stores quit employing blacks as clerks. In the 1960s when blacks were hired as clerks in most of the department stores in Lexington—including Graves, Cox and Kaufman's—most people assumed that this was another "first" when in reality it was the first time in about sixty years.

In addition to working as servants, Afro-Americans found a few other jobs in Kentucky's larger cities, though discrimination was always a problem. In Louisville and Lexington, for example, blacks found employment in the horse industry. Most of them were employed as laborers and grooms, jobs that paid better than average wages and offered the opportunity to travel. A handful of blacks acquired the experience and, most importantly, the confidence of wealthy white thoroughbred owners, and were hired in the lucrative position of trainer. Lexington's William Perkins was perhaps the best known black trainer around the turn of the century. Over the years he worked regularly for a number of the most prominent white horseowners in central Kentucky. William Walker of Louisville also made a very good living as a trainer. In the early 1900s when a local black newspaper did a feature on black homes, Walker's residence was described as being "the most brilliant and richly furnished home" owned by any of Louisville's more than forty thousand black citizens.[21]

Within the horse industry, however, far more blacks found employment as jockeys, a job that often led to instant wealth and fame. From the start of organized racing events in the antebellum period, a number of slaves had received training as jockeys. During the 1890s and for more than a decade thereafter, such black jockeys as Pike Barnes, Jimmie Winkfield, and John Hathaway were in great demand, making what were considered to be huge sums of money. According to one newspaper, Winkfield raced in Russia in 1905 for a guaranteed salary of six thousand dollars. The career of "Soup" Perkins demonstrated the possibilities available to talented black horsemen. Starting as an exercise boy, Perkins became a jockey in the early 1890s. Eventually, Perkins's services were in such great demand that he earned a salary of five thousand dollars a year. He purchased two homes in Lexington, one costing six thousand dollars, and at one time his reputed wealth was fifty thousand dollars. But the best-known black jockey was Isaac Murphy. The winner of three Kentucky Derbys, Murphy had a record of 628 wins in 1,412 races, a record which has never been surpassed. His racing exploits led to his being a celebrity, something akin to college basketball stars in Kentucky today. As one newspaper noted, "He amassed considerable money in his profession and a few years ago retired from riding and purchased a handsome home on East Third in Lexington."[22]

Of course, only a handful of blacks secured employment in the horse industry, and the same proved true in the more traditional industries. By employing blacks in certain limited capacities, managers had a source of cheap, easily exploitable laborers, which enabled them to keep labor costs at a bare minimum. A very revealing statement was made by the Louisville Industrial Foundation when listing a number of reasons why the presence of black workers made the city an attractive market for industry: "It is generally considered. . . . that the availability of negro labor has been a favorable factor in industrial development. For common labor and many kinds of semi-skilled labor, the negro in Louisville is well adapted. The Louisville negro is a tractable, dependable worker who applies himself to the job and works faithfully and constantly. There are many local instances where negroes have been on a company's pay-roll for ten, twenty, and thirty years."[23] This straightforward statement by the Industrial Foundation was accurate; because of their limited options, blacks, at best, were relegated to industrial jobs as common laborers or semi-skilled workers. A few advances were made in Louisville during World War I, but after the wartime emergency had ended, blacks were once again excluded from jobs in most industries. Nevertheless, opportunities for industrial employment for Afro-Americans were better in Louisville than elsewhere in the state, a clear demonstration of the dismal prospects they faced when seeking such jobs in other Kentucky towns.

Indeed, outside of Louisville they rarely found jobs in industry prior to the Great Depression. When pressed why they refused to hire blacks, white managers repeatedly responded with stock answers: they lacked skills, they were untrainable, they were lazy, and they were unreliable. As the manager of a large brick-making plant in Paducah claimed in the early 1900s, "Most of the negroes won't work, and what few will can live easy on about two or three days work in the week." He added that he had been unsuccessful in hiring black workers: "I will venture to say that I have asked 300 colored men if they wanted work . . . and all but three of them with grins on their faces answered in the negative. Several said 'dat their woman was working in de white folks yards and save them the chicken.'" The manager had a simple, but effective, solution to compel all black men to work: "If the basket-carrying could be completely stopped among negro cooks and housewives every negro in Paducah would have to go to work or starve to death in a month's time."[24]

Managers were reluctant to admit the primary reason for the exclusion of blacks from the labor force: the unwillingness of whites to work beside them; that all too often they threatened to strike or resorted to violence to protest the presence of black workers. In the small community of Olive Hill in 1917, several hundred white laborers at the brick-making General Refractories Company threatened to strike unless recently employed blacks were dismissed. After first refusing to meet with the leaders of the disgruntled workers, the company managers acceded to their demand and fired all the black workers. Violence occurred on a number of occasions when white workers attempted to oust blacks from their jobs. One of the most widely known of these episodes happened in Corbin around November 1, 1919, when a mob of at least 150 heavily armed whites ventured into the black neighborhood, forced more than two hundred black railroad workers to the train depot, and then ordered them to leave town on a train bound for Knoxville, Tennessee. Another occurred in Ravenna several months later when more black railroad workers were forced to leave their jobs and the community. Again in November 1924 at the Dix River Dam project, which was located near Harrodsburg, some eight hundred blacks were run off the work site. In both Corbin and Ravenna officials for the Louisville and Nashville Railroad Company (L&N), completely yielding to the will of the mobs, never returned black workers to either area. By contrast, within twenty-four hours of the outbreak at Dix River, the L.E. Meyers Company had encouraged state officials to send the Kentucky National Guard to Mercer County. Under the protection of the state troops, the black workers returned to the construction site.[25]

Racial discrimination in industry proved to be even worse for black women. To be sure, practically all women laboring in industries were exploited, but white women usually were paid weekly salaries, while black women were paid on a piece-rate basis. Some factories, most notably the woolen mills in Louisville, refused to hire blacks in any capacity while employing large numbers of young white females. Furthermore, rigid enforcement of segregation in the workplace of black and white women ensured that black women were relegated to the very worst jobs. In 1911 Governor Augustus E. Willson appointed a commission to investigate the conditions of working women. Comprised only of whites, the commission investigated 186 factories (ranging from clothing, woolen, and cordage mills, to candy and chewing gum manufacturing, and tobacco factories) that employed 25 percent (11,048) of the women working in Kentucky's industries. The investigators decided that a salary of $6.50 a week was the absolute minimum required by a woman for subsistence. Their findings revealed that roughly 65 percent of the women made less than that amount with fully 25 percent making less than $4 per week. "This wage will hardly keep the body and soul of the worker together, but it is a matter of equally common knowledge that many of these women receiving this wage or less have children, parents, and other dependents to support in addition to themselves." The report repeatedly mentioned the deplorable working conditions and pay of black women. In the clothing industries, for example, black women worked in areas that received no direct sunlight. Tobacco factories, consistently the largest employer of black females, lacked adequate ventilation. Also, the tobacco concerns were notorious for refusing to provide toilet facilities for black women. Even when a number of short-lived breakthroughs in industry occurred for Afro-American men during World War I, nothing changed for black women.[26]

Reports conducted by the National Urban League revealed that the exclusion of black women and men from industry continued during the 1930s and 1940s. Throughout the Great Depression, the director of the Urban League attempted without success to persuade industry officials to hire blacks, especially in skilled positions. League workers grew optimistic that industrial breakthroughs would finally occur in 1941 after President Franklin D. Roosevelt signed an executive order mandating the hiring of blacks by companies receiving government contracts. They quickly discovered that most of the large industries simply ignored the executive order. As an Urban League report of March 1942 explained, "Industries in Louisville . . . (are) making little or no effort to comply with the President's Executive Order of June 25, 1941. Ten of the industries reporting used Negro workers as janitors and porters only. Six industries employed Negroes for several semi-skilled operations. In two industries there were no Negro workers and the managers declined to consider the employment of Negroes." The Urban League's comprehensive survey of black employment in Louisville, completed in 1948, reached the same conclusion. "Prior to World War II some industries had built up a tradition of not hiring Negro labor in any capacity excepting possibly as menial workers. In many industries this tradition had been followed for so long that it became a fetish and symbol which was highly regarded by both employer and employee." The report concluded that it seemed highly unlikely that Afro-Americans would make any inroads in industry now that the war had ended.[27]

When one considers that black workers actually found more opportunities in Louisville than elsewhere in the state, it is very clear that very few changes occurred for them in employment during the first half of this century. Indeed, what Thomas L. Dabney of the National Urban League observed in Bowling Green in 1928 is illustrative of small communities all over Kentucky. Almost 85 percent of the gainfully employed blacks in Bowling Green worked as servants in the homes of whites or as common laborers in tobacco factories, stone quarries, and lumber mills. Also, as in most other cities, blacks were largely excluded from labor unions. Only ten of Bowling Green's five hundred organized workers were Afro-Americans, Dabney concluded. Though commenting on the limited employment opportunities for blacks on the eve of the Great Depression, his report could have been used to describe conditions in the next two decades as well.[28]

Instead of working as servants or industrial laborers, a small number of Kentucky blacks operated businesses of their own. While the vast majority of these black-owned businesses existed for only a short period of time before collapsing, the more successful ones traced their beginnings to the 1870s and 1880s and remained in existence for almost fifty years, until the Great Depression of the 1930s. In Owensboro, the sixth-largest city in Kentucky in 1890, blacks owned barbershops, groceries, and saloons. For more than a decade the city had several black-owned restaurants with the largest one, Amos and Sweatley, catering to both white and black customers. By the end of the 1890s, Owensboro had a new black business, Fite's Studio, perhaps the only black-owned photographic studio in the state. When applauding the existence and perseverance of Fite's business enterprise, G.F. Richings, a national chronicler of black businesses and educational progress, explained how whites had tried to undermine the existence of the black photographer: "Mr. Fite had a hard struggle when he first located at Owensboro, because of the unfair means used by the white men engaged in the same line of work to defeat him. But he has more than won the fight, and stands at the head as an example of what push and pluck will do." As an out-of-state newspaper noted, the small central Kentucky town of Versailles also had several black businesses in the late 1800s: "Versailles, has a livery stable, grocery store and clothing and gent's furnishing store owned by colored men." Paducah also had the usual assortment of independent black businesses, especially a large number of grocery stores. As Richings informed his readers, J.W. Moore operated "a very large grocery store; in fact, one of the best in the city. He has something to show for his labor, in the way of some eight houses, seven of which are rented." Where most small towns were fortunate to have one black physician, Paducah had three, and they eventually formed a partnership and opened the W.H. Lancaster Pharmacy to better serve their black clientele. In Princeton, a small town in western Kentucky, Afro-Americans operated grocery stores and ice cream parlors, and several black building contractors enjoyed the patronage of whites.[29]

But it was in Henderson of all the cities with total populations under 25,000, where an impressive number of successful black businesses existed. For more than fifty years black entre-

Benjamin F. Spencer and his wife Sue. In March 1878, he became the first former slave to be accredited as a teacher in Kentucky. He later owned a boot-making shop in Frankfort.
University of Kentucky Special Collections

preneurs were located in the heart of the city's business district. Black tailors, shoemakers, and, of course, barbers successfully competed with their white counterparts for white customers. According to a Kansas newspaper that often highlighted successful black enterprises, Henderson had, in the mid-1890s, "a drug store run by an Afro-American." To a degree not found in other small cities, the black business enterprises in Henderson, because of their ideal location, adequate financial backing, and the patronage of both blacks and whites, remained open until the 1940s.[30]

Louisville and Lexington, the cities with the largest number of Afro-Americans, had the greatest number and variety of black enterprises. At the turn of the century Lawrence Harris, a young black businessman in Lexington, published a pamphlet to inform the community of businesses being operated by blacks and to encourage both whites and blacks to patronize these enterprises. Harris listed twenty-five barbers, far and away the single largest business. Lexington could also boast of having eight physicians, three dentists, four lawyers, two undertakers, and two real estate agents. To make sure that the public was very familiar with the city's black entrepreneurs, Harris included biographical sketches of H.A. Tandy, a contractor who worked on the construction of Lexington's new courthouse, and John C. Jackson, the city's most influential black attorney and undertaker. The number of black-owned businesses continued to grow, so that by the 1920s Lexington had a black central business district on Deweese Street, consisting largely of saloons, poolrooms, and beauty and barbershops.[31]

The "Derby City" could boast of having an even greater number of black-owned businesses and professionals than Lexington. Louisville, in fact, by the turn of the century could rival most cities north and south, even cities with considerably larger black populations, in the number of black enterprises. Successful draymen, tailors, and furniture dealers were already well established in the city by the 1890s. Several black barbers, with shops in Louisville's most elegant hotels, were envied by white barbers. Louisville, unlike other Kentucky cities, had several black weekly newspapers that existed for a year or more, a long life for the average black weekly of that day, with two newspapers enjoying incredible success. *The Ohio Falls Express* was published for more than two decades by Henry Fitzbutler, the first black physician in Kentucky and an unsuccessful candidate for office on several occasions in the late nineteenth century. William H. Steward, the Afro-American most often consulted by Louisville whites regarding racial matters, the most highly respected Kentucky black throughout black America, and a friend of Booker T. Washington, founded *The American Baptist* in the 1880s. Steward served as editor of this religious newspaper (he often wrote editorials on secular affairs) for more than fifty years, and *The American Baptist* is still in existence today, surely one of the longest-running black newspapers in the entire nation. In Louisville several funeral directors acquired modest fortunes, becoming the wealthiest blacks in the community. The city also had more than its share of black lawyers and doctors, but because of a lack of white patronage and the refusal of some blacks to seek their services, these professionals found themselves struggling for financial stability. When highlighting Louisville's black-owned businesses, Richings mentioned People's Drug Store as being one of the most important, an enterprise that would surely play a role in blacks' being uplifted: "Of all stores that would be helpful to the colored people a drug store would be one of them, from the fact that the business could be carried on by educated people, and the more of that class who can be brought into prominent places the better for the entire race."[32]

Continuing in his complimentary assessment of Afro-American businesses, Richings explained that, in the person of Miss E.B. Slaughter, Louisville had a rarity—a young black woman successfully operating a business enterprise. A graduate of the Armour Institute of Chicago, Slaughter was engaged in the millinery business. Right from the start, her business benefitted from having both white and black customers. They were attracted to her store because of its ideal location, its neat appearance, and the wide selection of goods on hand. Richings believed that Slaughter's enterprise might "inspire some other young lady to start in business of some sort." And, as he also explained, the treatment of Afro-Americans, and especially the respect accorded them by whites, would be byproducts of successful black-owned business ventures: "When colored people, and especially ladies, are engaged in different business enterprises, . . . white people will then be compelled to see them not only as cooks and washerwomen, but as business women and competitors. Then, too, when colored ladies can operate successful millinery stores, that in itself will at least have a tendency to make white women engaged in such business treat their colored customers with more consideration."[33]

In 1906 Cary B. Lewis wrote an article promoting the black business enterprises found in Kentucky's largest city. The article contained biographical sketches on more than twenty of Louisville's successful black tailors, doctors, lawyers, teachers, newspaper editors, grocery store owners, and undertakers. Lewis discussed in great detail the career and business acumen of David L. Knight to illustrate what blacks could accomplish through hard work and sacrifice:

> One of the most substantial and successful businessmen in the city is Mr. D.L. Knight, who was the first man of color in Kentucky to establish a transfer line. He began his career in a brickyard and by working regularly and saving his money, purchased a horse and wagon. Today he owns eleven wagons. This equipment is styled "The Lightning Transfer Line." From the profits of his business he has purchased many and large holdings; he is a large tax payer on several pieces of property in the most desirable sections of the city. He puts into the hands of his race hundreds of dollars each month in wages and is regarded by the entire citizenry as a successful business man, and an exemplary citizen.

To prove that Afro-Americans were contributing to the development of Louisville, Lewis mentioned their personal financial wealth and the large amounts of taxes they paid on all of their properties. His assessment of the city's successful businessmen and professionals led to an optimistic conclusion: "The culture, intelligence, economic and industrial activity of the Louisville Negroes are winning for the race a place secure and high in the life of the city."[34]

The years between 1915 and 1930 witnessed the launching, often with much fanfare, of additional black business enterprises in Louisville. Two insurance companies, Mammoth Life and Domestic Life, wrote policies in Louisville and all over Ken-

The Mammoth Life and Accident Insurance Company Baseball Team, 1917. Founded two years earlier, Mammoth became Kentucky's largest black-owned business. Among those on the team were W.T. Merchant (top row, far left) and Charles H. Parrish, Jr. (top row, second from left).
University of Louisville Photographic Archives

tucky. Within five years of starting, both companies had acquired several large buildings in which to conduct their ever-growing businesses. Where blacks in most cities relied completely on whites for financial institutions, Afro-American businessmen in Louisville successfully started and operated two banks, First Standard Bank and American Mutual Savings Bank, and a number of savings associations. Both banks existed for a decade, closing during the Great Depression after the collapse of their depository bank, the National Bank of Kentucky. Several blacks tried their hand at operating cab companies, which required huge expenditures for automobiles, gasoline, repair stations, and mechanics. Launched in the mid-1920s, the cab company owned by Will Miles quickly surpassed its competitors. By the start of the next decade, he operated twenty cabs and had at least twenty-five employees. According to a boastful black newspaper, "Within six years the Empire Cab Company has grown to be the leading business of its kind owned and operated by Negroes in the United States." Continuing its praise of the owner, the paper concluded: "Mr. Miles is intensely interested in building business and making opportunities for the boys and girls of his race." A survey of Louisville businesses in 1944 showed that in addition to Miles's cab company, blacks still operated Mammoth and Domestic insurance companies, and scores of junkyards, second-hand clothing stores, small restaurants and taverns, beauty and barber shops, and moving and hauling concerns.[35]

Afro-American leaders of the early 1900s firmly believed that the ownership of businesses would go a long way toward resolving the problems faced by the race. At the very least, they argued, blacks by owning businesses provided jobs for members of the race thereby increasing the wealth of the community. Going further, black leaders believed that successful business enterprises proved that blacks were capable of conducting financial affairs and gave additional evidence that Afro-Americans as a group had "advanced" since emancipation. Also, because they keenly resented the racial insults members of their race experienced when patronizing white establishments, such as being prohibited from trying on clothing and shoes before making their purchases, they looked toward Negro-owned businesses as providing the same services with courteous treatment as well. Following the lead of Booker T. Washington, black leaders in Lexington and Louisville in 1903 started branches of the National Negro Business League to promote businesses owned by members of their race. H.A. Tandy in Lexington and David L. Knight in Louisville gave speeches championing the value of black ownership and chastising blacks for nonsupport. Clearly, no group played a greater role in promoting business enterprises than black newspaper editors who did so because their own businesses depended entirely on the race for support and also from a genuine belief that only through the ownership of businesses could Afro-Americans achieve economic independence. As W.D. Johnson, editor of the Lexington *Standard*, explained at the turn of the century, "business is a solution of the so-called Negro problem. When the Negro begins business for himself, and accumulates wealth and intelligence the problem will then be solved, business is the watchword."[36]

This promotion of black businesses reached a peak in the 1920s, during the "New Negro" period, a time when Afro-Americans expressed great pride in their race and its accomplishments. All over Kentucky the opening of a movie house, clothing store, or any business was proclaimed as a step forward for the race. Quick to take advantage of this trend, black businessmen, calling their enterprises "race ventures," repeatedly urged the race for support, not because they provided the best service or superior products, but merely because they were Afro-Americans. Despite all of the hoopla over black-owned businesses, most of these enterprises enjoyed at best only modest success and growth, with most, of course, being very small and having little impact in the black community. For these businesses the major problems remained a lack of sufficient capital and their dependence on Afro-Americans, often the poorest people found in a given area, for support. Perhaps the most positive achievement of these businesses was in giving members of their race pride in the fact that blacks indeed operated enterprises of their own, be it ever so briefly.

Finally, one field of employment merits attention because it often held out the opportunity for equal pay. Starting around the turn of the century, many blacks found jobs in the state's bituminous coal industry. Racial discrimination excluded them from management, but because of a severe labor shortage in the coal industry, they were welcomed—in fact, highly sought after—paid equal salaries, and had some opportunity to advance on the job. In a recent study on black coal miners, Ronald L. Lewis notes that coal company managers very early saw the value of an integrated workforce, of having a "judicious mixture" of the races in the coal mines: "This policy was founded on the notion that an ideal labor force was composed of a particular mixture of native whites, Afro-Americans, and foreign workers. Each operator applied his own variation of the formula but always to the end of achieving maximum control over the labor, and, hence, the costs associated with production." In 1900 the 2,206 black miners comprised 23.7 percent of the 9,299 miners in Kentucky. By 1920 the number of black coal miners had more than tripled to 7,407, though their percentage had declined to 17 percent of the state's 44,269 miners. The Great Depression in the coal region ushered in the start of a gradual decline in the number of black coal miners, eventually reaching a low of 2,965 in 1950.[37]

Many of the first black miners came as strikebreakers. As Lewis astutely observes, the prevailing racist beliefs of that day led many coal companies to assume that black workers were docile and not given to joining unions or striking to extract higher pay or better working conditions. This made black workers all the more attractive to them for they could be used to keep the wages for all miners low or to replace striking whites. During a strike in Hopkins County in 1900, coal companies brought in blacks from the Deep South. From then on, a sizable number of blacks worked in the mines of western Kentucky. Thousands of black southerners, primarily from Alabama, were lured to the eastern Kentucky coal fields beginning around 1910. The coal companies sent labor agents, some of whom were Afro-American, to entice men to the mines. In 1916 alone the Consolidated Coal Company of Eastern Kentucky hired more than 2,000 blacks to work at their operations in Jenkins, McRoberts, and Fleming. Also in 1916 at least seven hundred blacks from Alabama were hired by coal companies with operations in western Kentucky. The Blue Diamond Company of Earlington gave the black coal miners an interest-free loan to construct a church, a step the company hoped would encourage the miners to remain in the area.[38]

On average coal miners worked fourteen-to-sixteen-hour shifts and were paid by the ton; during good times this could be as high as thirty-four cents per ton or, at worst, as little as eighteen cents. Black and white miners alike were required to furnish their own picks and shovels, and this undoubtedly cut into their wages. Working in the mines proved to be extremely dangerous, with the risk of serious injury or death a constant possibility. Yet, given the limited employment opportunities found elsewhere, black immigrants from the South spent their entire working careers in the mines of eastern and western Kentucky. After a decade or so it was common to see the sons of miners laboring alongside their fathers. The Great Depression, of course, idled many workers, and the advent of machines reduced the number even more. Decades earlier, operators had needed every available hand to work in the mines and had, therefore, allowed blacks to work many of the same jobs as whites. But with machines now doing the work of a dozen men, companies became far more selective—discriminating—in choosing workers. This meant that all too often blacks were denied the training given whites to operate the machines.[39]

The discrimination that Afro-Americans faced in virtually every area of employment led many of them to leave the state for what they believed would be better job opportunities in the North. Though exact figures are lacking, the first three decades of the century witnessed blacks, by the tens of thousands, migrating to Indianapolis, Gary, Chicago, Detroit, and especially Cincinnati and other parts of Ohio. Just like members of their race migrating northward from the Deep South, the blacks leaving Kentucky were undoubtedly the more ambitious and those most dissatisfied with the status quo, resulting in a loss of black talent in Kentucky. Indeed, there is much truth to the widespread belief among Kentucky blacks that members of their race who have accomplished the most made their "marks" away from home. A study completed in the 1920s of Cincinnati's black leaders noted that a number of ex-Kentuckians were employed in the police department and other positions in city hall. A far greater number, however, worked as professionals, primarily as lawyers, doctors, and ministers. Many of them had migrated to Ohio to attend the white universities, which unlike Kentucky's public and private colleges, had long admitted blacks as students. The life of Dr. John C. McLeod was typical. A native of nearby Covington, McLeod had attended Cincinnati's public schools and the Cincinnati Veterinary College.

Upon graduating, he remained in the city and opened his own business, which according to the historian of Cincinnati blacks, resulted in his eventually enjoying a lucrative practice. Though most ex-Kentuckians living in Cincinnati had migrated from towns the size of Georgetown or Maysville, a number were natives of Louisville and Lexington, demonstrating that while employment opportunities were better in the larger cities than elsewhere in the state, many blacks were nevertheless dissatisfied because they had been restricted to certain jobs in these two cities.[40]

Just like people found anywhere, the lives of Kentucky blacks cannot be fully understood by looking only at the jobs which they held. Their daily routine, recreational activities, schools, and church functions—what they chose to do in the hours away from their jobs—most surely made their lives meaningful. During the early years of this century, several observers noted that because of isolation and the great distances involved, people living in different parts of the state had completely different social and cultural activities. This was most pronounced when describing the residents of eastern Kentucky. In the 1910s when large numbers of blacks were moving to eastern Kentucky, the Young Men's Christian Association (YMCA) sent a representative to Benham to explore the possibility of establishing a branch. He was far from impressed with the black coal miners he encountered: "The miners are made up of ex-convicts and desperadoes from a half a dozen states. . . . Here we have the worst element of the Negro race gathered at one place. . . . There is little hope for them." A decade and a half later an official for the NAACP made the following observation about Appalachian blacks: "I find the miners to be a very peculiar class of people: it is so very hard to get these people interested in anything that is uplifting, very long at any time. Miners are the most unstable class of people I have ever met. They are always on the go, from place to place, without any good reason for going except to be moving and finding if others are doing better in any respects than themselves."[41] These impressionistic statements, actually nothing more than stereotypes, are far from an accurate depiction of the blacks found in the region. In reality, eastern Kentucky blacks shared many if not all of the same values as the lowlanders. They formed the same types of clubs and fraternities, worshiped in the same kinds of churches, and in fact often served with other Kentuckians in a number of statewide organizations. In other words, blacks (and the same is true for whites as well), regardless of where they lived, shared the same values. Without question, the people of eastern Kentucky, who have often been described as "different," really are not, and the same is true regarding people living in other areas across the Bluegrass State.

Clearly, most of the institutions and activities found in black Louisville existed in the state's other cities as well. The two decades after 1865 witnessed the launching and sustaining of welfare institutions for orphans, the aged, and the infirm. As a continuation of their civic responsibilities, black leaders established a YMCA branch in the late 1880s to assist young men. Any number of cultural and literary societies existed, capped off in the early 1900s with the creation of the first all-black library branch in the nation. Virtually every fraternal and social club imaginable existed in the city. Afro-Americans from all over the state traveled to Louisville for church conferences or education institutes and then returned home and formed similar organizations. In short, with but few exceptions, such as attending a professional baseball game, going to the opera house, or spending the day at the amusement park—all recreational and cultural activities that blacks usually were excluded from enjoying by local custom anyway—the leisure-time pursuits enjoyed by Louisville blacks were available to those living in Kentucky's smaller communities.

The varied religious and recreational activities engaged in by Maysville blacks were quite similar to those found in the Afro-American communities of Louisville or Lexington. Maysville's five black churches were either Baptist or Methodist, which proved to be the case elsewhere since these two denominations comprised 90 percent or more of Kentucky's black churches. In the opinion of a local reporter, most of the black citizens of Maysville attended church regularly and were honest, hardworking people. Reluctantly, the reporter admitted that even this city, where Christian beliefs and practices were obviously widespread, had its share of blacks intent on making a living without working: "While we have no rich colored people here, we have some that are 'hustlers from way back.' " The reporter chose, however, not to focus on the few undesirable citizens but on the "positive," the many black social clubs and the city's small but influential group of elite black teachers, ministers, and businessmen who prided themselves on their high standard of living. The newspaper noted that Mrs. Bell Yancy owned a fancy cottage on the Fleming Pike which cost $1,000, but that high price had recently been surpassed by the new $1,500 two-story frame house of Mr. and Mrs. Charles Walker. Just as in Louisville, the annual graduation ceremony at the Maysville Negro high school was an important event that attracted an audience so large that in 1890 it had to be moved from the school to the city's opera house.[42] Similar activities took place in Frankfort, in Hopkinsville, which had a sizable black population, and in the small towns and hamlets around Muhlenberg County or Hardin County. Clearly, blacks living in small towns and rural communities enjoyed a rich and varied life style.[43]

Celebrations in honor of Emancipation Day occurred throughout Kentucky, with the residents of Louisville and Lexington, perhaps more than blacks elsewhere, turning January 1 into their most significant occasion for remembering their past, and especially the struggle to end slavery. Consistently, the "who's who" of these two black communities led the parades, gave speeches, and read aloud the Emancipation Proclamation. As a white Lexington newspaper noted, the program held on January 1, 1899, was outstanding in every respect. "Tuesday was virtually the colored people's day in Lexington. It was the anniversary of the emancipation of their race and it was celebrated in befitting style by a parade and ceremonies at the theatre. Practically all of the churches and fraternal orders were involved in the program. A long parade was part of the program, with the parade being led by carriages carrying the black community's leading citizens." Lexington had an even larger celebration on January 1, 1914, for the Fiftieth Anniversary of the Emancipation Proclamation. A black printer prepared a souvenir program for the occasion. It seemed as if every segment of the Afro-American community were represented at the formal program. Mrs. Lizzie B. Fouse, the wife of the principal of the local Negro high school and a person active in a wide range of civic affairs, had the honor of reading the Emancipation Proclamation, the high point of the program. Despite the importance of this celebration in black communities, the holding of Emancipation Day programs ceased in most parts of Kentucky around 1920. By the next decade Louisville blacks probably stood alone in carrying on this tradition. By that time the local branch of the National Association for the Advancement of Colored People (NAACP) was in charge of the program, and the organization had changed the date of the program from January 1 to the first Sunday of the year. The Emancipation Day program sponsored by the NAACP in 1935 included the usual assortment of black participants, and to the surprise (and dismay) of traditionalists in their midst, the program featured presentations and discussions from several white women of the Kentucky branch of the Southern Women for the Prevention of Lynchings.[44]

For more than fifty years the celebration of Emancipation Day in western Kentucky took place on August 8 instead of the first day of the year. By taking place at the height of the summer, the celebration tended to be a festive occasion, a black version of the Fourth of July, with picnicking, games, sporting events, and a dance the order of the day. Little or no emphasis was placed on the obligation of Afro-Americans to work hard, to uplift themselves, or to safeguard their freedoms. Indeed, in all likelihood the reading of the Emancipation Proclamation was not included since a formal service was no longer part of the activities for the day. Though programs were held all over the region, the largest crowds usually congregated in Henderson, Hopkinsville, or Paducah. Some twelve thousand Afro-Americans arrived in Paducah on August 8, 1906, with many coming by railroad and steamboat. Two different sites, the old fairgrounds and Rowland Park, were selected to hold the numerous games and activities of the day. Three decades later, the railroad companies with depots in Paducah did a booming business, running excursion trains from Louisville, Chicago, St. Louis, and Memphis. Festivities were held throughout the black area of town, highlighted by a carnival with concession booths lining the streets and a dance at the ball park. When commenting on the occasion, I. Willis Cole, editor of a black newspaper in Louisville, proclaimed the Emancipation Day celebration a great event in Paducah and western Kentucky, though no one knew why August 8 instead of January 1 was the date selected to commemorate the end of slavery.[45]

Among the state's black citizens, the holding of annual fairs rivaled Emancipation Day in popularity. Nowhere was this more evident than in Lexington. Started in 1869, the Lexington Colored Fair attracted thousands of blacks to the city and was so successful that it was held annually until the Great Depression. Some twelve thousand people were in attendance on the opening night of September 17, 1890, many having come from different towns and hamlets in the state. The large crowd was impressed by the numerous exhibits, including floricultural displays, and most of them stood in line for several hours to sample the dishes prepared for the cooking competition. A popular attraction at the fair was always the band competition, with the musical group from Georgetown being considered the best. The total attendance at the fair in 1890 and again in 1891 exceeded forty thousand. By the end of the century, the Lexington Fair had grown even more. Racing events, especially the trots, had been added to the program and proved to be very popular. The directors of the fair eventually decided that gambling would be prohibited on racing and all games of chance. Nevertheless, thousands of people still came to the fair. As a writer for the Lexington *Morning Herald*, a white newspaper, noted with a small degree of admiration, "Yesterday the town was crowded with the descendants of the second son of Noah. This fair annually brings thousands of colored people to Lexington from all over the country, and is doubtless the greatest organization of its kind the race affords." Commenting almost twenty years later, W.E.B. DuBois of the *Crisis* applauded the continued existence of the fair, which he concluded was "one of the most successful colored fairs in the United States."[46]

Perhaps the most favorable story about the fair was published by the Indianapolis *Freeman*, often a booster for black enterprises in Kentucky. The paper explained that the original purpose of the fair, officially named the Lexington Agricultural and Mechanical Association, had been to show how far the race had advanced in the scale of education and business pursuits, and that this goal had most surely been achieved over the years. As explained by the reporter in minute detail, at its inception in 1869 the fair had the backing of thirty-five members, each of whom had invested twenty dollars to finance the inaugural event. Twenty-three years later, this initial investment had grown to 108 shares, each valued at fifty dollars. According to the reporter, the fair turned a profit for its stockholders each year, having paid as high as 500 percent in dividends some years. In what turned out to be a wise business decision, the fair's directors, instead of returning all of the profits to the stockholders, had invested a sizable portion of these funds in property on the principal business streets in Lexington. By 1890 the value of the property owned by the association was estimated to be fifteen thousand dollars. The company's stockholders also purchased controlling interest in the Intelligence Publishing Company and the Lexington *Standard*, a weekly newspaper, which when combined with the property holdings increased the total worth of the company to almost twenty-five thousand dollars. The reporter ended this feature story with highly complimentary biographical accounts of the nine men responsible for the successful operation of the Lexington fair.[47]

Sponsors of the Lexington fair added new attractions over the years to ensure that out-of-towners continued coming. To maintain the interest of rural Kentuckians, one entire day was reserved for farm exhibits and demonstrations. "Louisville Day," another annual event, showcased the goods produced by that city's black entrepreneurs. For many years the fair featured racing events, and in the early 1900s the most popular one of all—the Colored Fair Derby—was inaugurated. Run at a mile and a sixteenth, the race quickly attracted the leading black jockeys and trainers. The winner of the race received four hundred dollars and a silver trophy. Black celebrities came to the fair. On one occasion, former heavyweight champion Jack Johnson drew a huge crowd for a boxing exhibition. Oscar DePriest of Chicago, the only black member of the United States Congress, was the featured guest in 1929. Given the large numbers of people in attendance, white Republican politicians came to the fair. Though issued an invitation, representatives of the Democratic party refused to come until 1904. That year, all the Democratic officials in Lexington and Fayette County were entertained at a luncheon and fair directors served champagne in honor of the occasion. Several Democrats expressed the hope that this occasion would lead to a new relationship between blacks and the Democratic party.[48]

The fair was held at a considerable loss in 1930. With unemployment increasing, the directors decided to cancel the event the following year.[49] Though the intention was to resume the fair once business conditions improved, it was never held again. During its sixty-one-year history, the Lexington Colored

Fair more than accomplished its initial goals of being a successful money-making venture and showing what Afro-Americans had accomplished since emancipation.

Around the turn of the century, when the Lexington Colored Fair and Emancipation Day programs reached their peak of popularity and community support, was also the time when scores of middle- and upper-class blacks established voluntary clubs to help uplift the race. With encouragement from the National Association of Colored Women, a number of clubs active in cities all over the state formed the Kentucky Association of Colored Women's Clubs in 1903. The motto agreed upon by these elite women clearly expressed their aim: "Looking upward, not downward; Outward not inward; Forward, not backward." Miss Alice E. Nugent, a Louisvillian who dedicated her life to working for improvements in the Afro-American community, eventually wrote a song to capture the spirit of these club women:

> We honor Kentucky Women,
> O, grand and noble is their call,
> They wave the banner of elevation,
> O'er every being within their wall,
> O join us, till from the wayside,
> Shall start the echoes—a wise God rules,
> Till every family
> Within our borders
> Will join in praises of which they're due.
>
> —CHORUS
> Kentucky Women, Kentucky Women,
> Kentucky Women, Kentucky Women,
> Kentucky Women, Club Women
>
> Oh! honor Kentucky Women,
> Kentucky Women, a home so true,
> That they are willing to leave their firesides
> To do with eagerness
> What they might do.
> Now hear us those who may differ,
> To what we're saying and our rubs,
> You'd better join us for home and honor,
> And push our slogan, Kentucky Clubs!

Oh! honor Kentucky Women,
Who are so charming and so brave and true,
Who fly Old Glory for elevation,
Unfurling the colors—red, white, and blue—
We ask then co-operation
From all the mothers of our time,
From all the fathers and their relation,
To push our motto—'Life as we climb.'[50]

As their motto and song clearly stated, members of the Kentucky Association of Colored Women believed that their efforts could make a difference in the quality of life enjoyed by blacks. In cities both large and small, they worked to improve health standards in black neighborhoods. They urged city officials to establish free, easily accessible clinics. Members of the association encouraged out-of-state black doctors and nurses to move their practices to Lexington or Louisville, and once these professionals arrived, the women assisted them in obtaining and furnishing offices and laboratories. But perhaps more than anything else, they lectured to, pleaded with, and chastised blacks in an attempt to persuade them to take the initiative and clean up their own neighborhoods. By doing so, they forcefully argued, the spread of disease could be arrested. Like other civic-minded Afro-Americans, these sincere women had another reason for urging blacks to uplift themselves; they optimistically believed that improvement in decorum, health conditions, and especially the neighborhoods where their race predominated would lead eventually to the breaking down of racial barriers in society. In short, blacks would show whites they were indeed worthy to be treated as equal citizens.[51]

Providing for children and women, two groups often considered powerless in the community, seems to have been another major concern of the Kentucky Association of Colored Women. Following the example of Louisville's black women leaders, the association called for the opening of day-care centers for the children of working mothers in several different cities. In the early 1930s the Woman's Improvement Club of Lexington started a day nursery that provided care for more than one hundred children. Affiliates throughout the state eventually duplicated the work of the Lexington organization. Keenly aware of the need for higher education for blacks, the women established a scholarship fund to pay the expenses of females to attend the Negro normal college in Frankfort. As part of this effort, the teachers of Lexington's black high school held an annual play to raise money. The women of the association eventually realized that many changes needed to protect working women in industry and to regulate child labor could only be achieved in the political arena. Therefore, in 1918 they formed a committee to lobby the state legislature in the interest of women and children.[52]

By the time of its fortieth anniversary in 1945, the Kentucky Association of Colored Women had eighty-two clubs still claiming membership and making positive contributions in black communities. In terms of longevity, one of the oldest affiliates was the Georgia A. Nugent Improvement Club of Louisville which, because of having been founded in 1896, actually predated the association by seven years. Another old and revered member of the association was the Married Ladies Industrial Club of Owensboro, which had been active since 1904. "Its aims were to help build better homes, to educate youth, support worthy causes, and to organize Junior Girl's Clubs." To better serve Owensboro's Afro-American community, the Married Ladies purchased property, erected a home for the aged, and gave annual contributions to the hospital. By the 1940s the club received funds from the local community chest which enabled it to hire two matrons and a housekeeper at the nursery. The Domestic Economy Club of Frankfort, founded in 1919, continued to assist the aged and the sick by raising donations for the Winnie A. Scott Memorial Hospital and the Infantile Paralysis Fund. This group sponsored kindergarten training classes for teachers, operated the first day nursery for blacks in the city, and provided a number of volunteers to work with juvenile offenders. The association remained active in politics, working with the state's only black representative, Charles W. Anderson of Louisville, whose mother was a past president of the organization. With the solid backing of these prominent Afro-American women, Anderson led the state legislature in passing several pieces of legislation concerning child welfare. Also, the commitment of the women to black education continued over the years. The statewide organization succeeded in having two books on black history and culture approved as part of the course of study for all schools in the state. And, as they had done for more than a decade, the members of the association continued raising money for scholarships for female students.[53]

Perhaps even more than the various community activities of women's organizations, black Kentuckians have been united by the activities and programs of churches. Without question, Kentucky's black churches, comprised largely of Baptists, were independent, with only the members of a congregation being allowed to vote on the selection of a minister, express opinions on how the money raised by the church was to be spent, and to decide on community activities (if indeed any at all) of the church. Though churches often competed for members and status, they also worshiped together on many special occasions. (It is difficult to downplay the intense competition that often exists among the state's black churches. In Lexington, for example, First Baptist and Pleasant Green each proudly asserts that it is the oldest black church in the state and has—despite the claim to exist only in a Christian spirit—strongly castigated the other for making the same claim. To strengthen their assertion, First Baptist has returned to its original name, First African Baptist Church, and Pleasant Green now goes by the name of the Historical Pleasant Green Baptist Church.) The spirit of unity among the churches started immediately after slavery when the Baptist churches worked together to establish a college and then sustained their school for more than fifty years. This sense of working together is further evident through their statewide organization, the General Association of Negro Baptists. For more than seventy years, that body has met on a regular basis and been active in a wide range of religious and secular endeavors.[54]

Historically, the churches have rallied together to protest racial discrimination. In the early 1890s blacks in Owensboro, Lexington, and Louisville met in churches in their respective communities to protest the passing of Kentucky's Jim Crow railroad law, and they eventually marshalled their efforts and created a statewide organization comprised largely of religious leaders. From their first protest against streetcar segregation in the 1870s to the open-housing rallies led by Dr. Martin Luther King, Jr., in 1967, black Louisvillians have attended meetings at Broadway Temple African Methodist Episcopal Zion, Plymouth Congregational, and several Baptist churches where they first discussed their problems, decided on a course of action, raised money for the cause, and then proceeded from the churches to begin the work of ending the latest racial indignity. As crucial as the church has been to the black struggle for change in Louisville, it might have been even more significant in smaller towns where it was often the only institution of any strength. Louisville blacks always had a number of black leaders and newspaper editors willing to denounce the establishment, and by the 1910s the city had the NAACP, the National Urban League, and the Commission on Interracial Cooperation. Meanwhile, blacks residing in much smaller towns, and especially rural areas, had few options besides turning to the church and its leaders for advice and support to resolve a racial crisis.

Just as black churches were a part of the community, so too was the presence of many "shady" characters and their illegal activities. An untold number of vice joints and houses of prostitution existed in Afro-American communities all over Kentucky. Though it must be viewed with caution, a white newspaper, the Paducah *News-Democrat*, documented the presence of a "red light district" in that city's black community. On one occasion, the paper informed its readers that "Tom Kelly, a notorious local negro, known as the 'King of the 900' is in trouble again." Kelly, a reputed gambler, was arrested after a man complained to the authorities that he had been swindled out of his entire weekly salary. About a month later, the police arrested Della Griffle, Kelly's girlfriend, for killing a man in a bar. The paper headlined this incident: "Black Amazon Adds to Casualty List of Famous '900' Sector." Six months later the Paducah police made yet another raid on gambling joints in the black community. The paper noted that in this last sweep the police arrested "Gold Tooth Annie" Tolliver, "a negress whose police record runs into antiquity. . . ."[55] Again, given the blatant racism of most white Kentucky newspapers when describing black people, the *News-Democrat* probably overstated the extent of black illegal activities in Paducah. Nevertheless, it would be naive to discount totally the presence of gamblers and con men in Paducah and other Kentucky cities.

The problems of vice were amplified in Lexington and Louisville where the presence of horse racing and gambling brought the "gaming" crowd to town. Under both Democratic and Republican administrations, saloonkeepers ignored closing laws, sold liquor to minors, and allowed prostitutes openly to advertise their trade. In Lexington in January 1905 as a way of stopping the spread of illegal activities in the black community, a meeting was held at the First Baptist Church. Coming out of this initial meeting was the formation of the Good Citizen's League. Something had to be done, members of this new organization explained in a statement to the press, because "there are more of our colored boys annually going to the penitentiary than attend our colleges; more of them going to Judge Hiley's court than are enrolled in our schools." The black leaders focused on "drink" as the root of many problems, noting that most of the blacks in jail awaiting trial for murder and assault were under the influence of alcohol when they committed crimes. Members of the Good Citizen's League complained that numerous illegal dives operated openly throughout the black community, with the tacit approval of police officials. One of the dives, they pointed out with obvious dismay, operated within a "few hundred feet of the police station. Black children were allowed in these places, while in the white community the dives kept the young people out." The league closed by saying, "There are here today ten saloons to every church, and it is in these dives and gambling dens that the young members of our race are permitted to be fed on the fire of hell. Remove this idleness and these other causes of vice, and the colored people will grow into a stronger and better race."[56]

Like most voluntary groups, the league's sincere attempt to remove vice from the black community proved to be short-lived. Though its efforts won the endorsement of the local white press, the league was, nevertheless, an all-black organization, which meant in early twentieth-century Lexington that except for a few comments by city leaders that they were committed to ending illegal acts, virtually no support was forthcoming from city hall. Not surprisingly, the problems described in January 1905 continued. City fathers finally felt compelled to act a decade later. In November 1914 the mayor named a group of leading citizens to the Lexington Vice Commission with a strong mandate to investigate prostitution and the situation of the unfortunate women involved in the practice. Their report, which highlighted in graphic details the work of prostitutes, noted that several of the most blatant houses of ill repute existed in close proximity to a black elementary school. "A little negro girl of six was seen being kissed and fondled by an inmate of one of the houses. The child is familiar with the women of the district, runs errands for them and uses vile language to answer the women and their customers." Members of the vice commission concluded their report with a list of recommendations calling for stricter prison sentences for women convicted of prostitution, the warning of known prostitutes to leave town, and ending the practice of health officials' being required to give examinations to prostitutes. Calling medical examinations a "farce," the commission explained, "That the certificate of health in the hands of the prostitute would give a false sense of security and thereby increase practice of the vice and therefore disease."[57]

Yet, after outlining a number of specific steps to end prostitution, the reformers seemed to reach the conclusion that the practice would continue. As they explained at length in their final recommendation, prostitution had always existed in "the segregated district of the city," but at present many houses existed in other parts of Lexington as well. Authorities should, they strongly advised, "take all possible steps to close immediately all such places outside of the segregated district and to punish all occupants of the same." Going further, the reformers explained that within the segregated district a "place" (they chose not to call it a house since that term described where prostitutes worked) should be provided for these women, and "we pledge ourselves to use all efforts to provide for the establishment, under proper management, of such place where such women may be received, as wish to be received therein, when they are compelled to give up their practice of prostitution." Not surprisingly, Lexington's segregated district, where prostitution had always existed and in the minds of the reformers would always exist, was located within close proximity to black neighborhoods, a phenomenon that existed in other cities throughout the country. In the eyes of the reformers, therefore, the real concern over prostitution was when it grew outside of that neighborhood. To be sure, the failure of these prominent citizens to call for a ban on prostitution everywhere in the city was not the ultimate reason that very little changed in Lexington concerning crime and vice, but their attitude strongly indicated a lack of total commitment on the part of city fathers to end such problems.[58]

In Louisville's "red light district" numerous illegal acts were carried on in the open. By the late 1800s prostitution was so widespread that a man by the name of Wentworth published a small book that listed the names and addresses of the various madames and provided detailed descriptions on the types of girls available and the "services" they offered. Surely, only male visitors needed Wentworth's "little black book," since any Louisvillians interested in such activities undoubtedly knew the locations of houses of prostitution. It became a common practice for black leaders to complain about vice and for city fathers to initiate a new campaign drive to eliminate crime. In 1907, after the usual complaints by blacks over the "red light district" adjacent to their neighborhoods, the police responded by arresting more than one hundred Afro-Americans and ordering many of them to leave town. Yet, a long, detailed account from the *Courier-Journal* in 1913 clearly showed that illegal activities remained unchecked. Well-known houses of prostitution abounded throughout the area near the black community. Opium and other illegal drugs remained easy to obtain from the many "joints" scattered throughout this area. Though operating independently of Lexington officials, Louisville's mayor named a group of leading citizens to investigate vice in 1915. Six months later they issued their report, which documented for Louisville the same kinds of problems highlighted in Lexington. Though undoubtedly disappointed that crime and vice remained a part of their neighborhood, Louisville blacks were probably not surprised that city fathers failed to act on the report of the vice commission. Occasionally thereafter, black leaders took the initiative and called on city fathers to adopt a tougher stance to wipe out crime and vice in black neighborhoods. For instance, in July 1927 a group of businessmen, educators, and ministers formed the "Colored Citizens of Louisville," and said they were tired of the "bootlegging, gambling, and prostitution that are openly carried on," and the other deplorable acts that had become part of the daily life in their community. Acting as if these complaints were being made for the first time, police officials expressed their shock over the extent of crime and promised to rid the community of illegal activities. Very little, however, besides the arrest of a few well-known pimps and prostitutes, occurred. In a sociological study completed in the 1920s discussing various problems found in Afro-American neighborhoods throughout the country, the author, Thomas Jackson Woofter, included numerous examples from both Louisville and Lexington.[59]

To acknowledge the presence of thriving "red light" districts in Kentucky's Afro-American communities is not to impugn the character of blacks but to illustrate how blacks lived and the obstacles they encountered when attempting to eradicate problems during the late-nineteenth and early-twentieth centuries. First of all, with racial discrimination closing off many avenues of employment, a handful of blacks (who, because of their high visibility, always seemed greater than their actual number) chose crime and vice as ways of making a living. The unwillingness of the white authorities to end illegal activities in or near black neighborhoods clearly indicated how white officials ultimately viewed blacks. Historically, a significant portion of the crime in black neighborhoods has been committed by whites largely because city officials and the police allowed white drug dealers, gamblers, and prostitutes to go unscathed as long as their vice activities occurred in black areas. So often, instead of destroying the "red light" district entirely, whites responded by placing the burden on blacks, saying that the continued presence of these criminal acts showed that blacks were unconcerned about vice and that such an attitude among blacks, not the indifference of city fathers, proved detrimental to ending illegal activities.

Significantly, in both Lexington and Louisville, whenever they finally felt compelled to act against crime, city officials appointed all-white boards, refusing to name any blacks. This exclusion of black social workers, ministers, and teachers from the vice commissions and other concerned organizations was consistent with what whites did elsewhere, but such a narrow attitude, first of all, shows how racial prejudice continued to hamper any efforts to end community problems, and, secondly, reveals that whites thought blacks incapable of contributing constructively to ending problems, even in their own communities. In reality, of course, far more than whites, black leaders were greatly disturbed by the presence of crime in their neighborhoods, saying that it reflected poorly on them. Therefore, in Louisville, Lexington, and all over Kentucky, they formed various organizations to combat crime. Though failing to end crime in their communities, these efforts demonstrated that blacks were indeed committed to making improvements for themselves. That the ultimate response of blacks and whites to the problem of vice and crime differed was natural and predictable. By discriminating in employment opportunities, failing to be concerned by problems in black neighborhoods, and, as will be shown in the next chapter, by adopting numerous formal and informal measures to keep the races separate, Kentucky whites had long revealed their determination to keep Afro-Americans at the bottom of society.

Two

Race Relations

THOUGH blacks already lived in a segregated world, the Kentucky legislature passed laws after 1890 ensuring this fact. During that decade members of the general assembly passed laws segregating the races on interstate railroads and in state-supported institutions for the mentally insane and the blind. Racist legislation reached high tide in the early 1900s with passage of the Day Law, ousting Afro-American students from Berea College, a private school that had admitted blacks for over thirty years.

Racial discrimination not only limited the access of Afro-Americans to schools, restaurants, and theaters, but also led to their being denied justice in the eyes of the law. For a black to be accused of a crime, whether in Louisville or in the most isolated county in the state, was nearly the same as being found guilty. Prior to 1938 when the United States Supreme Court ruled in the case of *Hale* v. *Kentucky* that blacks must be included in the pool of potential jurors, they had been systematically excluded from serving on jury trials in Kentucky. Not surprisingly, laws were stringently applied to blacks, and they were often convicted of offenses for which whites would not even have been charged. White newspapers and various state reports reveal clearly that from 1880 on, a majority of the inmates in the Kentucky penitentiary were black. In the legal sphere, racism reached its peak with more blacks than whites being sentenced to death by the state. More than half of the people put to death between 1890 and 1940 were Afro-Americans.[1]

In forming numerous ad hoc organizations to protest Jim Crow laws, legal discrimination, and other injustices, Kentucky blacks refused to submit passively to the white majority. The mere formation of these organizations proved significant because any act by Afro-Americans suggesting a challenge to the racial status quo could be viewed as "militant" by whites, which could then lead to increased hostility. Kentucky blacks also turned to the political arena, and especially the Republican party for support. To a certain degree this proved successful, with several Republican governors—from William O. Bradley in the 1890s to Edwin Morrow in the 1920s—taking steps to end racial violence in the state.

During these years racial discriminations existed on practically every front in Kentucky. It seems as if the vast majority of whites within the state and elsewhere agreed that blacks were "different," which meant "inferior." In reaching this negative conclusion about Afro-Americans, whites totally ignored the better educational and economic opportunities which society afforded whites. The view of black inferiority was held just as firmly by upper-class, educated whites as by those who were illiterate. President Theodore Roosevelt, an educated, enlightened man, had a blind spot when it came to racial matters, and he, like those of his generation, succumbed to the general stereotypes about blacks. He and other white Americans felt secure in their racist beliefs in part because the "scientific findings" of a host of white scholars provided further evidence that blacks were inferior. Within Kentucky, James H. Letcher, a physician in Henderson, said that blacks were most surely different from whites, basing his belief on having been "a close observer of them." Unlike whites, who relied on rational thinking and common sense, blacks were superstitious, putting faith in voodooism and folk medicines, he opined. Life would be less stressful for whites, Letcher acknowledged, if they could acquire one quality that characterized black people: "oftentimes have I wished that I possessed their unchanging optimism, their 'happy-go-lucky' nature, the trust, hope and confidence, not only in the sweet bye-and-bye, but in the now-and-now. I know of no race of people more religious than the negro." Journalist Arthur Krock, who considered himself to be a sympathetic friend of Afro-Americans, also believed that blacks were different. In his memoirs Krock noted with amazement that blacks were great crapshooters, having a natural ability at this game of chance, something akin to genius for them.[7]

Whites reasoned that the inferior blacks could not be assimilated into white society and that racial segregation ensured peace between the races. If blacks accepted "their place," many whites believed, then genuine love could exist between the two groups. An illustration of this attitude can be found in a letter written by "a Kentucky Woman," to the editor of the New York *Times* in the early 1900s. The *Times* had written an article about the directors of the Lexington Colored Fair entertaining a group of prominent whites. The only way the whites could fully show their appreciation, the *Times* reporter reasoned, would be by inviting the black leaders into their homes. When considering the almost universal agreement by whites on racial segregation in social activities, many whites undoubtedly refused to take the suggestion very seriously, simply viewing it as an absurd, facetious comment. But this woman was not amused by the *Times'* suggestion. In her reply to the idea of blacks and whites socializing, the "Kentucky Woman" expressed the following sentiment:

> It has always been the custom of Kentuckians to encourage the festivities of the colored people. At weddings, 'baptizings,' Christmas festivals, and all the functions that fill the negroes with pride, it has never been unusual to see white friends, kindly and interested, more or less amused, and assisting substantially in the finances.
>
> This was never understood on either side as social equality, but as the kindness of the superior to the inferior, in a word, the feudal relation. We might visit our old nurses in their homes, sit down and talk with them, write to them, but we did not—nor did they—ever think of invitations to dinner. It is these outrageous and cruel ideas that bring discord into the relations between white and black. If the negro is taught by certain Northerners to demand social equality, we shall be less able to extend kindness to them, for we, too, are free.[3]

Since racial segregation was clearly the norm, nothing more offended whites and was held in more contempt than the thought of interracial marriage. The statute laws of Kentucky endorsed this position: "Marriage is prohibited and declared void between a white person and a negro or mulatto." For performing such a marriage, a judge or minister faced imprisonment of up to twelve months and a thousand-dollar fine. The same penalties applied to any clerk who knowingly issued a marriage license to an interracial couple.[4]

In 1906 Henry Clayter, a twenty-six-year-old Afro-American, eloped with Ora Gardner, a fifteen-year-old white female. In describing Clayter, a white newspaper explained, "he is an unusual negro, both regarding appearance and manner. He is mulatto, having almost white skin with a tall military bearing and an excellent manner. He served over two years in the regular army in the Philippines, and rose to a non-commissioned officer." After an exhaustive search, Gardner's family eventually discovered the couple living in Chicago. Both were then arrested. Fearful of violence, the legal authorities had the couple sent to Louisville for safekeeping instead of returning them to the small western Kentucky community of Irvington, in Breckinridge County. The girl's father and brother said that under no circumstances would she be allowed to remain with Clayter, that she would be sent to a convent. Local whites were in an uproar over the incident, with a group of them openly calling for the lynching of Clayter upon his return to Irvington for trial. In response, a group of Irvington blacks boldly stated that if Clayter was killed, the blood of white lynchers would flow in the streets. As tension increased, a white man drew a revolver on a black, warning him and all other blacks to stay off the street.[5]

Under extremely tight security, Clayter stood trial at the October term of Breckinridge County Circuit Court. The all-white jury wasted little time in finding him guilty of carnal knowledge of a female under the age of sixteen and sentencing him to the maximum sentence of twenty years in prison. Almost immediately after the trial, a number of friends and relatives of Clayter called upon the governor to commute the sentence. In April 1909, after Clayter had served three years, Governor Augustus Willson reviewed the case and decided that a twenty-year sentence had indeed been too harsh and commuted the sentence to five years. Clayter was freed exactly two years later in April 1911. Given the numerous lynchings that occurred in Kentucky when a black had been accused of sexual intimacy with a white woman, when in fact no proof existed that any relationship had occurred, Clayter was fortunate to escape a lynch mob and serve only five years in prison. It is probably safe to conclude that after being released from prison,

Clayter chose not to return to Breckinridge County.[6] The Paducah *News-Democrat* was adamant in its condemnation of interracial marriage when discussing the relationship of Henry Clayter and Ora Gardner. In preradio and television days, both daily and weekly newspapers were widely read, thereby helping to express and shape the views of the general public on most issues. White newspapers in that day of "yellow journalism" consistently played up any crime attributed to a black person. Indeed, even before standing trial, blacks were found guilty in the white press, denounced in very harsh and derogatory terms. Newspaper editors called for severe punishments for blacks as the only effective deterrent to other blacks with criminal tendencies. On other occasions, white newspaper editors ridiculed black activities and attempts at respectability and ignored for the most part the serious and pressing concerns of black leaders.

Even editor Henry Watterson of the highly respected Louisville *Courier-Journal* denounced attempts by Afro-Americans to end segregation and to become involved in political activities. In this respect Watterson was consistent throughout his journalistic career; he criticized blacks in the 1860s and 1870s and continued to do so in the twentieth century. For instance, in 1901 the venerable editor chastised a London, England, hotel owner for admitting blacks. "In those parts of the United States in which negroes are numerous and for the most part undesirable guests, the proprietors have no choice but to exclude this class of customers or to close their houses. It does not make the least difference whether they think this is due to unjustifiable race prejudice or not. . . . Were English hotel-keepers confronted with similar conditions they would do precisely as the Americans do in the same business. When they talk about their superior liberality they are indulging in a bit of cant that costs them nothing, but which deceives nobody who is capable of thinking intelligently upon the subject." Given all of his public statements about blacks and the way he consistently ridiculed them with his "darky" jokes, that Watterson was often called by his contemporaries a "friend of the Negro" is remarkable. For instance, though claiming to oppose racial violence, he understood and often sympathized with whites who felt compelled to lynch Afro-Americans. In all fairness to Watterson, he did denounce lynchings in 1898 and again in 1915, but on balance his numerous negative comments about blacks clearly outweighed his few positive statements.[7]

White newspaper editors and reporters refused to give blacks any measure of respect. In several white newspapers it seems as if the word "darky" was a synonym for the word "negro." The word "coon" was often used when discussing a black man, while "negresses" described black women, and the term "pickaninny" referred to young blacks, usually girls. The Mayfield *Monitor*, a paper given to extreme racist views and to justifying the lynchings that occurred in that area, printed a poem in Negro dialect as part of an advertisement for the J.I. Burge Company. How the poem, which was entitled "That Sly Old Coon," had any connection with selling sewing machines is unknown. The poem, by an anonymous writer, told of a black going coon hunting, and, after the successful hunt, the irresponsible blacks celebrated by dancing the night away.

> As I was going to Sandy Point
>   De udder afternoon.
> Dis nigger's heel cum out ob joint
>   A runnin' uv a coon.
> I thought I see him on a log,
>   A lookin' might quar,
> But when I cum up to de log,
>   De coon he wusn't dar.
> I blow de horn, I call de dog,
>   An tell him for ter bark.
> We hunt all night in de holler log,
>   But de coon he still keep dark.
> At las' I hear de ole coon sneeze;
>   De dog he fly aroun',
> An' onto him he den did freeze,
>   An' pull him to de groun'
> De ole coon lay upon de groun'
>   As stiff as any post;
> I knock him den upon de head,
>   An' he giv up de ghost.
> We take him tu de ole log house
>   As soon as he usupire.
> He look jus' like a little mouse,
>   An we roast him on the fire.

De peepful dey all cum aroun',
An' kick a kind ob splutter,
Dey ete de coon an' clar de groun'
Tu dance de chicken flutter.
Dey dance all night tell de brake ob day
Tu a tune on de old banjo,
An' den dey all did go away
Befo' de chicken crow.

During the 1920s several white newspapers featured "Hambone," a cartoon caricature about blacks speaking in Negro dialect. Though most of the derogatory drawings, poems, and stories about blacks appeared in newspapers in small towns, the white press in the state's larger cities were not immune to the virus of racism. In 1935 the Louisville *Leader*, a black newspaper, complained about the abusive language used in the *Courier-Journal* and *Times* toward Afro-Americans attending the Joe Louis fight at the Louisville Armory.[8]

Perhaps no white Kentucky newspapers exceeded the Paducah *Weekly Democrat* (which was later changed to the *News-Democrat* after becoming a daily) in its use of abusive language when referring to blacks, especially alleged criminals, and in its attitude of ridiculing Afro-Americans. The day before the annual Emancipation Day celebration in 1916, the paper's headline proclaimed: "Safety Commission Prepares for the Usual Bellicose Festivities." As a reporter explained, some "8,000 or 10,000 of the dusky men and women are expected to make the annual pilgrimage here." This was most surely cause for alarm for whites, and to make the situation worse, Paducah's blacks were getting ready for the big day as well: "Local negroes have done everything in preparation for the reception of the visitors, from setting up drink and food booths to whetting their razors." The day after the celebration, the *News-Democrat* informed its readers that, as anticipated, the blacks had been rowdy, leading to thirty-six arrests. The paper noted only in passing, however, that nine of the thirty-six people arrested were whites, with one of the whites being charged with the murder of a black man. The paper also mentioned from an anonymous but reliable source that at least three thousand of the ten thousand blacks celebrated Emancipation Day by getting drunk.[9]

There were at least two exceptions to the overt racism of the vast majority of white newspapers. The Louisville *Commercial*, a Republican newspaper, called for fair—which in the context of the late nineteenth century meant separate but equal—treatment for blacks and denounced lynchings and other forms of lawlessness. On occasion, however, the writers in the paper referred to blacks in the same derogatory manner as was common in the Democratic-controlled newspapers.[10] Though strong supporters of the Democratic party, the editors of the Lexington *Herald* were far more consistent than the *Commercial* in calling for an objective assessment of the "race problem" in Kentucky. Perhaps the most remarkable example of this attitude was an editorial rebuking President Woodrow Wilson for being rude to Monroe Trotter and other black leaders who were concerned about the growth of segregation in the federal bureaucracy. The editor, Desha Breckinridge, explained that the Negroes (written with a capital "N" which in itself was an enlightened gesture in a white newspaper) were merely asking the president to treat black people with respect and give them the same employment opportunities enjoyed by other American citizens. Given the time and place, this is an enlightened editorial, one showing that Kentucky whites were not of one mind in how blacks were to be treated.

> Does the President of the United States believe that as a matter of governmental policy, citizens of African extraction should be treated differently from citizens of Anglo-Saxon, Teutonic, Slav or Latin extraction? Is the President of the United States, the Chief Executive officer of the greatest republic in the world, that has opened its doors as a refuge for the oppressed of all nations, willing to stand before the peoples of the earth as giving the sanction of his great personality and high office to the prepetuation of race prejudice? Is it to be the policy of the government of the people, by the people, for the people, that any race is to be set aside as distinguished from another race?
> At what point will the government as government stop the segregation of different races? As we conceive the purpose of this government it is to treat every individual as equal before the eyes of

the law—black or white, red or yellow, Jew or Gentile, Protestant or Catholic—whatever the breed, whatever the creed matters not, at least should matter not to the public official charged with the duty of serving all the people.

We are distressed that the President has allied himself with those who believe in the perpetuation of race prejudice and justify race passion. As a private citizen, every man has the right to determine his own course; as a public official, the higher the office the greater the obligation to act with justice and treat with patience those who must look to the public officer for the protection of the law."[11]

James C. Klotter, the biographer of the Breckinridge family, explains that although far from being racial egalitarians, newspaper editors W.C.P. and Desha Breckinridge strongly opposed the rising tide of racial hatred and consistently called for equal treatment before the law for Afro-Americans. In 1897 George Dinning, a black farmer in Simpson County, shot and killed a member of the mob that had surrounded his house and had threatened to beat or kill him. Though clearly a case of self-defense, Dinning was sentenced to prison by the all-white jury. W.C.P. Breckinridge responded with a front-page letter to the governor, urging an immediate pardon for Dinning. The letter said, "Dinning is a negro; he is poor; he was a slave; he may be unworthy; but he is a citizen, a man, a husband, and a father, and it was his home and he was its defender. There are six whites in Kentucky to every negro. The whites have been free, rich, educated for centuries, the negroes have been slaves, poor illiterate. Manliness, courage, charity unite to make outrages on them cowardly and unspeakably base." Upon assuming control of the *Herald* in the early 1900s, Desha Breckinridge continued to speak out against the unjust treatment of Afro-Americans. In 1906 he roundly condemned Thomas Dixon's *The Clansman*, pointing out that the novel said nothing new and would only tend to worsen race relations with its appeal to prejudice and passion. Several decades later, after a white man raped two young black girls in Lexington, Breckinridge called for equal and firm justice, for handing down the same death sentence to a white man that blacks received from all-white juries for raping white women. To disregard the law, the editor said, even when blacks were the victims, bred disrespect and lawlessness.[12]

In addition to expressing views about equal justice under the law for blacks, both Breckinridges called (in paternalistic terms) upon whites to assist blacks in making progress in other areas. Though most of the details are unknown, it is obvious that W.C.P. Breckinridge aided William Hart, a black lawyer (and possibly other blacks as well), in his pursuit of a career as an attorney. In 1911 Desha Breckinridge called for improving and expanding the programs available to black youths in the Lexington public schools. Referring to himself as a friend of the Negro race, Desha Breckinridge expressed a desire to see Afro-Americans "as independent politically and financially as any white man."[13] Yet, in what seems to have been a contradiction but was not to the whites of their day, both Breckinridges expressed a strong belief in white superiority and the conviction that segregation must be maintained. Desha went further than his father, calling for the elimination of blacks as voters, a view motivated by an intense disdain for blacks as loyal Republicans. As pointed out by Klotter, to aid the Democratic cause, he often resorted to overt racist statements and the use of racist cartoons near election day. In the final analysis, a few of the views expressed by the two editors of the *Herald* resulted in their standing apart from the vast majority of Kentucky whites regarding the subject of race. But clearly most whites agreed with the Breckinridges when they explained that segregation of the races was the norm and the exclusion of blacks was not only necessary but desirable.[14]

Journalist Arthur Krock's childhood interactions with Afro-Americans in the western Kentucky community of Glasgow—which largely shaped his views as a benign racist—were probably experienced by many other whites of that day, not only in Kentucky but all over the nation as well. One of his earliest remembrances was of his "black mammy," whom he affectionately called "Aunt" Courtney, and of her husband "Uncle" Armistead. In his memoirs Krock spoke of his love for these people, who were, he proudly proclaimed, part of his extended family. When desiring some special delicacy, he would go to Aunt Courtney's house. "I would arrive to find a table covered by a gleaming white cloth and a single chair drawn up to it. But, though the children of the household were not permitted to dine with even so unworthy a member of the master race as I, they would stand around and watch me devour every morsel. This undoubtedly whetted their appetites for the special dishes they would shortly inherit."[15]

Krock indulges in wishful thinking when stating that the black servants were treated with respect by the whites for whom they worked. "The Negroes served, yes, but also they were called into confidence on equal terms on matters affecting the household, agriculture, and the security of the community from racial violence. For at least in our community, the responsible Negroes possessed in exceptional measure the instinct for wise solutions of such problems." But after saying that blacks were treated with dignity in Glasgow, he then contradicts himself by pointing out something that was common everywhere, including his hometown; that blacks most surely were not accorded the respect given whites: "Yet we did not refer, in speech or print, to Negroes as 'Mr. and Mrs.' and in public assemblage they sat apart. The detestable blight of slavery was also still manifest in such practices as segregated public transportation."[16] Krock, a widely acclaimed journalist, was at a loss to explain why the good, solid, responsible Negro citizens of his community were treated by whites with disdain. He concluded that was simply the way whites treated Afro-Americans.

As Krock's memoirs clearly show, in all their dealings with whites, blacks were made to feel inferior and were segregated. As the historian of Paducah explains, by the early 1900s that city had a rigid form of segregation. "Public facilities for blacks were separate but not equal. Train . . . stations had separate waiting rooms, rest rooms, and restaurants for white and black patrons. Black women would not be welcomed to try on clothing in Paducah stores. Blacks went to their own schools and churches. Even the funeral parlors were separated by color." All over Kentucky, the hotels, restaurants, and theaters owned by whites excluded Afro-Americans or, at best, afforded them a Jim Crow section. Churches most surely drew the color line. As explained by an Afro-American newspaper, two "highly respected" black women entered the white Baptist Church in Maysville one Sunday and sat on the back seats. The sexton, a black man, ordered them to leave the church immediately. This incident could have occurred anywhere in Kentucky and during any time period from the 1880s to the 1970s.[17]

All over Kentucky blacks were prohibited from entering the public libraries. For a number of years around the turn of the century, Louisville blacks complained to city officials about their exclusion from the library, often noting with bitterness that as taxpayers they should have the right to enter any public facility. Library officials eventually grew tired of their complaints and began working with black leaders to secure financial support from Andrew Carnegie to open two black libraries. Meanwhile, they continued prohibiting blacks from the library's main branch, a practice that remained in effect until 1950. The Henderson Public Library opened in 1904. Right from the start the board of directors believed that allowing Afro-Americans to have access to the reading rooms and to borrow books "would totally destroy the usefulness of the Library to this community." To end black complaints about being excluded from yet another public institution, library officials moved a few books, which were "suited to the needs of the colored population," to the Eighth Street Colored School. Library officials viewed this dual system as an ideal arrangement: it would satisfy blacks by providing them with a library but, more importantly, as their report frankly stated, "it would leave the white population of the city undisturbed in their use of the Library building." Henderson's libraries were separate but far from equal: the white main branch had far more books and received far more of the city's tax dollars. For example, between 1916 and 1920, $3,151.24 was spent on the white library compared to the pitiful sum of $234 (or about $46.80 a year) at the black branch.[18]

Kentucky's black citizens were excluded from public hospitals even in life-threatening emergencies. Unquestionably, if blacks had received equal treatment at white hospitals, any number of lives might have been saved and much suffering would have been alleviated. In 1911 a black man was struck by a railroad train in Frankfort. Carried to the white hospital, the man was refused admission because of his race. He was then transported to the workhouse and left to die. On one occasion while responding to an alarm, several black firemen in Louisville were injured in a car collision. After being denied treatment at the public-supported white hospital, they were taken to the all-black Red Cross Hospital. Unlike their counterparts elsewhere in Kentucky, Louisville blacks were fortunate in having their own hospital. Even Lexington blacks did without a hospi-

Louisville's Red Cross Hospital (left), founded by black physicians in 1899.

University of Louisville Photographic Archives

Among the founders of the Red Cross Hospital was Dr. W.T. Merchant.

University of Louisville Archives and Records Center

tal and usually received treatment and examinations by black physicians at a small "clinic." If admitted to the public hospital they were segregated and assigned to white doctors. In Paris, after all attempts failed to persuade city fathers to admit blacks on an equal basis to the white hospital, a group of black leaders launched a long and ultimately successful campaign to raise $15,000 to build a Negro annex to the white hospital. The black ward finally opened in 1918.[19]

Hospitals and libraries were far from being the only public facilities that relied on taxation for support yet denied equal access to Afro-Americans. Louisville, Lexington, and several smaller towns operated segregated orphan homes. From its inception in November 1894, the Colored Orphan Industrial Home of Lexington received yearly appropriations from both Lexington and Fayette County governments. Nevertheless, the funding was far from adequate, and the facility compared unfavorably in every aspect to the orphanage for white children. Among other institutions, the state operated separate schools for the white and black blind, and as was common in all of the state-supported institutions, the school for blacks lacked much of the equipment found in the white school. Kentucky law called for segregation of black and white mentally ill patients at Eastern State Hospital in Lexington. A report of the state inspector of asylums in 1911 concluded that the building for black patients was a disgrace to the state. With the building being so overcrowded, many patients slept in the basement, a place that was dark and damp. The building was kept up by props, "and should a heavy wind strike it, it probably would collapse."[20]

Integration probably existed in city parks throughout the nineteenth century with segregation occurring in the first two decades of the new century. It is especially difficult to determine the situation in some of the small cities, places like Georgetown and Mayfield, that usually maintained rigid lines of segregation in other areas of society. In Henderson, for instance, blacks and whites coexisted in Barret Park for years, but in 1903 white city officials and civic leaders called for limiting Afro-Americans to a specific area within the park. Black leaders, unclear on why whites were now pushing for racial separation but well aware of the reality of segregation in most areas of black-white interaction, reluctantly agreed with the request. "We, the undersigned colored citizens . . . while not assuming

Children (above) pose outside Grace Community Center at Jackson and Lampton streets, Louisville, in April 1899.
University of Louisville Photographic Archives

This rare image (below) from a glassplate negative shows residents of Frankfort's Feeble Minded Institute, 1913. Photograph by Gretter
Kentucky Historical Society

to limit the colored people of the city[,] feel we voice the sentiments of the great mass of said people in accepting the proposition of August 30 to occupy that end of Barret Park next to the city wharf. We will ourselves most cheerfully acquiesce in said request and will urge all colored people to do so and we believe they will do so. We do not believe our people could ask for more than what is contained in said request."[21] Hopkinsville, with its large black population, instituted park segregation in the early 1900s by designating three playgrounds and two parks for whites and one park for blacks. Racial integration existed in all of Lexington's parks up to 1916. But that year Frederick Douglass Park opened in the far west end of the city. Given its location, the park was practically inaccessible to all but the few blacks who lived in that immediate area. Nevertheless, this would be their only park, though there were several playgrounds scattered throughout the city for Afro-Americans. For decades white and black Louisvillians shared the same parks, which usually had swimming pools, tennis courts, and baseball fields. Between 1910 and 1920 the city opened a few all-black parks. Afro-Americans were still admitted to other parks, though they were now prohibited from the swimming pools and tennis courts. Park segregation officially started in July 1924 with the passing of an ordinance. Despite the denouncements of blacks, the ordinance remained in place for thirty years.[22]

The evidence is often contradictory as to whether or not Afro-Americans lived in segregated communities. Obviously, many rural blacks working as tenant farmers lived in close proximity to whites. But white landowners and black tenants were far from being "neighbors" in any sense of the word. Housing patterns varied so greatly within the cities that it is often difficult to determine whether or not the races lived in the same neighborhoods. For instance, just because the local newspaper, city directory, or county historian referred to a neighborhood as the "Negro district" did not mean that the area was an all-black community. Perhaps it is safest to say that throughout Kentucky blacks lived close to but not in white neighborhoods, that some marker—the railroad tracks or businesses and warehouses—usually separated black residential areas from white neighborhoods. Krock nostalgically recalled the "Kingdom," the black neighborhood in Glasgow: "The houses were superior to many of those where the 'poor whites' lived, and the yards and gardens more carefully tended. The churches . . . were meticulously clean, airy and handcrafted with skills enhanced by religious devotion. Whatever Glasgow in those days had of what could be termed a slum, it was not the Kingdom." By contrast, the comments by Thomas J. Woofter concerning the black communities of Lexington and Louisville were far from complimentary. Referring to Lexington and other places, he said, "Even the smaller towns do not escape these bad, poorly, housed colonies. Poor drainage, few if any city services. No child who lives in such an environment has any decent chance, and the adults are beyond redemption."[23]

Whites in several small cities took steps to make certain that blacks remained excluded from white residential areas. In Henderson a deed restriction written into a 1913 mortgage said: "It is understood and agreed that the property above conveyed is not to be transferred by sale or lease to a person or persons of color." Another deed restriction contained the following clause: "No sale shall be made to a colored person for 99 years, or any residence erected on any of said lots used or occupied by a colored person, other than for strictly servants use of the person occupying or owning said residence."[24] According to the *Crisis*, Madisonville, a city where blacks comprised 40 percent of the population, was one of a dozen cities throughout the nation that enacted residential segregation ordinances between 1910 and 1914. Madisonville's housing ordinance remained in effect for several years, being overturned by the Supreme Court's ruling on the Louisville Residential Segregation Ordinance in 1917.[25]

From the end of slavery, many of Lexington's Afro-Americans resided in all-black neighborhoods (such places as Pricetown, Cadentown, Little Georgetown, Uttingertown, Fort Spring, and Davistown) on the outskirts of the city. Within the city, although blacks often found housing on the same streets with whites, the largest number tended to live in predominantly black neighborhoods in the eastern part of the city. Though there would be some expansion of black neighborhoods (for example, a housing project and two subdivisions were built in the west end); this housing pattern persisted in Lexington until the mid-1960s.[26]

By the 1890s Louisville blacks lived in two large ghettos that bordered the city's central business area. In the early 1900s their neighborhoods experienced numerous problems related to being near the city's "red light district," and a number of blacks began purchasing homes west of the downtown area. With the prices of the homes being rather expensive, only the elite—black lawyers, doctors, teachers, newspaper editors, and ministers—moved into what had previously been all-white neighborhoods. Whites responded nevertheless by passing the Louisville Residential Segregation Ordinance that prohibited blacks from moving into designated all-white streets and whites from moving into all-black districts. Even though housing segregation ordinances passed in other states had been declared unconstitutional, city leaders believed that theirs would be upheld because it discriminated equally against whites and blacks. After a long three-year battle through the courts, the ordinance was overturned in November 1917 by a unanimous vote of the United States Supreme Court. Yet the court's ruling did not lead to equal housing access because blacks still confronted a number of obstacles, ranging from deed restrictions to overt violence, when moving westward. It would be during the civil rights movement of the 1950s and 1960s before substantial numbers of blacks penetrated neighborhoods in Louisville's far west end, but even during those years they faced strong opposition when attempting to move into other parts of the city.[27]

While neighborhoods in Louisville and Lexington were most often separated by race, segregation in public accommodations was probably less rigid, with many places often open to blacks. Clearly, economic reasons accounted for blacks' being admitted in restaurants and shops in these two cities. During the course of a year both cities, especially Louisville, often hosted black religious, educational, and business conventions, and white businessmen found it beneficial to put aside their race prejudices temporarily. In 1909 when Booker T. Washington and the National Negro Business League held its conference in Louisville, city officials and local businessmen agreed to relax the city's segregation policies that prohibited Afro-Americans from eating in restaurants, staying in hotels, and going to the theater. Washington's group was so impressed by the warm reception of city leaders that they incorrectly believed that this open access might extend to individual blacks coming to Louisville to conduct business. By contrast, that same year Washington, upon his arrival in Hopkinsville, was compelled to stay

Street scene in Frankfort's black residential district, 1913.
Kentucky Historical Society

and dine in a black hotel and lectured in an auditorium where the races were segregated. By 1912, a time when racial segregation seemed complete in most places in the South, a few restaurants in Lexington admitted blacks on an equal basis with whites. In fact, when forming the Kentucky Commission on Interracial Cooperation after World War I, director James Bond complained that very few people joined the commission in Lexington because they believed that race relations, in the sense of blacks having the right to enter white establishments, seemed ideal in their city.[28]

Unquestionably, if given a choice, blacks preferred the fluid racial patterns of Lexington and Louisville compared to the more rigid form found in most other places in the state. Yet having access on occasion also meant there was a flip-side, times when blacks were unwelcome in white establishments or relegated to Jim Crow sections. Blacks must have found it unsettling that neither city adopted clear, firm positions on integration in public accommodations, which probably led to humiliating occasions when they were forced to leave a restaurant because their presence offended white customers. As a general rule, blacks could attend the theaters and other places of amusement in both cities but were forced to use separate entrances and sit in segregated areas. As Woofter explained when discussing the theaters in Louisville, "the entrances to the second balconies are located on dark alleys, one of them being on an alley behind the theater almost half a block from the street." Similar conditions existed for Lexington blacks: "one of the vaudeville houses has its entrance in the rear of the building almost facing the city jail." Racing officials in both cities reserved segregated areas for blacks at the race tracks. In Lexington during the early 1900s, blacks were often admitted to the same saloons as whites but relegated to a Jim Crow section. But after a series of shooting incidents involving whites and blacks resulted in the deaths of two whites, a total ban on blacks began.[29]

Likewise, though most department stores lacked a firm policy of racial exclusion, they most often discriminated against Afro-Americans. The newspaper advertisements of Crutcher and Starks Men's Clothing Store announcing that its sale on children's clothes would be for "white parents only" was a type of advertisement that Louisville blacks were accustomed to seeing. Also, upon opening for the first time, some clothing stores in Louisville firmly rejected potential black customers. As Ed Perry, the manager of DuRand Perry, a store handling ladies lingerie, hosiery, and shoes, said, "We don't cater to the colored people. If some of these white people should come in here and see some colored person trying on some of these things they would get mad." Yet, segregation was never complete. For instance, several Louisville department stores adopted the policy of excluding blacks after having once admitted them on an equal basis with whites. In 1925 the Kresge store refused to serve blacks at lunch counters after having received numerous complaints from white patrons.[30]

On occasion Louisville blacks targeted a particularly hostile businessman for his policy of discriminating against blacks. In 1924 editor I. Willis Cole of the militant Louisville *Leader* urged blacks to quit shopping at the bakery owned by George Wiegandt. Also, in the 1920s blacks grew agitated over discrimination at the Kentucky Derby, because over the years the area reserved for them had become considerably smaller. Their protest proved unsuccessful. In 1933, during a concert by Duke Ellington at the Louisville Armory, over one hundred blacks walked out to protest the Jim Crow seating arrangements at a social event that normally was not segregated.[31]

In contrast to Lexington or Louisville where blacks often enjoyed limited access to restaurants, saloons, and places of amusements, segregation in a very rigid form existed for the Afro-Americans living in the mountains of eastern Kentucky. Right from the start the coal companies strove for order, which in the context of race relations meant separation. However, a 1921 article by W.K. Bradley described black and white mountaineers not only as working together but often socializing on the Fourth of July and other occasions and attending the same churches. These activities among the races in eastern Kentucky, Bradley explained, were "a standing challenge to the statement that whites and blacks cannot live together on terms of mutual respect and absolute amity." He did admit that some separation did exist: "Though there is separation among the blacks and whites in the mountains to a certain extent, there is nothing like real segregation." This impressionistic account was published by the NAACP, an organization that had built a reputation on thoroughly investigating racial discrimination.[32]

Recent scholars have reached a far different conclusion about the race relations in eastern Kentucky. As explained by Ronald Eller: "Coal operators usually segregated the black population into 'Colored Towns' consisting of the least desirable houses in the camp. Schools and churches, where provided, were segregated, as were recreational facilities, restaurants, and saloons." Ronald L. Lewis further documents the extent of Jim Crow practices: "Jenkins, Kentucky was segregated . . . with blacks living in their own hollow and usually in the worst housing. The same pattern prevailed in nearby Dunham and McRoberts. Both towns also had two recreation halls, one in town for whites and one on the hill for blacks." Going further, Lewis points out that company officials in Wheelwright took steps to ensure that no racial contact occurred outside of work. The town's police force included a black deputy who worked in the black community only. Wheelwright had three boarding houses, one for blacks, one for foreigners, and one for native whites. Company officials established segregated elementary schools for both races and then clearly discriminated against blacks by providing a high school for whites while ending schooling for Afro-Americans after the sixth grade.[33]

In an attempt to end discrimination, blacks in the Bell County communities of Middlesboro and Pineville formed an NAACP branch in 1940. As the secretary of the newly created branch explained to the national office, the work of the NAACP was essential for blacks living in the mountains. "Negroes in small towns suffer more from the effects of segregation without equal accommodations than those of larger cities." The Bell County NAACP pointed out that all of the local businesses, recreational facilities, and hospitals were closed to the seven hundred Afro-Americans in the area. As a result, blacks were required to travel to either Knoxville or Lexington—both considerable distances away—for vital services. To indicate further the unfair treatment to which blacks were subjected, the Bell County NAACP sent a report detailing discrimination at the theater and at the bus depot:

Schines Manring Theater in Middlesboro

Section for Whites
Cushioned Seats on main floor and balcony

Effects of Air conditioned system
Lobby and rest room for both sexes.
Vitaphone distinctly heard
Floors covered with soft rugs.
Cool water to drink
Choice of selecting any seats.

Section for Negroes
Hard uncushioned seats
So far up and in rear cannot feel effects of air condition system
No rest room for either sex, no lobby
Can't hear vitaphone clearly due to being so far back
Floors bare
No water fountain
Have not the opportunity to pay for better seats and accommodations.

Greyhound Bus Service in Pineville

Waiting Room for whites
Running and drinking water
Cooling system
cushioned seats
Negroes in the majority of cases must wait until all whites are served first before they can purchase tickets or get on bus.

Waiting Room for Colored
No running or drinking water
No cooling system
Hard wooden seats
Negroes pay same price to ride bus are forced to sit in back over wheels and roaring exhaust pipe.[34]

The efforts of the Bell County NAACP failed to end these obvious forms of discrimination. Given the lack of power of blacks versus the area's rigid Jim Crow policies, coupled with the awesome power of the coal companies, their protests had little effect on ending racial barriers. Nevertheless, a group of blacks had contacted the national office of the NAACP, had signed up enough members to form a branch of the civil rights organization, and had courageously challenged racial discrimination. In this regard eastern Kentucky blacks demonstrated that even in areas where blacks were greatly outnumbered and, more significantly, where practically all of them relied on whites for jobs, support of their schools, and the like, they still found the will to denounce racial injustices.

Just like blacks in the mountain region, blacks all over Kentucky consistently challenged racial discrimination. Their movements were led by several leaders, men actively involved in the struggle for decades. To be sure, when identifying someone as a leader, there is always the risk of omitting other people who made significant contributions and thus deserve credit, and undoubtedly in Kentucky there were any number of men and women who dedicated their lives to the cause of racial justice. Yet, three blacks stand out as "race men" (people devoting most of their time to making improvements for blacks) around the turn of the century. In central Kentucky, the most active black resided not in the much larger community of Lexington but in the state capital. Physician Edward E. Underwood, a native of Mount Pleasant, Ohio, compiled a long list of accomplishments prior to moving to the Bluegrass State. The son of a prominent African Methodist Episcopal (AME) clergymen, Underwood attended the Mount Pleasant elementary school for Negroes, and succeeded in becoming the first black to attend the local white high school. Upon graduation he accepted the principalship of the Afro-American school in Emmerson, a nearby community, where he remained for seven years. Though committed to educating other young people, Underwood also pursued a second career, joining his father as a minister in the AME denomination. Affectionately referred to as the "boy preacher" (he had received his license to preach at the age of ten), Underwood served the church primarily as a teacher, first in Mount Pleasant and then at the St. John's Sunday School in Cleveland. He was eventually named secretary of the Ohio Sunday School Institute of the AME Church. In a move similar to other successful black leaders of that day, Underwood became involved in politics. In 1887 he was elected to the Mount Pleasant Republican Committee, and one year later he won a seat on the city council, beating out three whites in a community where blacks comprised only 10 percent of the population. As if being heavily involved in church work and local politics were not enough, Underwood felt another "calling" as well. He enrolled at Western Reserve Medical College in Cleveland. Upon graduating in 1891 with credentials as a physician and surgeon, he moved immediately to Frankfort. His choice of Kentucky's capital city as his new residence must have been something of a surprise, considering his strong church connections and political ties in Ohio.[35]

An Afro-American newspaper noted that "Upon his arrival in this capital city the citizens gave him a hearty public reception at the Corinthian Baptist church." Within a matter of months Underwood developed a thriving medical practice, won immediate acceptance in the black elite social circle (he would remain a bachelor for four years before marrying a school teacher), and though a "newcomer," he quickly became the leading spokesman for the Afro-American community. Contributing to his ever-widening circle of friends and business associates in Frankfort and throughout the state was his membership in several secret societies: the United Brothers of Friendship, the Grand United Order of Odd Fellows, the Knights of Pythias, and the Free Masons. As he had done in Ohio, Underwood served on local and state Republican committees. He also served on the executive committees of all of the boards formed by blacks around the turn of the century. Selected by Republican Governor William O. Bradley to the Kentucky State College Board of Trustees, Underwood became the first black to hold this position. Over the next three decades, he participated in every protest movement occurring in Frankfort; indeed, his support was essential for fund raising and ensuring a hearing before city fathers. After World War I he established the NAACP branch in Frankfort and served as its first president. In addition to practicing medicine, he published a newspaper, *The Bluegrass Bugle*, for more than ten years.[36]

Albert Ernest Meyzeek, the most outspoken black leader in Kentucky around the turn of the century, was employed by the Louisville school system, a position that normally curbed blacks from being "militant." A native of Indiana, Meyzeek arrived in Louisville in the early 1890s and almost immediately became involved in black protest movements. Believing that only blacks could solve many of the problems in their neighbor-

68 / A History of Blacks In Kentucky

Albert E. Meyzeek, "the most outspoken black leader in Kentucky" at the turn of the century.

University of Louisville Archives and Records Center

hoods, Meyzeek devoted time to the community by working with young people, helping create the YMCA, agitating for black library branches, and working diligently through the National Urban League. Above all, he clearly understood that racial discrimination was the primary obstacle faced by Afro-Americans. Therefore, he played a leading role in statewide protest organizations, often writing memorials expressing the group's sentiment against inequality. Within Louisville Meyzeek played a leading role when blacks protested police brutality, housing discrimination, and exclusion from the public parks.[37]

The best known black leader in Kentucky was William Henry Steward of Louisville, a man widely respected throughout black America. Steward became very powerful because of the wide circulation of his newspaper, the *American Baptist*, his connections in the Baptist church, and through associations in fraternal orders. Steward was viewed as something of a power broker for blacks seeking political jobs in Louisville and elsewhere in the state. In a career that spanned from the 1880s to the 1930s, Steward consistently demanded changes for blacks yet did so in a tone that was designed not to offend the white establishment. In that regard Steward's career as a race man often mirrored that of Booker T. Washington, a personal friend. Indeed, Steward somehow assisted blacks in challenging Jim Crow practices and yet maintained the support of white leaders, no easy task.[38]

One of the best-organized, most enduring struggles by Kentucky's black leaders related to discrimination on the railroads within the state. Beginning around 1890 a number of southern states passed legislation requiring racial segregation on intrastate railroads. Within Kentucky several newspaper accounts described racial conflicts that occurred on the railroads between black and white "roughs," and concluded that a segregation law was necessary to restore order on the trains. In reality, white Kentuckians were spurred into action by the same movements in favor of segregation that were occurring farther South. As explained by a leading scholar of railroad segregation laws, "legislators with small farm constituencies likely saw the legislation as a means of obtaining segregated cars for poor whites" who usually purchased tickets for the same compartments as blacks. Afro-American leaders received word in December 1891 that a bill would be introduced calling for segregation. They moved quickly into action, forming a "Committee on Correspondences," comprised of ministers, educators, and attorneys. Next, a large group of black men went to Frankfort on December 24 for two meetings, first among themselves and then with Governor John Y. Brown, a Democrat who had been elected to office despite black opposition. Led by Meyzeek, a large number of blacks met with the governor and read a series of resolutions urging him to go on record opposing segregated railroads. Brown assured the black leaders that he too opposed a segregation law. Somewhat suspicious of Brown despite his positive statement, blacks remained united and agreed to monitor all legislation proposed at the upcoming session. With the convening of the general assembly in early January, state senator Tipton A. Miller of Calloway County introduced a bill calling for racial separation on the railroads. Several days later Meyzeek arranged another meeting with the governor, and this time included within his group was a large delegation of teachers. On January 29, 1892, William H. Steward appeared before the Joint Railroad Committee of the House and Senate. He explained that a separate coach law would be a clear violation of section 204 of the United States Constitution which stated that common carriers were to be regulated in a way to avoid unjust discrimination. Closing with an emotional appeal, Steward pointed out that the law would give rights to foreigners while denying rights to native-born Kentuckians.[39]

The Colored Citizens Protective League of Lexington also sent delegates to Frankfort to inform members of the legislature about the injustices of Jim Crow railroads. Founded in the late 1880s to work for political rights, social changes, and education reforms, the Lexington group called for campaigning against local representatives if they supported the proposed segregation measure and for boycotting all businessmen who might come out in favor of the bill. Lexington school principal Green P. Russell and attorney Jordan C. Jackson began working with leaders from other cities to coordinate the efforts of blacks in their legal challenge to railroad segregation.[40]

Despite the efforts of Afro-Americans, it became clear that the segregation law would be enacted. The senate took up a bill on March 29, passing it by a vote of 18-10. Several weeks later blacks once again tried to forestall action, this time sending a group of prominent black women to address the joint committee of the house and senate. Their efforts proved futile as well, with the house passing the bill on May 14 by a vote of 59-25. Governor Brown, who had earlier assured blacks that he opposed the measure, signed the bill into law on May 29. The key provision of the Separate Coach Law stated that "Each compartment of a coach divided by a good and substantial wooden partition, with a door therein, shall be deemed a separate coach within the meaning of this act, and each separate coach or compartment shall bear in some conspicuous place appropriate words in plain letters indicating the race for which it is set apart." The law, of course, also called for equal facilities for blacks and whites: "That the railroad companies, person or persons, shall make no difference or discrimination, in the quality, convenience or accommodations in the cars or coaches, or partitions, set apart for white and colored passengers." Kentucky's Jim Crow railroad law, like those enacted in the Deep South, allowed black servants accompanying their employers to ride in the white compartment. As stated in the final provision, "employees of railroads or persons employed as nurses" were not required to be segregated by race. Failure to abide by the law would result in railroad companies' being guilty of a misdemeanor and fined between $500 and $1,000.[41]

Undeterred that their actions had not prevented the law from passing, black leaders formed two interrelated organizations, the Anti-Separate Coach State Central and Executive Committees. Led by William H. Steward and Edward E. Underwood, members of the organizations traveled the state to inform blacks of the segregation law and to solicit opinions on how best to challenge it. Many black leaders declared that the race should boycott the railroads rather than submit to Jim Crow seats. According to journalist Ida B. Wells, these leaders initiated a boycott which had an immediate impact on the railroad companies. "The railroads of the State are beginning to feel very markedly, the effects of the separate coach bill. No class of people in the State have so many and so largely attended excursions as the blacks. All these have been abandoned, and regular travel is reduced to a minimum. A competent authority says that the loss to the various roads will reach $100,000 this year. A call to state conference in Lexington, in June, had delegates from every county in the State. Those delegates, the ministers, teachers, heads of secret and other orders, passed the word around for every member of the race in Kentucky to stay off railroads unless obliged to ride." A boycott such as the one conducted by Kentucky blacks, she concluded, was an effective tool of protest for "the appeal to the white man's pocket has ever been more effectual than all the appeals ever made to his conscience."[42]

Regardless of whether the boycott was as successful as Wells stated, black leaders had intended all along to develop a test case to challenge the segregation law. On October 30, 1893, more than a year after the law had been in place, Rev. W.H. Anderson, a prominent minister in Evansville, Indiana, and a close associate of several leaders of the Anti-Separate Coach movement, sued the Louisville and Nashville Railroad Company on the grounds that on two occasions he and his wife had been denied the right to sit in the two first-class seats he had purchased. On the first occasion they had boarded the train in Evansville for a trip to Madisonville and entered the ladies' car. He and his wife remained in their seats "undisturbed so long as the train was without the state of Kentucky, but, when the train came into that state, the conductor required them to give up their seats." Refusing to leave the ladies' car, the Andersons were put off the train. Shortly thereafter, he purchased two first-class tickets in Henderson for a ride to Madisonville. Once again the Andersons seated "themselves in the car designated for whites, and . . . afterwards the conductor took their tickets and exchanged them for the usual conductor's checks, and then required that they should give up their seats and go to a compartment for blacks exclusively." For the second time, they refused to move and this time were put off the train at Robard's Station, thirty miles away from Madisonville. In short, the test case devised by black leaders challenged both interstate and intrastate segregation on the railroads.[43]

Anderson's suit was heard in United States District Court in Owensboro in December 1893. Six months later, on June 4, 1894, the presiding judge, John W. Barr, elaborated on two major points in explaining the ruling of the court. Kentucky did have the right to pass legislation requiring separate cars or compartments for white and black passengers when their travels started and ended in the state, but the Separate Coach Law was unconstitutional because it interfered with interstate commerce. Significantly, however, and ultimately to the detriment of blacks, the district court ignored the Fourteenth Amendment, with its guarantees against discrimination against blacks, when making its ruling. Despite the court's narrow ruling in rejecting the law, black leaders hailed the decision as a victory for their cause against Jim Crow railroads. In Louisville, Lexington, and Owensboro, victory celebrations were held in honor of the occasion. Attempting to view the outcome of what obviously was a mixed victory in the best light possible, a reporter for the Richmond *Planet* explained that Rev. Anderson and Kentucky blacks should be elated over the court decision even though he had sued for "$10,000 and the amount awarded was one cent and the costs. As this was a test case the result is highly satisfactory, inasmuch as it settles so far as this court is concerned the constitutionality of the act."[44]

As anticipated by the state's black leaders, their victory did not go unchallenged as the railroad companies continued to enforce racial segregation in the trains. Most of the railroad companies stated publicly their opposition to the law, citing the expensive cost involved in providing separate accommodations for their few black passengers. Nevertheless, the law's being declared unconstitutional placed the L&N in the position of appealing the court decision, in essence arguing for the law to be upheld. Immediately after the court decision, black leaders launched a fund-raising campaign to continue the litigation. From the central office of the Anti-Separate Coach headquarters, a letter was addressed to the "Colored Citizens of Kentucky," saying that previously $1,226.65 had been raised for attorney fees and other expenses, but "We must have Fifteen Hundred Dollars in the next 20 days." The black leaders concluded their financial appeal in a harsh tone: "Speeches and resolutions will not now fight our battles. Money alone is equal to this great task. Leadership at this time can only be measured by actual work and money raised to fight our way through the courts. The man who speaks, preaches, sings or prays against separate coaches, and then fails to go down in his pocket and respond to our call, plays a part of the hypocrite and traitor, and is unworthy of the confidence of leadership." To raise additional funds for the case, black leaders had a book published detailing their efforts to prevent railroad segregation in Kentucky. The book, which sold for $1.00, contained biographical sketches of a few black leaders, and a poem denouncing Jim Crow railroads written by E.G. Arnette, "an exemplary young man, a student of the State Normal School."[45]

Acting independently of the Anti-Separate Coach committees, several blacks filed suits after being forced to sit in Jim Crow sections on the trains. In March 1895 Minnie Myers sued, explaining that she had purchased a first-class ticket from Cincinnati to Lexington and upon boarding the train had been allowed to take her seat in the ladies' car. Once the train reached Covington, however, she was informed of the Separate Coach Law, removed from the ladies' car, and assigned a seat in the car partitioned off for Negroes. The outcome of this suit is unknown. Also in 1895, a black couple boarded a train five miles from Campbellsville. With a large number of whites occupying the car usually reserved for blacks, Thomas and Lula White were forced into a mail and tool car. They filed suit, not in protest over railroad segregation, but against a lack of equal facilities in the car provided for Afro-Americans. The Whites won in Taylor County Circuit Court. However, in state court, their case, *Louisville & Nashville Railroad* v. *Commonwealth of Kentucky*, was reversed, with the court ruling that "the company cannot be fined for an act of those whom it puts in charge of a train because they may have violated a penal statute. The failure to furnish the coaches for the transportation of white and colored passengers of the kind required by the statute is an affair of the company. . . . For the offenses of the company the conductor cannot be convicted and fined, neither can the company be convicted and fined for the offense of the conductor or those in charge of the trains, as is the result of this prosecution." In short, in the White case the court had reached a rather remarkable conclusion, that when enforcing the state's Separate Coach Law, neither a company nor its employees could be held responsible for the actions of the other.[46]

In the case of Cornelia Bailey of Barren County, the railroad company won before the court of appeals even though it had failed to provide separate but equal accommodations for black passengers. Instead of removing disorderly or drunken whites from the train, railroad employees often forced them to ride in the compartment assigned blacks. This practice was adopted by the companies in part because the Jim Crow car was often empty of black passengers. According to Bailey, she was in the car alone when the agents of the L&N did "willfully and wrongfully disregard" their duties by bringing three white men into the car assigned to blacks. Going further, Bailey noted that the men "used vulgar and obscene language, made insulting and indecent proposals to her, abused and threatened her, and otherwise mistreated her." From the witness stand, the three whites strongly denied Bailey's charges but did not dispute her claim of their riding in the compartment reserved for blacks. When making its ruling on January 13, 1898, the Kentucky Court of Appeals failed to comment on whether or not the L&N had violated the Separate Coach Law by placing the three whites in the area reserved for blacks. Instead, the justices concluded that when putting the white men in the car with Bailey, the conductor and other employees had not intended to harm her in any manner. Second, if any mistreatment had occurred, which was not proven to the satisfaction of the court due to the conflicting testimony of Bailey and the three whites, the railroad employees were unaware of it. In short, the court ruled, as it had in the case of Thomas and Lula White, that a conductor could not be held responsible for discrimination when carrying out the policy of the railroad company.[47]

In all likelihood the Anti-Separate Coach organizations took part in the suit of Robert and Fannie Lander of Hopkinsville. Lander, an attorney, was active in both organizations and had assisted in the fund raising for the Anderson case. On July 24, 1895, he purchased a first-class ticket for Mrs. Lander to ride from Hopkinsville to Mayfield on the Ohio Valley Railroad. She immediately took her seat in the ladies' coach. But, upon realizing that Fannie Lander was black, the conductor told her to move to the "smoker," the car reserved for Afro-Americans. Mrs. Lander testified that after refusing to leave the ladies' coach, she was seized by the conductor and three other men and roughly carried to the smoker, "a compartment . . . that was small and ill ventilated, and that was unclean, and equipped, and fitted with accommodations greatly inferior to the ladies' coach. . . . [The compartment] was occupied by Negroes of all classes, including smokers." The conductor denied the charges of brutality. He explained that immediately upon boarding, Mrs. Lander was told that the law compelled her to move to the area reserved for blacks. After she refused to move, he then personally carried her bags to the smoker. The conductor then returned to the ladies' coach and again—in a very polite manner—informed the plaintiff of the law. Mrs. Lander finally consented to move without any force or undue pressure's being applied. In closing his testimony, the conductor expressed his surprise over the entire incident because the compartments for whites and blacks were equal in every respect.[48]

The trial, which took place in Christian County Circuit Court, resulted in a verdict and judgment in favor of the Landers for $125. But in the Kentucky Court of Appeals their case was overturned, with the justices ruling that the Separate Coach Law did not conflict with the interstate commerce clause of the United States Constitution. Moreover, they explained, a railroad company had the right to separate its passengers if it chose, provided equal accommodations were available to both races. In making this ruling, the Kentucky Court of Appeals adopted a tone similar to that of the United States Supreme Court in the famous case of *Plessy* v. *Ferguson* of 1896. This statement by members of Kentucky's highest court clearly reflected the view of many whites regarding Jim Crow railroads, namely, that segregation was good for both races but especially so for blacks:

> The assumption by some colored persons, and by some of the white race, to the effect that the statute implies or assumes that the colored race is an inferior race, is not well founded. It is manifestly better for the colored race to be separated from the white race than to be placed in the same coach with white persons, with the result that the same would be offensive to the white race; for if this be true, it would reasonably cause disturbances, which would be alike disagreeable and injurious to both races. It seems to us that the law complained of is more necessary for the comfort, convenience, and protection of the colored race than of the white race; and it is to be regretted that the law has not been accepted by both races as designed and intended for the mutual benefit, convenience, and protection of both races.

There was, however, a dissenting opinion by Justice A.R. Burnam. Explaining that since both the Kentucky Court of Appeals and the United States Supreme Court had rendered decisions on railroad segregation, finally settling the question, he felt obligated "to dissent in this case. . . . Unwarrantable interference with the rights of railroad companies to conduct their business in the interest of the general public . . . is founded upon race prejudice, which tends to engender bad feelings between the races; and it is in its operation, prejudicial to the public welfare."[49]

On December 3, 1900, four years after the famous Plessy decision—which declared separate but equal accommodations for whites and blacks on railways within Louisiana constitutional, and for all practical purposes should have resolved the issue entirely—the United States Supreme Court made known its decision on Kentucky's Separate Coach Law. In the case of *Chesapeake and Ohio Railway Company* v. *Kentucky*, the justices by a vote of eight to one decided that the "separate coach law of Kentucky, being operative only within the State, and having been construed by the Supreme Court of that state as applicable only to domestic commerce, is not an infringement upon the exclusive power of Congress to regulate interstate commerce." The Supreme Court emphasized that its decision was being rendered only on *inter*state commerce not *intra*state commerce. Regarding the expense of adding a separate coach for blacks, the Supreme Court said the ruling was no more costly "than state statutes requiring certain accommodations at depots, compelling trains to stop at crossings of other railroads, and a multitude of other matters confessedly within the power of the state." In his dissent, Justice John Marshall Harlan (a native of Kentucky) explained that the Separate Coach Law interfered with interstate commerce, and that the state legislature had no right to classify citizens by color regarding where they could sit on the railroads. A black newspaper editor agreed with Harlan, calling the ruling the wrong decision. The editor proclaimed December 3, 1900, a "black letter day" for the Afro-Americans. "It is not the intent of the constitution to create classes of citizens," the editor concluded.[50]

Kentucky's black leaders fought for almost ten years to prevent segregation on the railroads. Though the Supreme Court upheld Kentucky's segregation law, they realized that their efforts had not all been in vain, that some partial victories had occurred along the way even though the final outcome was not to their liking. If nothing else, the long struggle against a Jim Crow ordinance had shown them the importance of working together; that they could, for example, rally their fellow black Kentuckians to contribute funds for worthy causes. Black leaders most surely found consolation in the dissent of Justice John Marshall Harlan, a former slaveholder and leader of the state's Republican party. In 1908 Harlan visited Augustus Willson at the governor's mansion. Invited to the reception were seventy-five black leaders. William H. Steward had the honor of giving the "Welcome Address" to Harlan: "During the years of your service on the court, it has been our comfort and our pride to know that we had at least one friend near the throne, who under any circumstances, was free from prejudice. . . . You stand heads and shoulders above your contemporaries on the Supreme Bench [because you recognize] the fatherhood of God and the brotherhood of man." Harlan gratefully thanked Steward and the other black leaders for coming, saying he was very surprised to see so many that he had first met many years ago.[51]

On two occasions in western Kentucky, several blacks refused to abide by the state's Jim Crow laws regulating travel by train. In April 1906 three blacks and two whites were injured in a fight on a train traveling from Cairo, Illinois, to Paducah. The blacks had purchased first-class seats in Cairo and refused to move to the "negro coach" when the train entered Kentucky. Several months later along the same route, Hardin Davis, described by the white newspaper as a "negro bully," shot a conductor and a passenger after being ordered to leave the car reserved for whites.[52] Given the reality of white violence and the oppressive white legal system that punished them for the smallest offense, most Kentucky blacks well knew the risk of resorting to violence to protest racial discrimination. That even a handful of blacks did so expressed the race's disdain for Jim Crow laws.

Far more common than resistance with force were the numerous protests by Afro-Americans to compel the railroad companies to abide by the law and provide equal facilities for the race. Prior to the 1930s, this was not a tactic on the part of blacks to break down the walls of segregation. Instead, it was a sincere attempt to obtain the use of sleeping car berths and toilet facilities when traveling on trains. Booker T. Washington, a frequent traveler on the Louisville and Nashville Railroad, complained to Milton H. Smith, the company's president, about the coaches reserved for blacks. "On train #1 between Nashville and Montgomery there is only one toilet for both men and women and no smoking room for colored men." Washington urged Smith to give the matter his immediate attention. Several years later, four Hopkinsville attorneys (two of whom were Afro-Americans) sought indictments against three railroad companies, the L&N, the Illinois Central, and the Tennessee Central, for unequal accommodations for white and black passengers. Though most of the details, including the court proceedings, are lacking, the lawyers representing blacks were victorious, with the L&N's being fined $500 in Christian

County Circuit Court. The company, unhappy over the high cost involved in providing equal services for its few black passengers, responded by equipping the Negro compartment with a smoking room and toilet facilities and by arranging for blacks to take meals after whites had been served. In the view of company officials, however, nothing could be done to solve the lack of sleeping cars for Afro-Americans. There were simply too few black passengers to justify this high expense.[53]

For years the L&N was confronted with how to comply fully with the concept of having "separate but equal" accommodations for blacks. In 1919 the carrier was ordered to provide an entire coach for blacks on each nonstop passenger train running between Louisville and Nashville. Up to that time the company had provided only half a coach for the use of Afro-Americans. Twenty years later, in 1939, blacks were still pressuring the railroads to improve conditions. Charles W. Anderson, the first black elected to the Kentucky state legislature, used his influence to extract a pledge from the L&N and other railroad companies to provide black passengers with air-conditioned cars.[54]

In addition to combating the Jim Crow railroad ordinance and other discriminatory measures, Kentucky blacks faced other severe challenges, with lynching perhaps the most consistent and troubling. The exact number of Afro-Americans lynched in Kentucky from the end of the Civil War to 1940 will never be known. At least 353 people died at the hands of lynch mobs during these years. Of this number, 258 or 73 percent were Afro-Americans. For the period beginning in 1890, 162 lynchings occurred, with black victims accounting for 127 or 78 percent of them. Though these figures on the number of people lynched seem high, they are unquestionably very low. During the years before 1890, especially the first decade after slavery, Kentucky probably had close to 300 lynchings. Furthermore, this number of 353 omits the many people who simply "disappeared" after being in the hands of law officers and the ones whose lives were spared by the mob on the promise that the state would quickly execute them.[55]

Lynchings occurred in all parts of the state in both urban and rural areas. Over 42 percent (149 of 353 lynchings) occurred in western Kentucky, the part of the state where blacks comprised a higher percentage of the total population. More specifically, the Jackson Purchase area, comprised of only seven counties, accounted for forty-nine lynchings. Within that area, Fulton County had at least twenty lynchings and Graves County had thirteen. Second to western Kentucky in lynchings was central Kentucky. Within a fifty-mile radius of Lexington at least 106 lynchings occurred. That western and central Kentucky had the most lynchings was a trend consistent with the South, where the areas of the greatest concentration of blacks usually witnessed the most lynchings. That lynchings did not occur (since the Reconstruction years) in either Lexington or Louisville was another trend consistent throughout the South, for very few lynchings took place in the largest urban areas.

With details available on more than three hundred lynchings, one can catalogue these mob murders at great length, giving very specific and gruesome details. Every atrocity imaginable happened in Kentucky, from a black's being totally innocent of any crime and being lynched for "general principles," to cases where the evidence was overwhelming that a black had, to use the phrases of whites taking the law into their own hands and meting out "justice," committed an "unspeakable revolting crime." Consistently, whether blacks were viewed as innocent or guilty mattered little to white officials who refused to protect their prisoners from lynch mobs.

During the 1890s a number of Kentucky lynchings received national attention. C. J. Miller was accused of the rape and murder of two young white girls in Bardwell in July 1893. Though all of the evidence suggested that the young black man was totally innocent and had never been within fifty miles of where the bodies were found, the mob's thirst for blood—anyone's blood—prevailed, and he was hanged with a huge iron chain before a mob of five thousand. Shortly after the lynching, the father of the girls, who had agreed to the mob's request to kill Miller though he had shown some "compassion" for the black man by insisting that they hang rather than burn him, all but acknowledged that the wrong person had been lynched when he urged local officials to continue the investigation.[56] Seven men died at the hands of mobs in western Kentucky during the week of December 18-26, 1896. Newspapers from all over the nation denounced the lack of law and order in the state, with one newspaper concluding, "In Kentucky this Christmas the favorite decoration of trees is strangled negroes."[57]

But perhaps the most widely publicized lynching was the last one that occurred in the nineteenth century. All lynchings were brutal, painful deaths that involved torturing the victims, and to say that one particular lynching was more painful than others is, of course, relative and impossible to prove, but clearly, this lynching was particularly gruesome. On December 7, 1899, Richard Coleman, a black farmhand, was burned at the stake in Maysville for rape and murder. News of his impending doom had traveled throughout northern Kentucky, and at least ten thousand people awaited his return from safekeeping in Covington for his "trial" in Maysville. While Coleman was slowly dying, hundreds of people, from little children to adults in their eighties, contributed to the fire by bringing small bits of wood. After the body had been totally consumed, the white mob made a mad rush for relics. All of the leaders of the mob were well known. Nevertheless, both the county judge and prosecutor said no charges would be filed, declaring they would have led the lynch mob if their wives or daughters had been raped and murdered by a black fiend.[58]

Yet, the very same years that witnessed these blatant lynchings also were the time when Kentucky officials passed an antilynching law. From the moment he took office, Republican Governor William O. Bradley, who had been elected with the solid backing of blacks, worked to end lynchings. Bradley gave numerous speeches denouncing mob law, and on several occasions he backed his words with action by sending state troops to areas where lynchings seemed likely to occur. In March 1897 he called the legislature into special session for the purpose of enacting a law to prevent mob violence. The burden of preventing lynchings, the governor informed the legislators, should be on the sheriffs and jailers, those in charge of the prisoners. For failing to prevent a lynching, a peace officer could be fined up to five hundred dollars and removed from office. Another proposal called for giving law officers the power to summon able-bodied men to help protect the prisoner and levied a fine against them for refusing to do so. The proposed law called for the governor and local officials to offer rewards to aid in the apprehension of members of lynch mobs. Bradley also proposed a radical measure, the arming of prisoners to protect themselves. "No mob," Bradley reasoned, "would be able to stand before the prisoner fighting for his life and the jailer or sheriff fighting for his office." Surprisingly, given how few lawmakers had publicly condemned lynchings, especially those occurring in their regions, the bill passed both houses with little debate and was signed by Bradley on May 11. Kentucky would be one of only eight states, three in the North and five in the South, that passed antilynching laws in the 1890s.[59]

It is difficult to determine how much credit should be given to antilynching laws for the decline in the number of mob murders. In Kentucky in the two years immediately after the law was enacted, at least thirteen people died at the hands of mobs. This high number of lynchings does not mean that Bradley failed to enforce the law but indicates the strong degree that "lynch law" existed in the Bluegrass State. Furthermore, by comparison with the early years of the 1890s, it can be argued that "only thirteen" lynchings for the remainder of the decade meant something of a decline in the brutal practice. Also, a number of instances occurred in which sheriffs protected their prisoners from lynch mobs even when a black had been accused of raping a white woman. Without question, the primary reason that the law of 1897 did not end lynchings all at once was one of enforcement. The governor, even one as committed to the cause as Bradley was (and this would not always be true of his successors), was forced to rely in part on county judges to enforce the law and apprehend lynchers. In too many regions in Kentucky, county officials and law officers remained at the mercy of outlaw gangs or citizens accustomed to taking the law into their own hands when they felt offended, especially by a black person. Therefore, in spite of the antilynching law, coroner's juries continued investigating lynchings and rendering verdicts that the victim died at the hands of unknown parties.

At least seventy people died at the hands of lynch mobs between 1900 and 1940. A lynching in the small western Kentucky town of Livermore in April 1911 made international as well as national news. Will Porter, a black man, shot a white man in self-defense. A mob took Porter from the jail, but, instead of hanging him near the courthouse (as was common), carried him to the local opera house. Admission was then charged to witness the lynching, with the people in the more expensive orchestra seats being allowed to shoot repeatedly at the suspended body. The New York *Times* and the Chicago *Tribune* gave extensive coverage to the lynching, and the incident was eventually featured in *Le Petit Journal*, a Paris, France, newspaper. Perhaps more than any previous incident of racial violence, the Livermore lynching led many white Kentuckians to acknowledge that such incidents, regardless of the offense attributed to the victim, undermined respect for the law and were therefore unacceptable. After roundly condemning the act, Governor Augustus Willson called on McLean County officials to identify and arrest the leaders of the mob. Nine men were eventually arrested and charged with the lynching. Held over to the grand jury, the men were acquitted by the all-white jury comprised of their friends and neighbors.[60]

The Livermore lynching became the impetus for a new antilynching law, though it took almost a decade before one was enacted. From its inception in 1914 the Kentucky NAACP worked for a law to combat mob rule. In 1920 after a lynching in Versailles, the Kentucky General Assembly, without a dissenting vote, passed an antilynching law. This new law, while largely copying many features of the 1897 antilynching law, did contain provisions calling for several severe penalities: all of the people involved in a lynching could receive life imprisonment or death. Where the intended was injured rather than killed, the penalty for the members of the mob varied from five to fifteen years. But perhaps the most significant feature of the law was the automatic removal from office of peace officers who allowed a prisoner to be lynched: "If any person, being a prisoner, . . . shall be taken from the hands of any sheriff . . . and lynched, . . . it shall be prima facie evidence of failure of the officer to perform his duty, and shall be prima facie evidence of neglect of duty on the part of such officer, and when such failure in, or neglect of duty, . . . is made to appear to the Governor, he shall at once publish a proclamation declaring the office . . . vacant." A feature such as this had been included in the 1897 law but for unknown reasons eliminated in 1902. At the ceremony signing the bill into law, Governor Edwin Morrow and members of the NAACP proclaimed the automatic removal of peace officers the most effective measure to ensure enforcement of the new law and optimistically concluded that lynching would end. The automatic removal of law officers was enforced after each lynching in the 1920s and 1930s. Nevertheless, though the number of lynchings declined in the state, the antilynching law once again did not totally eliminate mob violence. That local communities seldom arrested and never convicted their fellow citizens for lynchings undermined the new law. With lynchings continuing, officials of the NAACP argued in vain that trials of accused lynchers be removed to other communities.[61] Around 1940 the brutal phenomenon of lynching came to an end in Kentucky, and undoubtedly the law of 1920 had helped heighten public outrage over citizens taking the law into their own hands.

Afro-Americans deserve some of the credit for the decline in lynchings in Kentucky. From the end of slavery forward, blacks strongly denounced all acts of violence and challenged whites to live up to the principle that all men are innocent until proven guilty in a court of law. With whites often justifying lynchings on the grounds that blacks raped white women, Afro-American leaders produced data showing that most blacks had not been accused of, much less guilty of, rape. Though Afro-Americans have always well understood the risk involved in responding to white violence with violence, a few resorted with arms of their own to prevent lynchings or to express their disgust over lynchings. In Georgetown in 1891, in Paducah the next year, and in the Mayfield area in 1896, blacks responded to lynchings by carrying guns, starting fires, and threatening the lives of known mob leaders. These efforts by blacks produced mixed results, with the ending of lynchings in some areas, while in other places another black would be seized by whites. Regardless, the show of armed resistance from Afro-Americans clearly demonstrated their discontent with white oppression and a willingness to adopt drastic methods when necessary. Also, when considering that much of black protest has normally involved writing letters and petitions, holding indignation rallies, and forming local watchdog committees, then there has never been a period when they acquiesced in the face of violence.

Lynchings, because they were the most violent, spectacular manifestation of white hatred toward Afro-Americans, received far more attention than other forms of white brutal behavior toward blacks. Far more pervasive were many of the other forms of violence that blacks experienced in their local communities. Police brutality existed unabated in Louisville from the 1880s at least until 1940. In Lexington on March 31, 1925, a highly respected black woman, suffering from a severe attack of indigestion, was arrested and placed in jail where she eventually died. Calling the incident a tragedy, white leaders admitted that had the well-dressed woman been white, the police would have summoned a physician before assuming that she was drunk. In both Lexington and Louisville any black riding on the streetcars who refused to sit in the back stood a good chance of being beaten. On one occasion a Memphis newspaper printed the following headline concerning an incident in Paducah: "Assaulted by Vicious Negro: Mob Took After His Assailant and Another Darkey and Beat Them Terribly. Other Impudent Blacks Given Thrashing." According to white reporters, Gabe Fletcher, a black man, assaulted a prominent white doctor, J. W. Pendley. Informed of the altercation, a group of whites became outraged and responded by beating Fletcher, as well as a dozen or so other blacks they encountered. With whites accustomed to handling discipline matters involving their "people," corporal punishment still existed for blacks in the employ of whites, especially in rural areas. In several smaller towns the whippings of young black offenders often occurred. For instance, in Madisonville in February 1908 six young blacks were charged with committing a series of robberies and were given a suspended sentence on condition that they be given a public beating by police officers. Meanwhile, young whites who committed similar offenses were punished with stern lectures from police officials.[62]

For many Kentucky blacks, the Ku Klux Klan represented white violence. In the early years of the twentieth century, the Klan periodically attacked black farmers in western Kentucky, and though solid data is difficult to find—due in no small measure to the total disappearance of some blacks—the Klan was believed responsible for the murders of ten blacks in Butler County in 1915 and the deaths of an unknown number in other small towns. Throughout the 1920s the Klan occasionally became active in Kentucky's cities as well as in the countryside. By 1923 a number of firemen and policemen in Louisville had joined the Klan. Also, until banned by the mayor (with the prodding of the NAACP), the Klan held several parades in the Derby City. According to the *Kentucky Irish-American*, which consistently monitored the Klan because of the organization's penchant for making derogatory statements about Catholics, fully half of the men elected to the city council in Shelbyville in

1925 were members of the organization. After a series of rapes in the Madisonville-Earlington area in the mid-1920s, the Klan was determined to "clean up" the town. The organization remained on the scene until several blacks were arrested, convicted, and executed for the assaults even though no evidence linked the men to the crimes. Many local historians acknowledge the presence of the Klan in their community during the 1920s, but the authors quickly point out that the Klan was composed of the worst element of whites, had little support, and was soon disbanded by the cities' elites.[63]

Perhaps the most difficult violence that blacks encountered operated under the sanction of law. From the Civil War until the 1940s, if not later, any number of blacks were tried in hostile environments with judges and juries convinced of their guilt before hearing any evidence. A few "trials" took less than an hour before finding the defendant guilty and sentencing him to death. In Kentucky from 1890 to 1940, of the 187 people put to death under these circumstances, 106 were Afro-Americans. In other words, blacks, comprising no more than 10 percent of the population, accounted for 56.7 percent of those put to death.[64]

It is difficult to imagine a "trial" lasting a shorter period of time than that of a Clinton black man in October 1905. Though most of the details are unknown, Jim Hale was arrested and charged with the attempted rape of a white woman. To avoid a lynching, police officials had him removed from the local jail and carried to Paducah for safekeeping. Upon learning the date and time of Hale's return to Clinton for trial, a white mob made plans for a public lynching. In response, the county judge and prosecutor devised an ingenious maneuver, one designed to avoid a lynching; but their plan precluded protecting the right of the black man to a fair and impartial hearing. When the train carrying Hale arrived in Clinton, Judge J.R. Bugg and a special jury, which had already been selected, came on board and entered the baggage car. The judge quickly asked the defendant how he wanted to plead to charges of assault, and the man replied "guilty." Without any deliberation, the jury then handed down what had to have been a prearranged verdict of seven years' imprisonment in the state penitentiary. In all likelihood Hale decided to plead guilty to avoid being lynched. He surely must have known that a lynch mob was determined to seize him before he entered the courthouse to challenge the charges against him. When considering how the legal system usually operated against blacks accused of assaulting white women, Hale probably did not have the advice of counsel at his "trial." Furthermore, he was probably innocent of the crime of attempted assault; as a rule, a black charged with such an offense received a much stiffer sentence. The newspaper reported in regard to this case: "The trial was over in less than two minutes, and the train bore the negro on to the penitentiary."[65]

Scores of court cases indicate that whenever race was a factor in a criminal trial, the chances were very good that justice was far from equal. To be sure, numerous complaints were made that the law favored the wealthy or the politically well-connected. There are any number of cases in which miscarriages of justice occurred where a white killed another white in cold blood and then avoided prosecution. However, no one justified these acts as being fair. People did, in fact, strongly denounce the lack of fairness in court in particular counties that seemed to be controlled by gangs. But, the exact opposite proved true when blacks were involved; then, whites applauded themselves for having treated blacks fairly by allowing them to have trials before executing them.

Whether as victims of crime or as defendants, blacks surely must have known that prosecutors, judges, and juries had no sympathy for them. For a black to be found guilty of raping a white woman meant capital punishment, even though a conviction of rape did not automatically carry the death sentence. Meanwhile, no one, white or black, died for the rape of a black woman, which for all practical purposes was a noncrime in Kentucky. Instead of being tried for the rape of a black woman, whites usually stood trial (which was very rare) on charges either of detaining a female or assault, as if the woman had been beaten; and if convicted, they would be sentenced to a year or two in prison. Charles Falone, a white man with a long record of having committed brutal crimes, was charged with the rape and beating of a black woman in Louisville in 1926. After several mistrials, he was sentenced to five years in prison but paroled after serving less than a year.[66] For brutally raping and beating two young black girls in Lexington, Charles Merchant was sentenced to an insane institution rather than the hangman's noose.[67]

Courts at every level in Kentucky heard far more murder than rape cases, and very seldom, if ever, was a black given leniency for killing a white even in cases that clearly showed the defendant acted in self-defense. Although blacks were put to death for murdering whites, no whites were executed for killing blacks; in fact, they had little reason even to worry about standing trial for such an offense. Most often, after killing a black, all a white need say was that he had acted in self-defense, or that the black had threatened him, or, the best reason of all, that the black had made an offensive gesture toward his wife or sister. But what about other murder cases in which it was clear that the black had not been aggressive in any manner? Whites still received leniency that would have been inconceivable if the cases had involved blacks' killing whites. In 1894 a black newspaper in Kansas detailed the trial of Jeff Burdette, a white man charged with the death of a Henderson, Kentucky, black man. The newspaper was shocked by the verdict: "Yesterday evening at Owensboro the jury in the case of Commonwealth vs. Jeff Burdette, who two years ago struck a Negro over the head with a club, causing death, rendered a verdict of 'involuntary manslaughter,' affixing a fine of $100.'"[68]

Very little changed in the early decades of the twentieth century. In Franklin in late 1914, two white men killed a black woman, because, in their opinion, she had been unfaithful to them by going to a dance with a black man. The final outcome is unknown, but if they had received harsh penalties, the verdicts and sentences surely would have received extensive coverage in black and white newspapers.[69] According to the highly racist Paducah *News-Democrat*, Will R. Johnson, a white man, killed Orillia Singleton, whom the paper referred to as "a negress" and "his lover." They had been living together for four years and had wanted to marry but interracial marriage violated state law. Believing his common-law wife was having an affair with her boss, Johnson confronted Singleton at work, hit her repeatedly, and then pulled out a knife and attacked, almost severing her head. The sentence he received for this murder is unknown.[70]

In a story entitled "Equal and Unequal Justice," the Louisville *Leader* complained about the differences in how the law treated blacks and whites. Two men in Bardstown, one white and the other black, were arrested for the murder of a wealthy white farmer, the father-in-law of the white man. (Unfortunately the *Leader* failed to give the names of either defendant in the case.) The motive—the white defendant feared being written out of his father-in-law's will. Under oath, the black admitted seeing the white man commit the murder and that at gunpoint he was made to move the body: "If you don't go with me, I am going to kill you just like I killed him." Both men were given life sentences, even though only the white had a motive. Newspaper editor I. Willis Cole noted: "When a Negro plays a minor part in a case in which the white man is the major actor, it may be regarded as equal justice when the Negro's punishment is equal to that of the white man's in the case." But in the opinion of the editor, the justice for the black in Bardstown "is quite unequal."[71]

Black leaders denounced not only the discrimination members of their race encountered when appearing in court but also how the law consistently allowed white violence upon them to go unpunished. As a group of black leaders explained in the late nineteenth century, since the end of the war blacks had been tried in courts that were totally manipulated by whites. Of the hundreds of lynchings of blacks that had occurred, they pointed out, no white had been convicted of murder. More than anything else, however, they challenged the fact that no blacks ever served on juries in the state. "We are tried in courts controlled entirely by white men, and no colored man sits on a Kentucky jury. This seems no mere accident, but a determined effort to exclude us from fair trials and put us at the mercy of our enemies, from the Judge down to the vilest stubborn witness."[72] Protest in the new century would be just as loud, just as indicting, and, just as regularly, it fell on deaf ears. Consistently the Kentucky Court of Appeals, relying on several federal rulings, said that the absence of blacks from a jury did not mean that discrimination had taken place.[73] A successful challenge finally occurred in the late 1930s. Joe Hale of Paducah was sentenced to death by an all-white jury for the murder of a white man. After losing in the Kentucky courts, the NAACP won a unanimous decision before the United States Supreme Court by showing that within Kentucky for more than thirty years there had been "a systematic and arbitrary exclusion of Negroes from the jury lists solely because of their race or color, constituting a denial of the equal protection of the law guaranteed to petitioner by the Fourteenth Amendment." The court ordered the immediate inclusion of blacks into the pool of potential jurors.[74] Yet, when considering racial violence, blacks had far more success—limited as it might have been—in convincing whites that lynchings were unjust than in showing them that the legal system did not provide blacks a fair hearing. In other words, it is clear when mob lynchings ended in Kentucky; it is not so evident when blacks began receiving fair and impartial trials in the Bluegrass State.

In addition to protesting legal and illegal forms of racial violence, black Kentuckians turned to the political arena in their quest to end racial discrimination. The 1890s witnessed two significant trends regarding Afro-Americans and politics in the South. Beginning with Mississippi, the various southern states disfranchised practically all of their black voters, something they had been doing on a piecemeal basis since the end of Reconstruction. These disfranchisement efforts proved so complete that the number of blacks' voting in Mississippi, South Carolina, and Alabama declined by more than 90 percent. By 1912 all of the ex-Confederate states and Oklahoma excluded blacks as voters. Second, though blacks were no longer voting, their status was very much a political issue. Southern politicians often used race as "the" issue during election campaigns, with many candidates attempting to "out nigger" their opponents. Such a highly emotional issue, not surprisingly, caused many outrageous charges to be leveled against blacks, which in turn increased racial tensions and resulted in lynchings and race riots. Unlike their counterparts in the Lower South, black Kentuckians maintained the franchise during this period even though occasional rumblings were made in Frankfort about the necessity of eliminating blacks as voters. For the most part, however, instead of attempting to remove blacks from politics, Kentucky's Democratic party simply adopted the tactic of ignoring them, refusing to cultivate them as voters.

By contrast, Kentucky's three Republican governors between 1895 and 1930 addressed a number of issues of great concern to Afro-Americans. Elected in 1895, William O. Bradley appointed blacks to patronage positions in state government above the janitorial level in substantial numbers, a major breakthrough for the race. In his annual message of January 1898, Bradley surprised the state legislature by his "unequivocal recommendation" for repeal of the Separate Coach Law. As a reporter explained, "His appeal for simple justice for the struggling Negro race and picture of the great injustice of the present 'Jim Crow' car system in Kentucky is one of the best features of the message."[75] Perhaps more than any other Kentucky governor, Bradley denounced lynchings, condemned whites for making a mockery of the law, and called on county officials to indict and prosecute members of lynch mobs. As he said on one occasion, "Those who congregate and conspire to take human life are legally greater criminals than those whose lives they seek to take, for no crime is so base and repulsive as that committed under cloak of pretended vindication of law." In a step that probably no other governor from a southern state would have taken, Bradley traveled to Springfield, Ohio, and spoke before the Anti-Mob and Lynch Law Association in January 1898.[76]

Governors Augustus E. Willson and Edwin P. Morrow also exhibited a strong desire to end lynch law. Shortly after his election in 1907, Willson dispatched troops to western Kentucky to combat the raids by Night Riders on black and white farmers. In 1910 he pardoned eleven blacks who had been sent to prison for their involvement in a race riot in Dixon that resulted in the death of a white man and the wounding of another. In the statement announcing the release of the men, Willson said a grave injustice had occurred: "All men of ordinary sense know that negroes do not band together in such a county as this to mob white men. Yet, for attempting to prevent a lynching they were sent to prison while members of the lynch mob went free. It is a sorrow to every man who honors and loves Kentucky that such a story as this could be true in any county in Kentucky."[77]

Governor Morrow, in office from 1919 to 1923, received national attention for acting to end mob violence. In 1920, convinced that a mob would attempt to lynch a black man on trial in Lexington for rape and murder, Morrow dispatched state troops to the city and ordered them to fire if a move was made toward the courthouse. When this actually occurred, the militia fired, killing five and wounding as many as fifty people. Praise for Morrow came from all over the nation. The NAACP sent a telegram thanking him for taking such a courageous stand. The order to shoot upon lynchers became something of a model for other governors. Even before receiving national acclaim, Morrow had been active in the Commission on Interracial Cooperation, an organization established after World War I to lessen racial tensions. As governor, Morrow, who was William O. Bradley's nephew, lobbied the state legislature to pass the Anti-Lynching Law of 1920, and he took particular delight in signing the bill into law before a group of prominent blacks.[78]

While extremely appreciative of the positive actions of Republican governors, blacks at the same time remained frustrated by the overall attitude of the party of making only a minimal number of concessions to them. Republican officials had adopted such a view in the belief that only by distancing themselves from blacks on some issues could they hope to attract more whites to the party. Therefore, two pressing concerns of blacks were repeatedly ignored—increasing political patronage and party support for black political candidates. For example, on several occasions the Republican administration controlled city government in Paducah. Black leaders called upon the party to appoint members of their race to the police and fire departments, but just as consistently Republican leaders ignored this request, employing them only as custodians.[79] As a United States senator in the early 1900s, William O. Bradley, who had championed Afro-American rights a decade earlier, made public statements that disappointed blacks. While speaking on behalf of the Republican candidate in a heated mayor's campaign in Louisville where the status of blacks was a major issue, he made a number of patronizing comments towards blacks. Bradley concluded that though blacks deserved political patronage in the South, he approved of the Taft administration's policy of not appointing them to office in the state in which they lived.[80]

Blacks on two occasions seriously considered supporting Democratic candidates for statewide office to protest what they perceived as unfair treatment from the Republicans. In both cases, that of William Goebel for governor in 1899 and Augustus O. Stanley for the U.S. Senate in 1918, the Democrats had adopted a position calling for "fair" (as opposed to truly equal) treatment for blacks, a position that Republican leaders endorsed only under pressure. The nomination of Goebel as the Democratic candidate for governor in July 1899 led to a split within the party, with many of the party's established leaders deciding to support another candidate for the office. This split occurred at a time when the Republicans had won the previous governor's race for the first time. An editorial in the New York *Times* speculated that in a desperate attempt to win, Goebel might court the Negro vote. With blacks comprising one out of seven voters in the state, their support could well determine the outcome of the election. Throughout the fall campaign, Goebel made statements apparently designed to encourage blacks to support him. He called for equal accommodations on the railroads and in state-supported welfare institutions. Afro-Americans were not opposed to segregation, the candidate claimed, only to inferior facilities.[81]

Goebel's position on separate but equal facilities failed to convince black leaders in Louisville or Lexington to endorse his candidacy. He did, however, receive endorsements from prominent blacks in small counties who saw his position as enlightened. They were also hoping that Goebel could be persuaded to support other measures for blacks. The Reverend Reuben Goggins, a pastor from Somerset and vice-president of an organization called the Ex-Slave Pension and Bounty Association of Kentucky, openly took the stump on behalf of Goebel. That Goebel might win over any black voters became a concern to Republican leaders. Since state law prohibited Bradley from succeeding himself, the party selected attorney William S. Taylor as their candidate, a choice that greatly disappointed most blacks because of his refusal to call for the repeal of the state's Separate Coach Law. After newspaper editor Robert Benjamin of Lexington called on blacks to form an independent party or support Albert S. White, a well-known black attorney from Louisville, for governor, the Taylor faction took steps to pacify blacks. He made a vague promise, saying that he would be a "liberal governor," and with Taylor's blessing, Albert White was given a position working for the Republican party during the campaign.[82]

Because of the absence of voting return records from all over the state, it is impossible to know how many blacks switched parties and voted for Goebel; yet, even if the records existed, their accuracy would be questioned given the voter fraud in the election. With Taylor defeating Goebel by 2,383 votes, blacks undoubtedly played an important role in the election regardless of which candidate they supported. The closeness of the vote and the charges of voter fraud led to the election's being challenged and on January 30, 1900, the general assembly declared Goebel the winner. He, however, was struck down by an assassin's bullet.[83]

A.O. Stanley enjoyed some black support in his run for the United States Senate in 1918 and for re-election in 1924. As governor in January 1917 he had traveled to Murray and prevented a mob from lynching a black man accused of murder. The national media praised him for being a southern governor with the courage to denounce the lynch mob. Stanley was also applauded by Kentucky blacks, with several Afro-American leaders in the western part of the state endorsing his candidacy and citing his generous support of the black agriculture college in Paducah. Meanwhile, most of the black leaders in Louisville and Lexington called for the race to remain loyal to the Republican party. This seems to have been especially true in his second race for the Senate. I. Willis Cole, the outspoken editor of the Louisville *Leader*, said "Stanley is a good man. He has many colored friends in Kentucky. The *Leader* supported him six years ago." However, he added: "But not during his six years as a member of that body did he do one thing that entitles him to consideration of Negro votes for re-election in November. He did not support a single measure calculated to better the race relations of his country. . . . He voted against the Dyer bill, voted against appropriation to Howard University . . . and not withstanding his Kentucky Negro friends, and the votes they might cast in November, Senator Stanley is a Democrat, pledged to the Democratic caucus, and bound to vote with the Democratic South on all measures affecting the Negro." Stanley lost the election to Republican Frederic M. Sackett in a close vote.[84]

Except for the campaigns involving Goebel and Stanley, Afro-Americans, and especially their political leaders, were united in viewing Democrats as their opponents. And with good reason: the Democratic party consistently championed itself as the "white man's party," uninterested in the concerns of blacks. On more than one occasion the Democrats advised blacks to stay out of politics entirely if they wanted to cultivate the good will of whites. Perhaps more significantly, however, the Democrats very well knew the value of crying "Negro Domination" whenever the Republicans made overtures to attract white independent voters. As an anonymous Democrat said in the 1890s: "Why all we have got to do is to raise the cry of nigger, that

Attorney Albert S. White (left) lived at 2706 W. Walnut Street in Louisville.

University of Louisville Archives and Records Center

takes every time, and we can make even the Populists believe that story, and that means a gain of 25,000 votes for the state ticket."[85]

Indeed, whenever they felt threatened, Democrats informed white voters that a Republican victory would lead to black domination and integration. During the mid-1890s when the Republican party made its most serious attempt for the governor's Mansion, the *Courier-Journal* gladly pointed out to its readers how the Republicans were catering to blacks. But an even sharper attack came from a white newspaper in Lebanon. In an article entitled "The Spoils," the reporter noted: "A fact has leaked out . . . that will be a disagreeable surprise to many people who are supporting Col. Bradley for Governor." According to the reporter, if victorious, the Republicans had promised to divide equally with blacks all appointments of clerks and other positions in state government. William Ward, a Louisville black politician, would be named warden of a state prison, and Ed Lane, described as a "shrewd Frankfort negro," would be chief clerk in the auditor's office. In return, blacks had agreed not to push for black candidates on the ticket. The plan depended on keeping it a secret from the public, "upon 'keeping it dark.' Indeed, it is a dark subject." Furthermore, "The scheme has been working smoothly up to this time, and the white Republicans have been pointing with pride to the fact that they had no negro on the ticket. . . . Unfortunately, however, it looked like such a good thing that the negroes could not keep from talking."[86]

At the turn of the century, Democratic leaders strongly called upon whites to vote for them and to take measures to prevent blacks from using fraud to help the Republicans win. On two occasions in Louisville, in 1901 and 1909, the Democrats were victorious in close campaigns by convincing voters of impending doom if the Republicans won. In the early 1900s Lexington women were allowed to vote in school elections. When black women allegedly came out in larger numbers than whites, the Democrats responded by disfranchising all women to prevent black women from voting. Laura Clay, the state's leading suffragist, called for state instead of national legislation giving women the right to vote. Clay reasoned that southern states could enact safeguards giving the vote to white women while keeping black women disfranchised. By 1910 the Democratic party of Lexington and Fayette County, claiming to be working for the good of the entire community, began publishing the names of registered voters "as a matter of popular interest and information," and to help "detect the wholesale fraudulent registration." Party officials openly encouraged white citizens to scrutinize closely the names, "especially in their own precincts and neighborhoods" for "any doubtful names there, or note the absence of voters who ought to be registered on the special registration days." Democratic officials said that for the good of all involved, white citizens should look closely at the "City Precincts Having Heaviest Colored Republican Vote."[87]

The Fayette County Democratic Campaign Committee of 1911 produced a pamphlet that was surprisingly frank in denouncing black involvement in politics. Lexington blacks paid practically no taxes, Democratic officials argued, and thus relied totally on white support for their public schools. "And thus it is that while the white citizen pays a tribute of 98 per cent and gives the colored citizen every right and privilege he receives himself—protection of life and property, light, streets, schools, police and fire protection, etc., the colored citizen of Lexington is still not satisfied, but like the conquering Romans, hold it as their prerogative to govern and lord it over us besides." The second part of a pamphlet reprinted a letter to the newspaper from an irate white citizen, C.E. Merrill, which contained a direct call for violence to prevent blacks from voting and taking over the local government. In reality, Lexington blacks lacked the numbers to dominate whites politically, but this pamphlet, like many other acts of the Democrats, was obviously an effective tool to get out the white vote and ensure their party's victory.[88]

Lexington Democrats were far from alone in making racist appeals to white voters. An editorial in a white Hopkinsville newspaper in 1911 stated: "The last time the Republicans appointed a police force in Hopkinsville it had a negro on it. Are we ready for a second experience of that kind? Democrats stick to your own party and take no chances on having the prosperity of Hopkinsville given a backseat by Republican rule." Almost a decade later, the Democratic leader of Mayfield urged all white women to register and vote the party ticket in November. "The negro women will be there bright and early and late and the Kentucky white women should have enough patriotism and love for their glorious nation to let nothing keep them away from the polls. This is a time when it will be decided who shall name the president of the United States, the negro men and women or the white men and women." In the governor's race of 1923, Democratic candidate William J. Fields warned the voters that unless his party was elected, the state was in danger of black domination which would result in having social equality forced upon all whites by the Republicans and Negroes. He cited the recent hiring of Afro-Americans as policemen and firemen in Louisville as a move toward social equality. During the same campaign season, another Democratic candidate pleaded with "white women to go to the polls and vote to offset the votes of the 'nigger wenches' throughout the state and prevent social equality." Though avoiding such abusive language, Mrs. Herbert Ottenheim, president of the Kentucky League of Women Voters, strongly urged the white women of Kentucky to vote. The Ku Klux Klan applauded the call for white supremacy by Fields and the "better class" of Kentucky women. As one scholar of Kentucky politics has noted, the Klan claimed credit for his victory in the governor's race, and "three fiery crosses burned on the hills above Frankfort the night of Fields's inauguration."[89]

With the Democrats remaining totally unresponsive and the Republicans often adopting similar tactics, Afro-Americans felt the need to run candidates of their own race for political office. Blacks in several western Kentucky communities, where the race comprised as much as a third of the population, often stood a better chance of being elected than in Lexington or Louisville, the two places with the highest numbers of Afro-Americans. Starting in the 1880s, black Louisvillians campaigned for the state legislature, the city council, and the local school board. Repeatedly, the Republican party cautioned that the time was not ripe for them to be elected to office, that their candidacy would strengthen the hand of racist Democrats. Tired of the excuses of the Republican party for not endorsing black candidates, a group of young black leaders formed an independent party in 1921. They lost overwhelmingly at the polls, due in no small measure to the opposition of established black leaders. The threat of a black independent party did lead Republican officials to hire blacks as policemen and firemen and to increase the number of patronage jobs for the race, but the party still refused to support black candidates. On several occasions Lexington blacks campaigned for citywide positions, but they too were unsuccessful. As had happened in Louisville, the candidacy of a black tended to divide Lexington's black leaders.[90]

In all likelihood, the first election of blacks to office occurred in Hopkinsville and Christian County in November 1897. Surprisingly, instead of denouncing their election as the start of black domination, the Democratic newspaper simply stated that "The colored wing of the Republicans got three official positions in the distribution of the pie." They were Edward W. Glass, elected to the city council of Hopkinsville, James L. Allensworth, county coroner, and John W. Knight, constable in the North Hopkinsville district. All three took their positions without any protest. Of the three, Edward Glass served longest, remaining on the city council for the next twelve years. Glass's efforts led to a number of blacks' holding patronage jobs in city government. In the 1920s Walter Robinson, "a brilliant young lawyer," campaigned successfully for the city council in Hopkinsville. His election, just like that of Glass and the others, caused no uproar in the city. The Louisville *Leader* cited the election of Robinson to prove that Afro-Americans in Hopkinsville were far more aggressive than Louisville blacks in demanding changes in the political arena. Robinson remained in office for at least a decade.[91]

Afro-Americans also served on the city councils in several other cities in the early 1900s. Though details are sketchy, Shelbyville had a councilman by the name of Baxter for many years. During the decade of the 1910s, Mount Sterling had not one but two blacks on the city council. According to the Louisville *Leader*, James L. Donegy was a member of the city council in Danville for twelve years, beginning in the 1920s. Two blacks, W.R. Dudley and Edward Alexander, were candidates for the city council of Georgetown in 1929. In the Republican primary both men received the overwhelming support of the black community, with Dudley getting 129 votes, Alexander 126, and the closest white candidate only thirty-nine votes. Both lost in the general election, along with the entire Republican slate. That data is scarce on the political campaigns of most of these men suggests that racial tensions and the threat of violence did not occur on every occasion in which blacks campaigned for elective offices in Kentucky communities.[92]

However, in the city of Winchester the election of a black to the city council greatly upset the white community. In November 1913 Horace Colerane, a minister and plasterer, was elected to the city council from the predominantly black fourth ward by a majority of 193 votes. From the beginning the Winchester *Sun* speculated over whether Colerane would actually take his seat on the city council. Several years earlier a black had been elected to the council, but because of his failure to meet the two-thousand-dollar property qualification (which was obviously a good way to keep blacks and poor whites from office), he was not allowed to take his seat. "It is believed if Colerane attempts to take his seat it will be made very unpleasant for him by other members of the Council," the newspaper speculated.[93]

The new city council was to be sworn in on Friday, December 5. All week long Colerane was approached by prominent whites who urged him to step down. That Monday, however, he met with the city's notary public and gave proof of meeting the property qualification. Moreover, all of his public statements suggested that he would take his position. Behind the scenes he met with the other councilmen and presented a proposal, asking that he serve at the December and January meetings, and if any opposition remained thereafter, he would then resign. This won little support as seven of the nine councilmen signed a petition calling for his removal from office. The headlines of the Saturday edition of the *Sun* told the story: "Colerane Resigns Seat." As the paper explained: "One of the tensest situations in the municipal affairs of Winchester . . . was brought to an amicable close at the first meeting of the city council when Colerane resigned his seat without ever making his appearance in the Council chamber." In his written statement, Colerane resigned because of the agitation growing out of his election, and in "the interest of the peace and prosperity of the city." His suggestion of James N. Hisle to fill his seat was approved. A measure of how the white councilmen of Winchester felt about blacks can be gleaned from Colerane's lone friend on the council, Dr. M.S. Browne, who said that the entire matter had convinced him that "negro suffrage is a crime on civilization," and that he was now in favor of a limited suffrage.[94]

Several newspapers condemned the whites of Winchester for hounding Colerane from office. An editorial in the *Courier-Journal* said in part, "It seems rather a pity—and a reflection upon the majority—that a view so narrow was taken by the members of the Winchester Council." Though correct, this was a very self-serving statement from a newspaper that consistently called for blacks' remaining out of politics in Louisville. In a story entitled "Another Cringing Coward," editor W.E.B. DuBois of the *Crisis*, the journal of the NAACP, recounted the entire episode to his readers. From the safety of his New York office, DuBois berated Colerane for resigning and not fighting for his seat on the city council and harshly concluded: "So the colored gentleman resigned and named a white Democrat in his place, whom he describes as the 'Honorable James N. Hiles [sic].' No wonder our race is still in slavery."[95]

To an outsider like DuBois, the deplorable situation in Winchester probably became his gauge to judge race relations in Kentucky. Yet, by contrast, in several other cities blacks held positions on city councils and were beginning to receive political patronage. Also, first in Louisville, then later in other cities, blacks began to see the value of proclaiming themselves as independents in politics. Though the Democrats remained aloof, the Republicans continued to realize the solid base of support blacks gave them and listened to their concerns. There were, in other words, a few changes in politics by the 1920s that gave blacks reason to be optimistic.

Yet, when assessing race relations overall, it is highly debatable just how many positive changes had occurred in the state by the 1920s. Jim Crow and racial discrimination were widespread. For many Kentucky blacks the very best they could hope for would be a segregated hospital or YMCA, for the reality often meant total exclusion from white institutions. On the surface it seemed as if racial violence had been sharply curtailed in the state. Indeed, compared with earlier decades, the number of lynchings in the 1920s and 1930s had dropped considerably from earlier decades. Yet the number remained high. It is possible that the state had replaced the mob in carrying out the maximum punishment to blacks. On far too many occasions—one instance would have been too many—Kentucky blacks were sentenced to death in court proceedings that in no way resembled fairness.

A very positive sign for the overall struggle of Kentucky blacks was their consistent challenge of the racial status quo from 1890 forward. The anti-separate coach movement was only one of numerous organized efforts fighting to end discriminatory practices. Kentucky blacks came away from their battles with a sense that changes could occur, though they surely knew that ending discrimination would require a united effort, funds for litigation, and the support of white allies, usually in the political arena. Among their activities designed to end legal discrimination and lynchings, Kentucky's black leaders began forming NAACP branches during the 1910s and that organization ultimately played a leading role in the struggle for change in Kentucky.

Three

An Education: Providing the "Proper Kind of Training" for Blacks

IN his annual message to the general assembly in January 1898, Governor William O. Bradley deplored the quality of the public schools provided for the state's Afro-American citizens. Kentucky had made strides in creating a good system of graded schools for whites, he explained, but the black schools had been seriously neglected. Also, in spite of a law requiring the equal distribution of school funds, the money allocated for black schools was far from equitable; because, in practically every county within the state, the only funds being used to support their public schools were raised from the taxes paid by blacks themselves. Bradley quickly assured the legislators that he agreed that the races must remain in separate schools, "but equal privileges should be given the unfortunate people, who stand in such great need of educational facilities."[1]

Few Kentuckians could dispute the governor's assessment of black education. The schools provided for Afro-Americans were vastly inferior to those for whites in a state where the white schools were grossly underfinanced and ranked at the bottom when compared with white schools throughout the nation, even in the South. None of the black elementary schools and, even worse, none of the few black high schools had libraries but rather relied primarily on concerned teachers and citizens donating a few books to be used as reference materials. From Ashland to Paducah, schools for blacks were housed in old, dilapidated buildings that had outlived their original purposes. Prior to the 1930s in most Kentucky cities a high school education for Afro-Americans consisted of completing one or, at most, two years beyond the eighth grade, not the four years offered to white students. During these years normal schools were very important for the training of teachers, and most cities had created one of these institutions for whites. Meanwhile, Louisville had the only public normal school for blacks. Thomas Jesse Jones, who conducted a massive survey of black education for the federal government, could very easily have had the plight of Kentucky blacks in mind when he concluded that "Negro schools in the aggregate undoubtedly form the most impoverished group of educational institutions in the United States."[2]

The vast majority of Kentucky whites viewed black education as a burden, spending only the minimum required by law, if in fact that small amount. They most surely agreed with southern whites that an education for blacks should result in their being more useful to the dominant group. Above all, schooling should not equip blacks with the ideology or confidence to challenge the racial status quo. In a provocative study of black education in the South, James D. Anderson explains that southern educators and a number of highly influential northern philanthropists devoted their efforts and resources to developing the "right education," a system of training whereby blacks accepted their second-class status and willingly worked the menial jobs assigned them in southern society. That these whites failed to convince Afro-Americans of the importance of such an education is a credit to blacks who viewed an education as leading to full equality rather than making them content with the status quo. White educators in Kentucky applauded the efforts of their counterparts in the Deep South and agreed that the end product of black education should be the acceptance by Afro-Americans of "their place" in southern society. As superintendent of public instruction, George Colvin explained to Robert W. Bingham, owner of the *Courier-Journal*, it was essential for the state's black citizens to be educated in the South, not the North, because education in the North tended to give them false ideas about their importance and make them discontent with their menial jobs in the South.[3]

That Kentucky's public schools for blacks were grossly inadequate and poorly funded violated the law, for on April 4, 1882, the federal circuit court had handed down a most significant ruling regarding black education. In the case of *Commonwealth of Kentucky* v. *Jesse Ellis* the court ruled that "any fund created by the state for educational purposes must be equally and uniformly distributed among both classes, and neither in the raising of the fund by taxation, nor in the distribution of it, must there by any inequality or any discrimination on account of race or color." The ruling gave Kentuckians a choice: to integrate white and black pupils or to equalize the funds for black and white schools. The latter option was adopted—black schools would be funded on the same per capita ratio as white schools and would not be dependent on the taxation of the poorer blacks only. A year later, Judge John Barr of the United States District Court, who would read the court's ruling a decade later in the black suit against Jim Crow railroads, affirmed the law in the case of Edward Claybrook against the city of Owensboro for an equal share in the common school fund. Barr ruled that blacks must have equal privileges. He granted an injunction against the treasurer of Owensboro to prevent his paying out to the black schools only that portion of the school fund that had been paid by Afro-Americans.[4]

Despite these positive rulings, equal funding for black schools never became a reality under Kentucky's dual school system. In city after city white voters approved bonds to raise additional taxes for the white schools only. Blacks were prohibited from voting on these measures. When challenged in court, the bond issues for white schools were upheld on the grounds that whites had contributed to the Negro schools and at the same time incurred additional taxes for the benefit of white schools.[5] In most instances, however, whites simply refused to reach into their pockets for more money for public education and therefore failed to allocate an equal share for blacks. To justify their discrimination, whites often said that given the few blacks in their particular area, the cost of providing schools for them was beyond the financial resources of the county. When commenting on the laws mandating equal funding for black and white schools, an "Observer" in a black newspaper noted that "These equal school laws are a blind to most people when they come to observe their application to the situation," because in many districts with well-organized schools for whites there were none for black children, "although there are plenty of colored children of school age." Further, he explained that school trustees were often unconcerned about black schools, leaving it to blacks themselves to finance the construction of a school with private funds. "Trustees tell them if you get a house put up we will get you school money for two or three months."[6] Without question, under "separate but equal" as practiced in Kentucky, black schools, even in areas of large concentration of Afro-Americans, were greatly inferior to those being provided for whites. Louisville's black schools were located in old structures, usually buildings that whites had abandoned. These "schools" had no libraries or gymnasiums and often no playgrounds. Black educators and civic leaders complained for years about the deplorable building that housed Central High, while the white high schools—Male, Manual, and Female—all enjoyed modern facilities. Unfortunately, this was Louisville, which boasted of providing the best schools in the state for Afro-Americans.[7]

The law calling for equalization of school funds was consistently violated to provide far more funding for white schools. In 1925 the Commission on Interracial Cooperation conducted an investigation of Kentucky's black public schools with the goal of "securing local leaders[,] white and colored[,] to test these abuses [in the distribution of educational funds] in courts and secure the repeal of an amendment to laws creating this situation." The report, written by James Bond, emphasized that steps needed to be adopted immediately to ensure equality of education in Kentucky. The problem, the commission's report thoroughly explained, was simple—though blacks received a pro rata share of state taxes "many racial discriminations . . . have crept into our educational system; that there are some ten cities of the fourth class where by the act of the City Council, property of white people is taxed for white schools and property of colored people is taxed for colored schools. . . . That there are 250 independent graded districts in cities smaller than the fourth class where local school tax is levied upon whites to the exclusion of the Negroes and for the benefit of the whites to the exclusion of the Negroes."[8] Despite the thoroughness of the commission's report, nothing was done to halt the inequality in the funds' being appropriated for Kentucky's black and white public schools.

The discrimination in the dispersal of school funds, coupled with the refusal of some communities to provide any schools for blacks, and a host of other factors, resulted in a high rate of black illiteracy. In 1890 fully 56 percent of the state's

197,689 black citizens were illiterate. This declined over the years: 40.1 percent in 1900, 21.0 percent in 1920, and 15.4 percent in 1930. By comparison, the white rate of illiteracy was 16.1 percent in 1890, decreasing to 5.7 percent in 1930. Of fifteen southern and border states in 1900, Kentucky's black illiterate percentage of 40.1 percent ranked sixth best. This undoubtedly was little consolation to concerned educators and citizens within the state. Though the rate of black illiteracy dropped steadily between 1900 and 1930, there remained several counties where 25 percent or more of the black residents were illiterate: Hart, 26.3 percent; Washington, 26.8 percent; Henry, 26.9 percent; Jessamine, 28.2 percent; Marion, 29.2 percent; and Simpson, 29.3 percent. Most of these counties had very small black populations and provided next to no education for Afro-Americans. On the other hand, by 1930 Lexington's black illiteracy rate of 13.1 percent and Louisville's 9.8 percent were below average for the state.[9]

At the turn of the century eight counties (Campbell, Elliott, Jackson, Johnson, Letcher, Martin, Menifee, and Morgan) had no schools for blacks nor arrangements with other counties to provide an education for them. To be sure, Johnson and Elliott counties had only a handful of blacks, but Campbell and some of the other counties had five hundred or more Afro-American residents. Still other counties, while providing schools for blacks, had a much shorter school year for them than for whites. Also, given the overall poverty of the race, many families needed their children to work, especially in rural areas where harvesting the crops often determined the length of the school year. Regardless, no more than one-third of Kentucky's Afro-American students attended school six months a year and one-fifth attended less than three months, with most falling somewhere between.[10]

Two decades later most of Kentucky's school districts maintained the discriminatory practice of providing a much shorter school year for Afro-American students. In December 1923 Mrs. Emma Boyd of Reed (Henderson County) expressed to the NAACP her frustrations over the local board of education's policy of closing the black schools before the academic year had ended for whites. Though Mrs. Boyd's letter might have been poorly written, the sincerity of her message and the unjust manner in which blacks were being treated came through clearly: "Supt. N. O. Kimbler . . . has ordered the J. Boyd Colored School closed after teaching three and one half months and the teacher has a contract for seven months. We are paying taxes on nearly nine hundred acres of land, have bought books and clothes for 19 children [and] now they must grow up in ignorance. The Patrons are compelled to pay hundreds of dollars in school taxes. If these children get to school any more they must go down in their pockets. Just think of it three and one half months[,] such was never done before in the State of Kentucky. He has closed another colored school [in] Scuffletown. The teacher is still teaching although the Supt. has told her she would not get any money. We have appealed to the State Board of Education at Frankfort, Ky. for justice. We need help Dr. DuBois." Louisville and Lexington proved to be the exceptions in having schools for blacks that remained in operation for more than six months a year.[11]

The rate of illiteracy and the much shorter school year were not the only indicators that Kentucky's dual school system greatly shortchanged blacks. The annual reports submitted by county school superintendents to state officials further illustrate the extent of racial discrimination. On occasion the superintendents, instead of acknowledging that black schools existed without anything approaching adequate funding, resorted to making comments about how blacks as a race did not appreciate the importance of selecting highly qualified teachers. These comments are not a true indication of how blacks felt about education but stand as a strong indictment of the lack of concern of whites who considered themselves to be enlightened educators. The report from Barren County in 1891 explained: "The schools in the colored districts are in a deplorable condition financially—most of the schools being taught in colored churches; not one district in three owning a school house. A great many of the Trustees being unable to read and write, of course, could not judge the qualifications of the teacher employed. . . . Several districts are entirely too large for the children to be taught by one teacher. I visited all the colored schools and lectured to them, and I hope, by continuing to do so, lead them to see the importance of an education." That same year the superintendent from Boone County complained about black schools meeting in churches: "The colored districts are very large in area, owing to the assembling of the negroes in and around the villages. Without exception, the buildings used as schoolhouses serve for church purposes, and, in some instances, the members of the church endeavor to exercise an undue influence in school matters. I have tried to eradicate sectarianism, with what result I am unable to say." The report from the superintendent of the Gallatin County schools clearly showed that blacks did without adequate school facilities: "The colored schools are doing good work, considering the disadvantages under which they are compelled to labor. There is but one district in the county that has a house, and it is in very poor condition."[12] Finally, the comment made in 1901 by the superintendent of Caldwell County showed that discrimination in allocating funds to black schools still existed in Kentucky: "I find it impossible to devise plans for the colored people to build. They are too poor to build by taxation."[13]

A number of superintendents complained that many black schools met in churches; they were especially harsh in condemning the involvement in school affairs of black ministers in whose churches the schools were meeting. Without question, the "meddling" of a powerful local preacher could hinder the work being attempted by the teachers, but when criticizing the black schools for meeting in the churches, the superintendents were adopting the policy of "blaming the victim" for discrimination. This obscured the real issue of inadequate funding; in fact, Afro-Americans in many of Kentucky's small communities were fortunate that the churches had willingly opened their doors to the schools; for, without the cooperation of these churches, schools for blacks could not have existed at all since no other buildings were available for that purpose.

Blacks throughout Kentucky experienced the same frustrations as those in Muhlenberg County when it came to the establishment of public schools. It was not until the early 1900s that small schools which met in churches opened in several places in the county. From the beginning blacks living in the more remote parts of the county were required to furnish their own transportation to the larger "cities" within the county to attend schools. When engaged in this early form of school "busing" (or to be completely accurate, riding a horse), Muhlenberg's black residents passed a number of white schools along the way to the black schools. By 1908 there were eleven black schools in Muhlenberg County, with the smallest school having only fifteen students while the largest had one hundred students. A countywide high school for blacks opened in Central City in 1920, many years after a high school had been established for whites.[14]

School officials in Muhlenberg County were far from alone in dragging their heels when it came to opening schools for Afro-Americans. Public schools for whites began in Owensboro in 1871. Though urging school officials to open a school for them at the same time, blacks remained frustrated for an additional thirteen years. Then, when the black school was finally ready to open, it mysteriously burned to the ground the evening prior to the first day of classes. As a result, school started in the African Methodist Church. Initially, all of the teachers hired for black schools in Owensboro were black. Though the reasons are unclear, before the start of the second school year, the board hired whites to teach in the black schools. The board's decision to dismiss the black teachers led to a bitter debate in which some black leaders endorsed the change while others demanded the return of black teachers. Finally, in 1896 after nine years of using whites as teachers, the school board relented and hired blacks once again to teach at the Afro-American school. The superintendent explained: "I am satisfied that the change from the employment of white teachers to that of colored teachers in the colored schools, while at the time viewed with some well founded distrust, was a wise step, and if the same care be taken in the employment of colored teachers as has characterized the appointments so far, this wisdom will more and more show itself. While the white teachers we had employed in the colored schools were of excellent ability and training, and did their work with rare conscientiousness, yet I am free to say that the improvement along all lines, and in all departments of the colored schools is plainly manifest."[15]

Clearly, the "foot-dragging" of white school boards was most evident when it came to establishing separate and equal high schools for Afro-Americans. Except for the Louisville Negro high school which opened in 1874, no high school existed for black Kentuckians for more than a decade after the start of their elementary schools. By the 1890s public high schools for Afro-Americans were in operation in Covington, Frankfort, Lexington, Owensboro, Paducah, Paris, and Winchester. During this time, however, no high schools for blacks existed in either Henderson or Hopkinsville, both cities having sizeable black populations—surely sufficient numbers to justify the establishment of a high school—and active black leaders. Once in operation, the course of study offered black high school students tended to differ from the instruction available to whites. At white high schools, especially in the state's leading cities, students had the opportunity to study a wide range of courses, from those that provided preparatory training for college to courses geared toward vocations as skilled workers. Louisville, of course, went further along these lines with its three distinct white high schools: Male for those interested in attending college, Manual for industrial skills, and Female to prepare elite white women for traditional roles as homemakers and mothers, and working-class women for employment. By contrast, the city's Afro-American high school, Central Colored, offered basic courses in grammar, mathematics, history, and usually Latin. For decades blacks complained in vain that under separate but equal the city was required to establish a separate high school for black females based on the one provided for white females. Furthermore, Central Colored High School placed a strong emphasis on industrial skills; but, the skills blacks learned at Central differed dramatically from the ones whites learned at Manual High. The black school tended to prepare students for positions as servants and common laborers, while whites took courses in engineering.[16]

Without question, the decades after the Civil War were a time when influential whites advocated a different form of education for blacks, training that would make them "useful" in white society. As a leading scholar in Afro-American history explains, white businessmen desired a trained labor force, especially for jobs in the industries they hoped would be attracted to the South, and they were convinced that only through industrial education—a practical form of education—would Afro-Americans acquire these needed skills. Given such an attitude toward blacks and their "place" in society, white leaders felt comfortable in working with William J. Simmons and Charles H. Parrish, two Louisville black leaders who advocated industrial training based on the successful model of Booker T. Washington at Tuskegee Institute. That Simmons became a staunch advocate of industrial training is somewhat surprising; though born a slave in Charleston, South Carolina, he became one of the best-educated members of his race, acquiring degrees from Howard University and the Theological School of Madison University. In 1880 he was named the first president of Kentucky Normal and Theological Institute, a school which took pride in its collegiate program. Yet, while serving as president of a school that offered law and medical degrees, Simmons consistently wrote and lectured on the value of industrial education for Afro-Americans. Though blacks could gain from classical learning, he forcefully argued, true equality for them would occur only through hard work that made them useful in white society. Simmons extolled the virtures of their learning carpentry, blacksmithing, tailoring, cooking, and domestic services. These views led logically to Simmons's resigning from Kentucky Normal in 1890 and forming his own college, Eckstein Norton Institute. The funding for the school came entirely from white benefactors who agreed fully with Simmons that the school would stress practical education for Afro-Americans: "The object of this School is Industrial education for the colored youth. It teaches the dignity of labor, believing that industrial training is the trip hammer which will make many an opening to our people. The motto is 'The Heart, head and hand we educate.'" Without question, though the school's motto spoke of a total education for Afro-Americans, educating the hands—to the exclusion of training the mind—was to be emphasized at Norton Institute.[17]

Within weeks after Norton Institute opened, Simmons died of a heart attack and control of the school passed to his longtime friend, Charles H. Parrish. Like Simmons, Parrish had been born a slave. Also, Parrish, though a college graduate, had cultivated white friendships with his emphasis on the importance of industrial training for blacks. During the twenty-one years he headed Norton Institute, Parrish made numerous speeches on the value of industrial education, and on one occasion he published a detailed article on the subject in the *AME Zion Church Quarterly*. Parrish stated his theme clearly—industrial education was "an indispensable factor in the development of the Afro-American youth of this country." Far more than any other form of training, an industrial education "trains all of the faculties with which the Divine creator has endowed mankind, and prevents what might otherwise result in a one-sided development." In words that sounded similar to those of his mentor, Parrish dismissed a college education as being impractical for blacks while, by contrast, "Industrial education reduces the abstract theories of the school room to practical realities, and shows the actual and intimate relationship existing between book lore and the actualities of real life." All men cannot hope to be orators, statesmen, philosophers, poets, and men of letters, Parrish informed his readers. Classical learning would, therefore, cause many people to be dissatisfied with their vocations, while industrial training would ensure that every person was placed in "his own particular sphere, and each one in his sphere can accomplish the most good for the benefit of the whole." Parrish saved what he thought to be his most convincing point in favor of industrial education for the conclusion: "But the last, and to my mind the most important reason is the dignity that it imparts to labor. There must be something radically wrong about an education that defeats the very object for which it was designed; an education that causes a boy to vainly imagine that it is much more honorable to add figures in a musty back office at the munificent compensation of 'Three Dollars' a week than to lay bricks in God's open sunshine at 'Three Dollars' a day."[18]

Like Simmons and Parrish, school principal Green P. Russell was well aware of the willingness of whites to fund the "right kind" of education for blacks when he called for the start of manual training in Lexington's black high school in 1900. By this time a number of Louisville's black leaders complained that at Central High their youths devoted far too much time to industrial courses. Yet Russell, ever the astute politician, argued that the manual training popularized by Booker T. Washington instructed idle black children in how to work, thereby helping resolve many of the pressing problems of the black community. His proposal caught the attention of newspaper editor W.C.P. Breckinridge, who immediately proclaimed that, regardless of race, industrial training would benefit most of the youths living in Lexington. Breckinridge conceded that "Equity and expediency would decree, however, that the manual training school be first provided for the colored children of Lexington; for to them training in the combined use of head and hands is by circumstances made more obligatory." The editor had recently visited Hampton Institute, the Virginia school that Booker T. Washington had attended and had used as a model for Tuskegee Institute, and was impressed with the school's program for preparing black youths to be productive workers. Breckinridge noted: "I came away from the institution with a bundle of catalogues with a fixed intention of sending one other small Kentucky pickaninny in whom I took a special interest to that institution, if possible, and with a longing desire that such training—moral and manual—might be provided for the colored youth of my own state and town." Several days later a second editorial appeared calling again for industrial education for blacks. Breckinridge acknowledged that since the Civil War a small group of blacks had worked, saved, and progressed. Meanwhile, an even greater number had retrogressed, largely because they missed the contact with whites that they had enjoyed and benefitted from during slavery. These two editorials show clearly that in the minds of white Kentuckians, manual training would reeducate blacks in the important skills and customs they had acquired under slavery but had lost since freedom. The Lexington Board of Education endorsed Russell's proposal and introduced industrial courses into the black schools.[19]

While the merits of manual training were being debated for blacks, whites clearly realized the value of establishing high schools for all of the white youths of Kentucky. In 1908 the Kentucky General Assembly passed a law requiring each county to establish a public high school. Under the law a county school board could enter into a contract with a city to provide high school education for rural students in areas where the number of students were too few to justify operating a high school. This act had an immediate impact on white education, resulting in the opening of high schools in many rural areas for the first time. The County School Law of 1908 did not mention high schools for blacks, an omission which, during the heyday of racial discrimination, was an indication that the legislators were allowing school districts to ignore creating a black high school in every county. Indeed, that lawmakers failed to comment specifically on black high schools was surely not an accident. Most local school boards continued to be unconcerned about providing high schools for blacks even though under the concept of separate but equal blacks obviously were entitled to a high school education. In 1905 there were seven black high schools in the entire state—no more than had existed in the

1890s. By 1913, after the new law had been in effect for five years, the number had increased by one, and three years later another black high school had been established.[20]

Furthermore, despite the new law, blacks often constructed their schools without the support of school officials and local taxes. James D. Anderson calls this phenomenon a "double taxation," whereby Afro-Americans, after paying their fair share of taxes just like whites, raised additional funds, purchased or donated land, bought the building materials, and provided the labor for the construction of schools in their communities. In the early 1900s a group of blacks in Henderson called for the start of a high school. The school board finally relented in 1905 and appropriated funds for the hiring of several teachers for the black high school (which was named in honor of the black abolitionist Frederick Douglass) but refused to pay for the construction of the building. Classes at Douglass High then started in the same building that housed the black elementary school. After raising funds for several years, a group of black leaders purchased a lot and began building a separate facility for Douglass High. At this point the Henderson Board of Education allocated funds to complete the project. As long as Kentucky operated under the guise of separate but equal education, blacks in many other communities were compelled, just like the group from Henderson, to erect schools for their children or do without them. Professor Anderson's final comments on the system of double taxation reveal clearly that whites refused to allocate equal funding for black education:

> Although we shall never know the precise amount in cash, land, and labor contributed by black southerners to public school authorities, a vast quantity of primary sources indicates that the double taxation of black southerners was [a] widespread and long-standing custom. We see a certain fineness or heroism in the sacrifices made by such poor and ordinary men and women. . . . Yet the traditions of double taxation and extraordinary sacrifice had distinct limits, beyond which they were both unjust and dangerous. One limit was the point at which 'self-help' became unconscious submission to oppression. In vital respects, the re-

gionwide process of double taxation was an accommodation to the oppressive nature of southern society. It made the regular process of excluding black children from the benefits of tax-supported public education easier and more bearable for both whites and blacks.[21]

Thomas Jesse Jones made a number of comments about Kentucky's nine black public high schools in his 1916 nationwide study of Negro education. Though claiming to be high schools, in reality, only six of the nine provided four years of study beyond the eighth grade. Moreover, practically all of them, Jones noted, stressed industrial training to the exclusion of other subjects. His report, nevertheless, highlighted a number of positive accomplishments in at least three of the high schools. Investigators were favorably impressed with the high school in Frankfort, with its instruction in Latin, English, and mathematics, and with its physical plant. Overall, the program at Lexington was judged to be good, though "the courses in science and history need strengthening." According to the report, Louisville's black high school, unlike other black schools in the state, had a sufficient number of highly trained teachers. Indeed, the Jones report and practically all other observers concluded that Central High School ranked with the best high schools for Afro-Americans in the nation.[22]

Even though the report's comments about Central High were highly favorable, they must be viewed with caution. The white observers compared Central not with white public high schools but to black schools, which as the report repeatedly emphasized, were rated at best as only "fair" institutions. Unquestionably, because the school had a large pool of trained black professionals to choose from, Central High had outstanding, well-qualified teachers, something lacking in many smaller areas in Kentucky. Yet, Central High, which existed for decades in an old, deplorable building, did without the facilities and equipment considered necessary in white schools. In short, Central High School was a good "Negro school," but it could not be compared favorably with Male or Manual High Schools, which, like Central, were located in Louisville and relied on public funding.

With only nine black public high schools in operation by

Louisville Central High School Band.
Canfield & Shook Collection, University of Louisville Photographic Archives

the mid-1910s, the vast majority of Kentucky's black citizens either ended their schooling at the completion of the eighth grade or looked to other institutions to provide them with high school courses. All over the state Afro-Americans attended small private high schools run by religious denominations. In a real sense this also amounted to a system of double taxation. Atkinson Literary and Industrial College, founded by the African Methodist Episcopal Zion Church in Madisonville, Bowling

Green Academy, owned by the Kentucky Branch of the Colored Cumberland Presbyterian Church, and Wayman Institute, supported by the African Methodist Episcopal Church in Harrodsburg, were three of the better-known religious schools.

Founded around 1890, Atkinson (which went by several names, all of which contained the word "college," though this was never more than a high school) operated for more than a decade. Its very existence was due to the donations and continued support of J.B. Atkinson, president of the St. Bernard Coal Company, who did this to appease his black workers. Throughout its history the number of students remained small, usually ranging from sixty to a hundred, who were taught by a principal and no more than two teachers. Like other institutions, Atkinson College adopted a motto: "Thoroughness in all the branches taught." The school said, "We promise as good accommodations as are furnished by older and more pretentious schools." Though calling itself a college, the school offered a preparatory department which covered the grammar school course, and a normal department for the training of teachers. After functioning for more than ten years, this "college" had yet to offer college courses: "The full College course will be provided when a sufficient number of students shall justify an increase in our present faculty."[23] Named in honor of Bishop A.W. Wayman, the state's AME school had several departments: college preparatory, English, theological, normal, music, and domestic economy. In all likelihood, the latter was the most developed.[24]

The quality of education received by black students at these institutions was extremely poor, and the reasons were obvious: the schools had virtually no financial resources, lacked trained teachers, and their physical plants were totally inadequate. Nevertheless, the existence of these schools for decades was not only remarkable but further demonstrated that because of the unwillingness of white officials to provide separate but equal facilities, Afro-Americans had few, if any, alternatives for attaining high school educations. In a more positive vein, the very existence of Atkinson Literary, Bowling Green Academy, and Wayman Institute proved that Kentucky blacks attempted to uplift themselves. Unfortunately, most of the private black high schools found throughout the state were below the already low standards of these three schools and existed as schools in name only. However, such was not the case of the private high school for blacks in Lexington. Founded by the American Missionary Association of the Congregational Church in 1889, Chandler Normal School provided high school courses for many of the city's black students even though the Lexington Board of Education had established an Afro-American high school. Unlike most private black schools, Chandler enjoyed solid financial backing. As a result, the school existed for four decades and offered a wide range of courses, all of which, according to one survey, were "well done."[25]

Well aware that most private and public Negro high schools were so inadequate that they failed to meet the educational needs of the race, black leaders consistently tried to persuade white school board officials to upgrade them. In 1915 a group of Lexington blacks, comprised of ministers, doctors, leading businessmen, and educators, wrote a polite, cautious letter to the school board, pleading for improvements in their schools and for the building of a new high school. In their call for education improvements, Afro-American leaders assured white officials that they were not asking for an equal share of the school funds, as mandated by state law, just an increase in the amount reserved for black education. They stated:

> We, the undersigned committee . . . come before you in the interest of the educational facilities of our youths. We come not demanding, but asking that you give our petition a fair consideration. We are mindful of the fact that the school buildings we now have are inadequate to accommodate the present number of children and the yearly increase as shown by the census.
>
> Being interested as we are and as we believe you are to reduce the illiteracy of the Commonwealth of Kentucky, we are forced to come before you asking that you give us ample buildings to accommodate our 5,247 children of school age. The three school buildings we now have are overcrowded with the enrollment of 1,713 children, and since 3,736 are out of school entirely, we are compelled to ask you to complete the Forest Hill school as first planned. Give us a new high school

Basketball teams, Winchester, Kentucky, 1921. Photographs by A.J. Earp. *University of Kentucky Special Collections*

building and convert the Russell School into a ward [elementary] school.

The school census of 1915 shows 5,342 white children of school age and 5,247 colored children of school age. The white children have six school buildings and now a bond issue of one hundred thousand dollars is asked to erect two more buildings. We feel that if it will require eight buildings to accommodate 5,342 white children, then we should have at least five buildings to accommodate 5,247 colored children. If the 3,730 colored children are to remain uneducated because of the lack of school buildings, why have the State made appropriation for them?

Gentlemen, we beg you in the name of fairness and justice to add fifty thousand dollars to the one hundred thousand or give us one-third of the one hundred thousand for our second school. We are not asking for an equal share with you, but only that you give us buildings sufficient to educate our children, and that will be satisfactory to us.

The Lexington Board of Education ruled favorably on the petition. This, of course, was far from an enlightened move on the part of Lexington whites but a realization that far more funds had been allocated and spent on constructing modern facilities for white students. As requested by the black leaders, Russell High was converted to a ward school in 1922 with the opening of the newly erected Paul Lawrence Dunbar High School.[26]

Compared with blacks elsewhere in the state, Lexington blacks were unique in having local school officials cooperate with them in the upgrading of black schools. Louisville blacks called for the building of a new physical plant for Central High School for more than three decades before one was finally constructed on the eve of school integration in the 1950s. Throughout the state, black elementary and high schools were confined to old, run-down buildings, with few facilities. A very revealing statement about black schools was made after a survey had been conducted of the white schools in Danville in 1927: "If the situation in the white schools is described as 'bad,' it is almost impossible to find words to describe the situation in the colored school. . . . Crowding . . . has of necessity been reduced to a science, with every inch of available space and a good many inches that are not or ought not to be available used for accommodation of pupils." Without question, the comments about the Danville black school accurately described many of the Afro-American schools found in every section of Kentucky.[27]

The lack of schools, especially beyond the eighth grade, has often been cited as a primary reason why many blacks left Kentucky. Lena Beatrice Morton, a native of Flat Creek, Bath County, traveled to Winchester for elementary school, since no school for blacks existed in Bath County. After Morton completed elementary school, her family moved to Ohio so she could attend an accredited high school. (It is obvious that the Morton family valued an education. Morton's mother had attended Berea College before the passing of the Day Law which ousted blacks from that institution.) Lena Morton eventually obtained the Ph.D. and taught for years in a black college in Texas. But the point is clear—she was compelled to leave her native state for educational opportunities. Undoubtedly, many more Afro-Americans took a similar course, choosing to leave Kentucky to pursue an education. Indeed, Wendell Dabney's study of blacks in Cincinnati contains biographical sketches of scores of Kentuckians who moved across the Ohio River to take advantage of the superior education offered blacks in the Buckeye State.[28]

James Bond's 1924 survey of public education clearly documented that Kentucky's dual school system shortchanged black students and teachers. As director of the Kentucky Commission on Interracial Cooperation, Bond worked in every region of the state for the passage of bond proposals to help finance new schools for blacks and encouraged school officials to increase the salaries for black school personnel. Despite his determined efforts, and those of a number of influential white CIC board members, very little progress was made in improving educational opportunities and facilities for Kentucky's Afro-American citizens. His report listed fifty-one public high schools for blacks, a tremendous increase in the last fifteen years. But upon close investigation, only eight were fully accredited, while "forty-three others are listed as approved but not rated as standard high schools. Most of these forty-three are two year high schools." The salaries paid black teachers and principals were pathetic, often no more than 50 percent of the salary paid whites in the same school district. For example, the average salary paid the principals in the forty-three unaccredited black high schools was less than $900 a year, a wage considerably below that of a white teacher, meaning that the salary of a black principal was a small fraction of what his white counterpart of equal educational training and experience received.[29]

A report produced by a group of white and black civic and political leaders in 1945, twenty years after Bond's investigation of black education, showed that very little had actually changed under the state's dual system of education. "A survey of Negro schools in Kentucky reveals that educational facilities for Negroes, particularly in the rural areas, is scandalously poor. There is a great need for new school buildings and equipment, higher standards of Negro teachers, and an educational program adaptable to present-day economic and social changes." A serious problem was the lack of adequate schools for what was then described as the "problem of sparse and scattered rural Negro population." Yet, after graphically discussing the adverse effect of the state's dual educational system, the solution endorsed by these state leaders was perhaps predictable, given the view of most Kentucky whites on the subject of school integration: "A long range program should seek to establish several boarding or consolidated high schools in centers near the homes of pupils as is practicable."[30] In other words, admitting the few black students into the schools for whites in these areas was not considered as a solution by these Kentucky leaders.

In addition to working for the start of public high schools, Kentucky's black leaders urged state officials to start a college for Afro-Americans. They pointed out that black illiteracy could not be wiped out until sufficient numbers of teachers had been trained to teach the people. Black leaders also appealed for separate but equal treatment for the race, pointing out that a state university in Lexington had been created for whites. The Rev. William J. Simmons, president of a black Baptist college in Louisville, Rev. Charles H. Parrish, one of Louisville's leading black ministers, and school principals John M. Maxwell and John H. Jackson were the leaders of this movement. Their agitation bore fruit; on May 18, 1886, an act established a college for blacks: "The leading object of this school shall be the preparation of teachers for teaching in the colored public schools of Kentucky."

The first permanent building on Kentucky State's campus, Jackson Hall, as it appeared in a 1910 photograph by Gretter.
Kentucky Historical Society

Frankfort, located between Louisville and Lexington, was selected as the site of the school. Named the State Normal School for Colored Persons (in 1902 the name was changed to Kentucky State Normal and Industrial Institute for Colored Persons), the school first opened in 1887, with fifty-five students, increasing to eighty-seven by the second year.[31] As part of the program held in honor of the founding of the school, William H. Perry, a school principal from Louisville, wrote the "Dedication Poem."[32]

Dedication Poem.

Majestic hills that guard our honor'd State,
Break now your silence, help us to rejoice;
Awake ye silent sentinels, find voice;
Ye need no longer, like the hoary seers,
Keep watchful eye upon the coming years,
For we are a mid for what the years may bring,

An Education / 125

Are strong for effort, therefore with us sing
Ye smiling planes, assist us in our praise;
Ye winged songsters, lend your charming lays;
Aye: let us all unite, with might and main
Make known the burden of our glad refrain
Today we gather here to dedicate,
In name of Progress, our, growing State,
This Normal School, wherein we consecrate
A safe guard that will bless with fruits of peace
 increase
Our homes and State as swift the years
Here shall the minds true growth be clearly
 shown;
Truth be portrayed and Error overthrown;
The principles of thought shall be explored

Make known the burden of our glad refrain
Today we gather here to dedicate
In name of Progress and our growing State,
This Normal School, wherein we consecrate
A safe guard that will bless with fruits of
 peace increase,
Our homes and State as swift the years
Here shall the minds true growth be clearly
 shown;
Truth be portrayed and Error overthrown;
The principles of thought shall be explored
The teachers art to its high realm restored.
They who within these walls, shall knowledge
 gain
How they should childhood's _____ scent
 powers train
Shall to our Commonwealth protection be
Greater for peace and for prosperity—
More true to her high hopes and aims, by far,
Than all the arts and implements of war.

O Then Eternal One whose boundless pow'r
Holds us in life, this priceless dower
To us by Thee in gracious love is sent;
And we to Thee our thankful hearts present.

The Nature's glory and the State's reowned,
That constant joy and happiness that crown
The peaceful homes of our great prosperous
   land,
Shall we endure, if thy indulgent hand—

Scattering peace and comfort every where,
Shielding from dangers that the years may
   bear
Shall give us in the paths that lead aright
And guard us with Thy all subduing might.

And we would learn of Thee; Thou art the
   cause
Of all our joys, and these Thy wondrous laws,
Deep written in Thy works, that here abound,
Proclaim Thy wisdom matchless and
   profound.

Where'er we look, where'er we turn we find
New evidence of Thy creative mind;
Throughout creation, whereso'ever we scan,
Proofs of Thy goodness both to beast and man,
All testify of Thee, our spirits yearn
To know Thee more; and in Thy works discern
Thy truths—from Thee this lesson gain,
How we may beings noblest heights attain.

O may Thy blessings in the school descend
Protect it ever-against ev'ry all defend;
And may the lessons her in gain'd and taught
With rich result, with highest good be fraught.

Kentucky State started with very modest aims and some very serious, inherent handicaps. To gain admission an applicant had to be sixteen years old, of good health and character. Though labeled a college, the institution was in reality a high school until the 1920s, with most of the students completing two years of high school courses. Since the mandate of the school was to train teachers (tuition was free to any student who pledged to teach in Kentucky), the normal department was the first course of study established at Kentucky State. A legislative act of May 22, 1893, organized agricultural, mechanical, and domestic departments. These programs were viewed as essential for the growth of Kentucky's black population. Farmers needed to be informed of better techniques, black laborers needed skills, and, of course, from the white point of view, there was always a pressing need for good black servants. By the early 1900s the curriculum had been expanded to offer a few of the social science courses found in most of the colleges of that day.[33]

The state legislature gave financial support to Kentucky State very sparingly and only after funds had been allocated to the state's white institutions of higher learning. In the beginning the school operated on a state appropriation of $3,000 and continued to do so for about ten years. A second source of funds came from the Morrill Act of 1890, which gave federal dollars to the school's industrial and mechanical programs. In the early 1900s the state allocated $40,000 for the construction of dorms, an administration building, and classrooms. At no time, however, did the funding for Kentucky State approximate (in both terms of actual dollars and the per capita rate for students) the funds being allocated to the white state university in Lexington or even the white regional colleges at Bowling Green and Richmond. This is clear for the 1920s.

Funding for School Years

	1925-26	1929-30
University of Kentucky	$877,589.82	1,535,877.88
Western	357,317.19	587,533.40
Morehead	299,967.73	373,189.75
Kentucky State	47,250.00	211,058.84

In a study of state funding for higher education, John Taylor Williams concluded that blacks were greatly discriminated against in the allocation of funds and that "In reality, there is no budget system existing at Kentucky State. The president and Board of Trustees never know the approximate amount of funds which will be available until the state legislature sort out the funds in a haphazard manner."[34]

Because of its limited funding, Kentucky State operated with an inadequate physical plant. During the early years of the school, the library had only a few general books and no reference materials. A 1908 investigation of the school said: "In spite of a very recent addition of several hundred books, the library facilities are woefully inadequate. No books bearing upon the industries are to be found in the collection, and but few on science and education. Nor are there even any such set of books as teachers of reading and of general literature need to supplement and illustrate their work with their classes." In this regard, very little changed over the years. For example, a 1932 report on Kentucky State noted that the librarian, when asked about the number of books, declined to give this information. "This action was the result of the recent recognition of the institution as a four-year college and that it was required to reach a minimum number of books. It was feared by the administration that a report of the actual number of books might hurt its accreditation." The investigator speculated that the library contained no more than 4,000 of the 8,000 books required for accreditation. In the early 1900s Kentucky State lacked adequate laboratory equipment needed to teach courses in physics and chemistry. "For the work in chemistry practically no apparatus is provided. A few chemicals have been secured, but these like a part of the cost of the physics cabinet came out of the pockets of interested instructors." Finally, because of a lack of equipment in the mechanical department, students were not given practical application in the operation of machines. "What little machinery there is in the mechanical department stands idle for want of a boiler," the 1908 report concluded.[35]

Ultimately, the most serious problem facing Kentucky State during its early years of existence was not its "shoestring" budget or poor physical plant but a lack of good leadership and continuity in the office of president. Without question, several of the early presidents were chosen first because of their political affiliations and second for their educational expertise. The first president, John H. Jackson, was an exception. A graduate of Berea College and a teacher in Lexington, Jackson had worked consistently for educational improvements for the state's black residents. He served as president from the school's founding in 1886 to 1898, when he resigned to accept the presidency of Lincoln Institute in Jefferson City, Missouri. The board of trustees selected James Givens, of whom practically nothing is known, to succeed Jackson. For whatever reasons, Givens resigned after only two years. He was then followed by James S. Hathaway, a graduate of Berea who had taught at both Kentucky State and Berea. Hathaway, very active in politics, was president from 1900 to 1907. With the backing of Governor Augustus E. Willson, Hathaway was forced out, and John H. Jackson returned to Kentucky State as president for a second time. He served only three years, resigning abruptly in 1910. Within two weeks of Jackson's resignation, the board named Albert Ernest Meyzeek to the position. His appointment was a surprise; though an outstanding and innovative educator, Meyzeek had a well-deserved reputation for being uncompromising on race and difficult to work with in general. On August 1, 1910, before he officially took over, Meyzeek resigned the post, citing serious disagreements with the board on the future direction of the school. The board then turned once again to James Hathaway, whose second term was no more successful than his first. Not surprisingly, he was forced to resign after only two years.[36]

Around 1910 Clarence L. Timberlake, a black educator in western Kentucky, wrote a pamphlet entitled "Politics and the Schools." He called for changes in the law that restricted membership on the Kentucky State Board of Trustees to citizens of Frankfort. This had resulted in men with very provincial opinions controlling the school, causing much instability, especially in the office of president. "The colored Normal School has been established for more than a quarter of a century and it is the consensus of opinion of the best minds of the state that its vitality has been sapped and its usefulness impeded by the lack of a statewide board of Regents," Timberlake concluded.[37] For whatever reasons, when criticizing the composition of the Kentucky State Board of Trustees, Timberlake neglected to mention that no blacks had served on the board of this all-black school. It would be a number of years before Frankfort physician Edward E. Underwood became the first Afro-American appointed to a seat on Kentucky State's board.

In 1912 the board of trustees hired Lexington school principal Green Pinckney Russell as president. A great admirer of Booker T. Washington and his approach to black education, Russell quickly won the united support of the board of trustees and the governor. He also tried to emulate the Tuskegean by running Kentucky State with an iron hand. After a series of minor incidents, capped off by a shouting match at an assembly in October 1914, a break occurred between Russell and student leaders. Russell had told the entire student body that someone had stolen his suit and that the guilty party would be expelled. When the suit was discovered in a trunk owned by his nephew, Russell refused to take any action. Later, Russell's nephew and several other students drove his car without permission and caused a wreck. He punished all of the students except the one who obviously needed disciplining most, his recalcitrant nephew. Russell suspended the student leaders after they charged him with favoritism. He also had arrest warrants sworn out, charging them with rioting and carrying concealed weapons. Despite their pleas to the governor, the suspended students were not reinstated at Kentucky State.[38]

Russell survived as president of Kentucky State for seventeen years even though he came under constant attack from students, faculty, and alumni. (He was actually removed from office in May 1923 only to be reinstated by a new governor in April 1924.)[39] Disgruntled faculty knew not to challenge him openly for fear of being fired. Indeed, as a scholar of higher education in Kentucky explained: "In the three institutions for White people members of the various institutions have recourse to their Boards of Trustees whenever differences arise. In the Negro institution no provision is made for discussions of differences with authorities higher than the president." In 1924, I. Willis Cole, a prominent black newspaper editor from Louisville, called for Russell's resignation. Nothing was done until four years later when several Afro-American educators from throughout the state harshly condemned Russell's methods of operating the school. Their complaints convinced Kentucky State's newly appointed board members to investigate the president, especially his financial transactions. To the obvious delight of Russell's many critics, the board discovered a number of questionable financial practices. They were especially appalled upon learning that his wife and daughter were on the payroll as employees of Kentucky State's small library. He resigned under extreme pressure on March 1, 1929.[40]

Despite its many problems—relying on Kentucky whites who were largely indifferent to the idea of higher education for

Students at Kentucky State received both vocational and technical training. Photographs by Gretter, 1911.
Kentucky Historical Society

blacks, poor funding, lack of an adequate physical plant, often corrupt and incompetent leaders, and political interference—Kentucky State achieved its mission of educating black teachers. Furthermore, any number of future Afro-American leaders in other areas of Kentucky society were educated at Kentucky State. As will be discussed below, between 1879 and 1950, Kentucky had other schools of higher education for blacks, but none competed with this institution for the loyalty of blacks. Without question, Afro-Americans from all over the state saw Kentucky State—with all of its shortcomings—as their school.

Another institution actually has the distinction of being the first black college in Kentucky. Simmons University, known as the Kentucky Normal and Theological Institute when it opened in November 1879 and then as State University, was a private college, conceived and run by the General Association of Negro Baptists. The school offered theological training, elementary training, college courses, and, like most black schools, a smattering of industrial courses. Within ten years of its inception, Simmons had expanded greatly, offering courses of instruction leading to degrees in medicine and law. Along with Berea College, Simmons served as the primary source of black collegiate training in the state for more than decade. Indeed, when considering that Kentucky State existed as a high school until the 1920s, Simmons filled an important void in black education for many years.[41]

On the eve of the Great Depression, Simmons University, largely because of indebtedness, had to curtail sharply its program and sell most of its property. Contributing to the retrenchment of the school was the publication of a highly influential report by the Bureau of Education (then a branch in the United States Department of the Interior) that recommended that "the friends of the institution" withhold their contributions until Simmons existed on a sound financial basis and had reorganized and eliminated most of the courses of study offered at the school.[42] This event, however, coincided with the start of a black junior college in Louisville. As part of a political deal to secure black support of a bond proposal, the Board of Trustees of the University of Louisville agreed to operate a black branch of the university. In 1931 Louisville Municipal College for Negroes opened on the site where Simmons had existed for more than fifty years. Municipal College, conceived primarily as a liberal arts college, had a varied curriculum, athletic teams, and a number of outstanding teachers. The school continued to operate for twenty years, until the desegregation of the University of Louisville in 1951.[43]

Several black colleges were started between 1910 and 1930. The creation of a school in the western part of the state was a major concern to many blacks, since Simmons, Kentucky State, and other schools were convenient primarily for central Kentuckians. Dennis Henry Anderson founded Western Kentucky Industrial College (WKIC) in Paducah in 1910. He called for state appropriations for the school, something that was not forthcoming until 1918, when, led by Governor A.O. Stanley, the general assembly enacted the following legislation: "That there is hereby appropriated for the benefit of WKIC the sum of $3,000 annually, provided the college gives free tuition to colored teachers taking a training course to teach in the colored common Schools of Kentucky and free tuition to colored boys and girls who have attained the age of sixteen and have completed the common school course of this State." Despite the glowing predictions of several western Kentucky black leaders that the institution would play a major role in black education, Anderson's school remained small and never accomplished its goals of training teachers and assisting blacks in acquiring vocational skills.[44]

Unlike Kentucky State, Simmons, and Louisville Municipal College, this western Kentucky school failed to achieve accreditation, which proved to be a severe setback to its growth. Scholars, of course, must use caution when reviewing the reports of white investigators of black institutions, realizing that in the eyes of many whites all of the black colleges were inferior institutions, deserving at best very poor ratings. This extremely negative view was based more on the fact that black colleges were staffed by Afro-Americans rather than the poor facilities and inadequate funding with which the schools were forced to exist. Nevertheless, in spite of the sincere efforts of the founders of WKIC to aid the race, there is probably some truth to the reports of the shortcomings of the school. One particularly harsh assessment came from Oscar F. Galloway of the University of Kentucky: "Honesty, however, compels the statement that the school fails to measure up to any of the more commonly accepted standards of a junior college. The plant is inadequate, the funds available for current educational purposes are meager, the faculty is both poorly trained and underpaid, the educational program is one sided, the library is inadequate, and the students are allowed to amass credits at a rate so high as to leave grave doubts concerning standards of scholarship maintained by the school. . . . There is no good reason for the state continuing the support of an unaccredited institution."[45] Reports such as this convinced state officials to cut the appropriations to WKIC, effectively closing the school. In 1938 the legislature passed a bill establishing the West Kentucky Vocational Training School for Negroes, which was to be located on the site once occupied by WKIC. The purpose of the new school greatly resembled the old with its emphasis on black uplift through vocational skills. Western Kentucky Vocational remained in operation until the 1950s when integration opened the doors of the white schools in the area to Afro-Americans.[46]

Though sympathetic to what the black colleges were able to accomplish on their meager resources, the reports of black investigators often detailed the shortcomings of these schools. James Bond, in his report on black education in Kentucky, compared Kentucky State College and WKIC with the five state-supported colleges for whites. He documented at length the ways that either racial discrimination or inadequate funding contributed to these schools' being deplorable in many respects. Bond also noted that because racial discrimination kept Afro-Americans out of the white colleges and the overall quality of the black institutions was very poor, more than one thousand young blacks were forced to leave their home state to receive adequate college training. On the other hand, Bond explained, "The white people have four state teachers' colleges and a great university at Lexington as well as scores of private colleges." Another scholar, after reviewing the white and black colleges in the state of Kentucky reached a similar conclusion. "When all of the pertinent facts are taken into consideration it is apparent that, in spite of favorable legislation, Negro education on the secondary and normal or collegiate level has not enjoyed the development comparable to that of whites or conducive to the best interests of that class of the commonwealth's citizens."[47]

Lincoln Institute was another black college founded in the early 1900s. Whereas the other institutions of higher education

Members of the integrated Alpha Zeta Literary Society, founded at Berea College in 1894.
Berea College Archives

had been created at the urging of blacks, this one was established by whites, and its existence proved to be a controversial issue to many black leaders. On July 1, 1904, the Kentucky legislature passed a Jim Crow school law requiring racial segregation in all schools in the Commonwealth. This act was aimed at Berea College, an integrated school. Members of the school's board of trustees soon voted to establish a school for blacks based on the model of Booker T. Washington's Tuskegee. However, a few of Berea's supporters said this step was premature, that neither the Kentucky courts not the United States Supreme Court had ruled on the constitutionality of the Day Law. Nevertheless, plans for the new school, Lincoln Institute, went forward even as Berea College pressed forward in the courts its test of the Day Law's constitutionality. Following the program of the other colleges for Afro-Americans in Kentucky, the founders of Lincoln Institute conceived of their school as offering only a handful of traditional college courses with most of the work of the school's being devoted to high school courses and especially industrial training. Establishing a school that had its main emphasis on industrial education was an obvious appeal to potential white benefactors. Also, it reflected the paternalistic leanings of the white founders. When speaking on behalf of Lincoln Institute, President William G. Frost of Berea College explained: "Some such training as was given by masters and mistresses in the old days must be supplied now through the industrially trained teacher in the public school for the Negro." On another occasion he informed a white civic organization in words that they probably felt very comfortable in hearing about why the school was so essential for blacks' progress: "The colored people miss the training that some of them received in our best homes in the olden times, and in many cases they are not yet able to give adequate parental care to their children. We shall touch the seat of trouble if we can raise up a small army of colored teachers who shall be imbued with the industrial idea and who will teach the fundamental virtues of cleanliness, promptness, and desire to excel in skill and thriftiness."[48]

Frost's assumption that whites would support yet another black industrial school proved correct. Andrew Carnegie, a member of the Berea College Board of Trustees, pledged $200,000 if that same amount could be raised from other sources. Several New Englanders, also strong supporters of Berea, gave large donations. Within the state, the largest donations came from a group of white businessmen affiliated with the Louisville Board of Trade. When endorsing the concept of the school, the board of trade said: "We feel that proper industrial training for the colored race is essential." By February 12, 1909, the one-hundredth birthday of Abraham Lincoln for whom the school was named, $400,204 had been raised by the Berea board of trustees for Lincoln Institute.[49]

Though the white business community endorsed the creation of "the Tuskegee of Kentucky," the vast majority of their fellow white citizens were opposed to the school's being located in or near their community. In this regard, the members of the Lincoln board of trustees (men who had been associated with Berea College) had naively believed that whites would see the positive benefits of having a black college in their town. After failing to obtain a site for the school in either Lexington or Louisville, the founders acquired property in Anchorage, a small community in Jefferson County. But under intense pressure from hostile whites who believed that the presence of a black school would lead to criminal assaults and ultimately would lower property values, members of the Lincoln board of trustees yielded to these protests and abandoned their plans to construct the school in Anchorage. Still hoping to have Lincoln Institute located near a large town, the board then purchased a farm in Simpsonville, Shelby County, twenty-two miles east of Louisville. Whites who resided in this part of Shelby County, upset over the idea of a Negro school nearby, resorted to legal means to prevent the construction of Lincoln Institute in their community. Their state representative introduced legislation making it mandatory for three-fourths of the voters of a county to approve the building and location of any school erected in their county. The proposed bill, the second piece of legislation aimed directly at blacks' attending college, passed overwhelmingly but was declared unconstitutional on June 6, 1910. Despite the favorable ruling of the court, the school's founders adopted measures to allay the fears of whites that large numbers of blacks would move to Shelby County to enroll their children in the school. The Lincoln Institute board decreed that only students residing at the school would be admitted. In other words, students living in Shelby County were prohibited

Berea Hall at Lincoln Institute, the so-called "Tuskegee of Kentucky."
University of Louisville Photographic Archives

from commuting on a daily basis to the school. Founders of Lincoln Institute also resorted to a "friendly bribe" to win support of the school: Shelbyville's mayor, the owner of a construction company, was given a contract to help with most of the building of the school.[50]

What remained was black opposition to the school. A number of blacks were opposed to what they called "colored Berea," believing that President Frost had been behind the passage of the Day Law. In response to the complaint that no blacks were involved in the development of the school, two well known blacks, James Bond, a Berea graduate, and Rev. Charles H. Parrish, a Louisville pastor and president of his own black college, were named to the Lincoln Institute Board of Trustees. Yet, their appointments did not sit well with some outspoken black leaders since they viewed both Bond and Parrish as conservative, "safe" black leaders who worked very closely with whites. As a way of winning the support of reluctant blacks, members of the Lincoln Institute board escorted a party of twenty-five black leaders by excursion train to Simpsonville to see the school on September 1, 1911. According to A.E. Thomson, a Berea teacher who had been selected as the school's first principal, the tour was a success, with the black leaders' becoming highly enthusiastic over the construction of the school.[51]

Thomson's comments that the excursion ended black criticism of Lincoln Institute are highly suspect. Some blacks remained opponents of the school out of a sincere conviction that too much emphasis had already been placed on industrial education for blacks. Industrial education, they argued, ensured that blacks remained at the bottom economically because they learned skills that were rapidly becoming outdated. Julia Sohmers Young, of the *Kentucky Standard*, a paper published in Lexington, clearly expressed the view of these critics in a sharp attack on the proposed program of study at Lincoln Institute. "Are we to forever tamely submit to the prevailing idea that the Negro now must be educated as 'hewers of wood and drawers of water' for the more favored race, or shall we make a plea for the same kind of education every other race enjoys, telling those among us who elect, and whose minds so incline to hew wood and draw water to their hearts content." Without question, throughout its entire history, Lincoln Institute had any number of black critics.[52]

When considering that Lincoln Institute depended totally on whites for financial support, then it is not difficult to understand why industrial training was implemented at the "college." Indeed, the critics of Lincoln Institute failed to realize that industrial training was the only type of education that whites were willing to finance at a private college for Negroes. Kentucky State, a public institution, was in reality more of a high school than a college. Whites, by not adequately funding this state-supported school, demonstrated their unwillingness to pay for an equal education for the state's black citizens. But, in supporting Lincoln Institute, whites proved a willingness to fund an education that kept blacks in "their place." In short, given the time when Lincoln Institute was created—the early 1900s when racism was rampant—the alternatives for blacks' seeking an education beyond high school, especially in a private school, were extremely limited; it was either industrial training or no training.

Despite the concerns expressed by black intellectuals, Lincoln Institute opened on October 1, 1912. According to *The Lincoln Log*, an official publication of the school, graduates of Lincoln Institute became successful teachers, mechanics, farmers,

During his service as president of Lincoln Institute from 1936 to 1966, Dr. Whitney M. Young, Sr., increased student enrollment and received new and much larger contributions from donors.
University of Louisville Photographic Archives

nurses, and a few received advanced degrees, becoming lawyers and doctors. (It is not surprising that blacks affiliated with the school, when given the opportunity in the school's publication, boasted more often about Lincoln's graduates who became doctors and lawyers than those who were farmers and mechanics.) Yet, despite the school's success in educating many of Kentucky's black youths, the board of trustees would have closed the school during the height of the Great Depression in 1935 except for the timely intervention of Whitney M. Young, Sr., one of the first graduates of the school (and the father of Whitney M. Young of the National Urban League). Within two years of being named president of the school, Young had increased student enrollment, received new and much larger contributions from donors, and the school's farm showed a profit. Young remained at the helm of the school for over thirty years. In 1965, with most of Kentucky's schools integrated, Lincoln Institute became an institution for gifted but disadvantaged white and black youths. This program existed for five years, until the school was officially closed.[53]

Lincoln Institute grew out of Berea College, a school that, given its location in a southern state and the ever-rising tide of racism in the late nineteenth century, was involved in a unique educational enterprise. Founded in 1855 by abolitionist John Fee and Cassius M. Clay, Berea College started admitting blacks immediately after the Civil War and did so until the passage of the Day Law in 1904. To be sure, there was some racial tension at the school. A few students, for example, quit the school when the first blacks were admitted, but, on the whole, the school was relatively free of racial problems. Indeed, when trying to assess why whites called for segregation at Berea, *The Nation* stated, "Its offending may have been that its success in educating whites and blacks side by side was contrary to the doctrine of white superiority and tended to disprove the theory that equality of scholastic opportunity would mean the degradation of the white race."[54]

That practically all of the teachers and administrators were products of Oberlin College, one of the first schools in the nation to admit blacks, contributed greatly to the spirit of interracial goodwill at Berea. Moreover, Berea went far beyond tokenism in admitting blacks; by the 1880s blacks comprised a little more than 60 percent of the student body. Berea officials encouraged black enrollment by speaking before Negro organizations and placing advertisements in newspapers circulating in the black community mentioning the value of the school to Afro-Americans. Also, one black, James S. Hathaway, later to be president of Kentucky State, served on the faculty. A few black alumni were distressed that more members of their race were not added to the faculty, but in many respects Hathaway's appointment at Berea was an enlightened step in the South of that day. Considering the racism of America during the late nineteenth century, he might have been the only black teaching at a white college in the nation.[55]

Integration at Berea most surely offended white Kentuckians, even though the vast majority of them had no affiliation with the school and refused to contribute financially to its support. Black students representing Berea in extracurricular activities often encountered problems. On one occasion Berea officials had planned on sending black delegates to the YMCA convention in Paris, Kentucky. Several days before the students were scheduled to leave, school officials were informed that the blacks would not be accepted at the meeting. In July 1885 editor Henry Watterson of the *Courier-Journal* wrote an editorial denouncing mixed schools, specifically pointing his finger at Berea. The educators at Berea, he explained, were miscegenationists who were setting a bad role model for the youth of both races. Segregation at the school would benefit not only Berea but also the state, the Watterson editorial concluded. The editor of the New York *Freeman* denounced Watterson, reminding him that miscegenation was born and bred in the South and that the whites denouncing Berea were responsible for the rise of miscegenation in southern society.[56]

In 1889 Berea's president Edward H. Fairchild died, and three years later Oberlin professor William Goodell Frost was selected to head the school. To the surprise of some friends and alumni of the school (but not several members of the board who agreed with Frost), he urged that steps be taken to reduce the number of black students at the school, because in the eyes of some supporters Berea had become a "common high-school for colored students." As historian James McPherson explains: "Frost exaggerated the problem. True, enrollment had declined from its peak in 1886, but the total of 354 students in 1892-93 was on par with the average for the preceding decade. And while the number of white students from outside Berea had indeed dwindled, Frost's implication that the school was about to become all black was far from true. In fact, white enrollment had held steady during the preceding six years; the decline had occurred among black students, and the white percentage of the student body had increased from 39 to 46 percent." Frost believed, however, that the number of black students should be reduced even further, that the racial balance at Berea should reflect the state's racial balance which was about 80 percent white.[57]

The editor of *New South*, a black newspaper, noted with dismay that Frost, in a determined effort to accomplish his goal of increasing the number of white students at Berea, began telling them that upon enrolling at the school they would be required to associate with Afro-Americans "no more than you do when you work with colored people." The paper went on to say that Frost had two editions of the *Berea College Reporter* printed, one for whites and one for blacks. When asked why, he sharply remarked: "I do not send out of my front door what should go out of the back door."[58] During his first eleven years as Berea's president, white enrollment at the school increased dramatically while the black enrollment declined. Frost said this was more than acceptable because Berea's pressing concern should be the education of southern mountain whites.[59]

Despite his Oberlin background, Frost's words and actions revealed a strong belief in white supremacy. In the early 1900s he was quoted as saying that it was far more important to educate white youths than black youths. This public statement brought out the ire of Booker T. Washington, a black leader normally circumspect when criticizing whites. "I disliked very much to see you quoted stating that the white man should be educated before the Negro is educated. I regret also to note that other white men engaged in education in the South have been preaching the same doctrine recently. . . . I think it wholly unfair for anyone to make the statement that the white man should be educated first. There is but one interpretation to be put upon such a statement, and that is that the education of the Negro must be stopped while the education of the white man goes forward. A broader and more statesman-like thing would be to say that both races should be educated."[60]

Frost eventually forced James S. Hathaway, Berea's only

black faculty member, to resign. Hathaway had been hired as a math tutor in 1884. According to a member of the Berea board of trustees who supported Frost in dismissing the black teacher, Hathaway was unqualified, needing more education before he could be promoted to professor. "He fully expected further advancement but it never came, and both he and his colored followers were jealous and dissatisfied. . . . After a while the trustees, though not making him a professor, did vote that he must be invited to the faculty meetings." At some point, Hathaway approached President Frost about a leave of absence to pursue post-graduate work. Frost agreed to the leave, but implied that regardless of the outcome his position would no longer be available at Berea. A black newspaper editor sympathetic to Hathaway explained: "Comprehending fully the situation, and having opportunity to go into a more congenial field, Tutor Hathaway resigned his tutorship in Berea College, and accepted a professorship in the State Normal School, in the summer of '93."[61]

Though Frost's actions had led to a reduction in the number of black students and set the tone for several incidents of open racial hostility on the part of white students, the school had nevertheless remained integrated. But, as most scholars have speculated, when considering that Berea College was an integrated school during a time of rising racism in Kentucky and the South, it was inevitable that segregation would occur. In November 1903 Carl Day, a state representative from Breathitt County, an area with only a handful of blacks, toured the Berea campus and proclaimed his outrage at the sight of blacks and whites "living together." In January he introduced a bill directed only at Berea. The bill called for imposing a $1,000 fine with $100 per day penalty upon any institution which admitted both white and black students. All instructors at such an institution and students attending the school faced being fined as well. Frost and the board of trustees urged the defeat of the proposed Day Law. Frost gave a speech before the general assembly, pleading with the legislators to allow Berea to continue along its accustomed path, free of state control. The politicians assured Frost that though they personally opposed the measure, the bill would nevertheless pass. One member of the legislature candidly told Frost: "We understand that this proposed law is an outrage. The state has never contributed to the support of Berea College and it has no right to interfere in its affairs. I want you to understand that I have no sympathy with the law; but the facts are these: the law is going to pass. Now for me to oppose it would make it necessary for me to discuss the Nigger question in every political speech as long as I live. It would wreck my political future and so I shall be obliged to stay away when the matter comes up, or vote for the bill."[62]

The legislator was correct; the bill passed overwhelmingly on July 1, 1904. Several months earlier, Frost had written to Booker T. Washington (in confidence) for his advice on what actions Berea should take once the law was enacted. "Should Berea resist this proposed law to the utmost (of course in a christian spirit) or might we find a way to do as much good as now in a manner less offensive to the Southerners?" Interestingly, though phrasing a question to Washington, Frost then hinted at the action the school would eventually take: the starting of a separate school for blacks. He concluded: "My instincts are for 'standing pat' on platform vindicated by so many years. But I wish to know what others would say. Do you think Berea's advanced position ought to be fought for?" Washington, as he had been in his previous letter to Frost, was very direct: "I advise as strongly as I can, and that is every effort should be made to convince the members of the legislature that your present organization of the college ought not to be disturbed, and that no harm has taken place by reason of your present policy." As a letter from William H. Steward to Washington clearly demonstrated, while Frost spent considerable time weighing what steps to take once the segregation law was enacted, black leaders worked in a desperate attempt to prevent the passage of the Day Law. Their efforts, of course, ended in defeat. Steward informed "the Wizard of Tuskegee" that even though he and others had been working with sympathetic legislators for some time, given the strong desire by most whites for racial segregation at Berea, very little could be done to prevent the expulsion of black students from the school.[63]

Frost and the Berea board of trustees decided to challenge the Day Law through the courts. John G. Carlisle, a former Speaker of the United States House of Representatives and one of the most prominent lawyers in Kentucky, was selected as the school's attorney. Nevertheless, the Day Law was upheld in Madison Circuit Court October 8, 1904, and the Kentucky

Court of Appeals in June 1906. The appeals court said that under the police power of the state the school, a private corporation, could be compelled to segregate the races since the laws of Kentucky mandated the separation of the races in places deemed necessary. Furthermore, the Day Law, the court ruled, did not discriminate against either race. "The right to teach white and negro children in a private school at the same time and place is not a property right. Besides, appellant, as a corporation created by this state, has no natural right to teach at all. Its right to teach is such as the state sees fit to give to it."[64]

The case was appealed to the United States Supreme Court. In calling for the Day Law to be declared unconstitutional, Berea's attorneys, John G. Carlisle and Guy Ward Mallon, argued that "the right to maintain a private school is no more subject to legislative control than the right to conduct a store, or a farm, or any other one of the various occupations in which the people are engaged." The court's ruling, upholding the Day Law, was handed down on November 9, 1908. When approving the constitutionality of this Jim Crow law, the justices, by a vote of seven to two, agreed that "the state court determines the extent and limitations of powers conferred by the State on its corporations"; and second, "A corporation is not entitled to all the immunities to which individuals are entitled, and a State may withhold from its corporations privileges and powers of which it cannot constitutionally deprive individuals." Further, the majority opinion of the court said it was the settled policy of Kentucky to "preserve race identity, the purity of blood, and prevent an amalgamation of the races." Justice John Marshall Harlan wrote a lengthy, poignant dissent:

> In my judgment the court should directly meet and decide the broad question presented by the statute. It should adjudge whether the statute, as a whole, is or is not unconstitutional, in that it makes it a crime against the State to maintain or operate a private institution of learning where white and black pupils are received, at the same time, for instruction. In the view which I have as to my duty I feel obliged to express my opinion as to the validity of the act as a whole. I am of opinion that in its essential parts the statute is an arbi-

trary invasion of the rights of liberty and property guaranteed by the Fourteenth Amendment against hostile state action and is, if the Commonwealth of Kentucky can make it a crime to teach white and colored children together at the same time, in a private institution of learning, it is difficult to perceive why it may not forbid the assembling of white and colored children in the same Sabbath-school, for the purpose of being instructed in the Word of God, although such teaching may be done under the authority of the church to which the school is attached as well as with the consent of the parents of the children. . . . Again if the views of the highest court of Kentucky be sound, that commonwealth may, without infringing the Constitution of the United States, forbid the association in the same private school of pupils of the Anglo-Saxon and Latin races respectively, or pupils of the Christian and Jewish faiths, respectively.

Have we become so inoculated with prejudice of race that an American government, professedly based on principles of freedom, and charged with the protection of all citizens alike, can make distinctions between such citizens in the matter of their voluntary meeting for innocent purposes simply because of their respective races.[65]

In the wake of the court's ruling and the immediate steps undertaken by Berea officials to open Lincoln Institute, Frost was bitterly assailed in some circles as being behind the passing of the Day Law. Oswald Garrison Villard, the grandson of William Lloyd Garrison and one of the founders of the NAACP, pointedly told Frost that his public statement of being opposed to the law, yet his willingness to follow it, was "inexcusable." Other white supporters from New England accused Frost of turning his back on one of the primary missions of the school, the educating of blacks and whites at the same institution. They vowed to withhold their contributions from the Jim Crow school. A black graduate of Berea, Frank L. Williams, wrote a pamphlet attacking Frost and, though not blaming him for the enactment of the Day Law, concluded that Frost created the ideal climate for racial segregation. In a confidential letter to one of his benefactors, Booker T. Washington said that many Negroes (though he did not include himself) are of the opinion "that the present authorities have encouraged the separation." Many years later when reflecting back on the ousting of Afro-Americans from Berea, Carter G. Woodson, the school's most illustrious black graduate, said that he and most blacks believed that Frost had been the instigator in the actions of Carl Day.[66]

The debate over Frost's involvement in the enactment of the Day Law will probably never be resolved. As Professor McPherson and others have said, the passing of a Jim Crow ordinance directed at Berea College was natural, given the desire of Kentuckians and southerners to stamp out any vestige of interracialism. Undoubtedly, Frost can be indicted for the "moral climate" he created at Berea, for he did encourage a weakening of the racial egalitarianism that had historically existed at the school. It must be acknowledged, however, that Frost accomplished the goal he set when accepting the presidency—making Berea a first-rate school for mountain whites. Tragically, he accomplished his goal in part at the expense of Afro-Americans, and in that sense the story of Berea College is a capsule of what blacks experienced in the field of education in Kentucky. Whites firmly agreed on the necessity of separate education for the races. In doing so, they relegated the education of Afro-Americans to the back seat, and supported it only when it was the "proper kind" of education, one that made them useful to whites. Not surprisingly, the education available to Kentucky blacks was poorly funded and greatly inferior to that offered whites.

It is important to understand, however, that despite all of the obvious shortcomings resulting from racial discrimination in education, the schools were an important asset to the Afro-American community. Black schools provided educational training, leaders, role models, and, above all, race pride. It is striking that when reading the various local history books produced by blacks or the book by Alice A. Dunnigan, *The Fascinating Story of Black Kentuckians: Their Heritage and Traditions*, who interviewed countless people and traveled throughout the state, the people cited most for dedicating their lives to uplifting the race are school teachers. Unquestionably, as has been shown throughout this chapter, during the age of racial segregation, the black schools, especially the physical plants and equipment, were inferior to white schools at every level in Kentucky. But, because of the many outstanding, dedicated blacks teaching in these schools, the gap between the quality of the education—the learning experience—in the white and black schools was much smaller than most people perhaps ever realized. Blacks and indeed the entire state would have profited immensely if real equality in funding and other support had been extended to the black schools. Furthermore, as was wisely pointed out by R.R. Wright, Jr., in his study of black education, despite all of the failures and shortcomings, blacks had a right to be proud of their efforts—most surely their reliance on self-help—in combating illiteracy and in providing schools for the race. As R.R. Wright, Jr. has written:

> If it is proper to measure progress by the depth from which one comes as well as by the height which one reaches, the efforts at self-help in education by Negroes deserve praise. Their contributions have been far from adequate for even meagre education, and, to-day, half of their children of proper school age are not in school, and two-fifths of their race are unable to read and write. But the history of civilization does not show one other instance of a wholly illiterate race or nation reducing its illiteracy in half in a single generation.[67]

Appropriately, an organization of black teachers was responsible for many of the positive steps that occurred in black education. Founded in 1879, the Kentucky Negro Education Association (KNEA), comprised of principals and teachers of the public schools, and presidents and deans of the black colleges, worked for new buildings and substantial improvements in the physical plants of the schools, a longer school year, and increased funding for Afro-American schools. The KNEA annual convention highlighted a wide range of issues. At the Thirty-Sixth Annual Meeting, held in Louisville in April 1915, sessions were devoted to "Misbehavior in the Class Room"; "Negro Music and its Value in the Schools"; "Domestic Economy in Rural Schools"; "The Qualification of Teachers"; and "How to Keep Students in High School." As one president of the KNEA explained, the organization "not only champions the cause of education of the Negro but works for general social and economic progress of the Negro." Writing in the mid-1940s, Harvey C. Russell, the author of a study on the KNEA, applauded the enduring efforts of black teachers and administrators to bring about educational changes for the race:

> For seventy years the founders and their successors have carried on. In no small way the organization contributed its part to the establishment of the State Normal School and its successor, the State College. Through its efforts came the teachers' institutes, the state Parent-Teacher Association, the equal salary movement, the accreditment of Negro schools and colleges, and many other educational services. The issues of today are just as vital and challenging as those of former periods. Vast work remains to be done if Kentucky is to realize the K.N.E.A. slogan: "An equal educational opportunity for every Kentucky child."

To reach its goal of an equal education for every Kentucky child, the organization played an important role in the black challenge to Jim Crow education. In April 1940 the KNEA approved a recommendation from its committee on higher education to file suit if Kentucky refused to conform to the Supreme Court ruling in the Missouri case and admit blacks to the state's white universities.[68]

The willingness of the KNEA to consider litigation if blacks were refused admission to Kentucky's white colleges was clearly a step in a new direction. Previously, Kentucky blacks had called for improved educational facilities, increased funding, and in a few rare instances, they had even demanded that whites abide by the law and provide equal funding for white and black schools. But now, Afro-Americans agreed that though improvements had been made in the quality of education available to blacks, their goal of equal education was far from being achieved. Unquestionably, for decades white Kentuckians had grudgingly supported black education only when it had been demonstrated that schooling resulted in blacks' acquiring "useful" skills. While never agreeing with whites that the end product of black education should be docile workers who willingly accepted the jobs reserved for them, blacks had often acquiesced to the white view because of a lack of alternatives to segregated but inferior schools and because they lacked an effective way to protest. Indeed, the programs initiated in the black public high school in Lexington, at the state college for blacks in Frankfort, and in the small industrial colleges reflected the white view of a proper education for Afro-Americans. But, on the eve of World War II, members of the KNEA and other key black leaders, like their black counterparts in other states, were developing strategies to challenge the concept of segregated schools.

Four

The NAACP and the Quest For Equality

THE NAACP, founded in 1909, was the driving force of the Afro-American civil rights movement from the 1920s to 1954. Almost from its start, the organization had an active branch in Louisville. During its first ten years of existence, the Louisville branch protested lynchings and mob violence, Jim Crow public transportation, and discrimination in public education. The branch also successfully challenged the Louisville Residential Segregation Ordinance of 1914. Fighting this suit required unity, money, and perseverance. Overturning the ordinance did not entirely end discrimination in housing, but it was an important victory for the NAACP to build upon in both Kentucky and the nation. For years thereafter, when highlighting accomplishments, the national office cited the Louisville decision as one of its most significant victories against racial discrimination. By 1920 the membership of the Louisville branch was one of the largest in the nation.[1]

In January 1919 Walter White of the national office traveled throughout Kentucky, encouraging community leaders to form branches. White's message was timely, given the increase in racial violence that occurred during and especially immediately after the World War. His effort was extremely successful as blacks in more than a dozen cities, in all regions of the state, formed branches. In several small communities, most notably Maysville, the local black leadership applauded the work of the NAACP but feared identifying themselves as members of that organization. By contrast, however, at the formation of the NAACP branch in Earlington, several prominent whites, including the president of the St. Bernard Mining Company, publicly endorsed the work of the organization. In many places, though, after the fanfare over launching the branch subsided, the local affiliate did very little. Nevertheless, the very act of forming a civil rights organization had been important, showing publicly that Afro-Americans were disappointed with the racial status quo. Also, new recruits were required to pay a membership fee of one dollar, and this money, pouring in from Kentucky and elsewhere, was extremely important to an organization in desperate need of financial resources to continue its activities.[2]

After its inception in April 1919, the Frankfort NAACP became for almost a decade second only to the Louisville branch as a "watchdog" over black rights. Led by Dr. Edward E. Underwood, who had been active in the Anti-Separate Coach Movement in the 1890s, this organization worked not only in Frankfort but all over the state. Members of this branch took the lead in championing a state anti-lynching law. On several occasions when national office officials received letters from Afro-Americans awaiting trial for rape or murder in small Kentucky communities, they referred these cases to the Frankfort branch. The branch helped prevent the execution of black men in Richmond in 1923 and in Lynch in 1924, but the death of Underwood and the start of the Great Depression greatly hindered the program of the Frankfort NAACP. During the Great Depression the national office unsuccessfully attempted to resurrect the branch.[3]

NAACP branches in several other cities also proved helpful to blacks whose civil rights were being violated. During the late 1920s, the NAACP became involved in a case in the small community of Allensville in western Kentucky when a precinct official refused to allow a black man, Samuel Smith, to cast his ballot in the primary election. Smith contacted the NAACP. With the aid of the national office, Smith secured the services of a white attorney from Russellville. A court date was scheduled, but in return for Smith's dropping the suit, the defendant agreed to pay the plaintiff's attorney's fees and court costs, and promised not to restrict him or other blacks from voting. Thus, the NAACP claimed another important victory in Kentucky.[4]

The Covington branch aided Afro-Americans throughout northern Kentucky by providing legal counsel. On one occasion members of the branch assisted Charles White of Newport, who had been arrested and charged with reckless driving after

154 / *A History of Blacks In Kentucky*

Women at the polls in Louisville, ca. 1920
Canfield & Shook Collection, University of Louisville Photographic Archives

his automobile struck the car of a white man. Though a relatively minor offense, White had remained in jail for a period of time. The intervention of the NAACP brought the matter to a conclusion.[5] An even more serious case started on March 6, 1930, when a white woman said she had been raped by a black man. Suspicion was immediately focused on Anderson McPerkins, a native of Georgia who had arrived in the area after jumping from a freight train. He had been seen begging for food in the vicinity of the woman's home. At his trial, which was attended by a large number of angry whites, who demanded a quick verdict, McPerkins was found guilty and sentenced to death. After visiting the condemned black youth in jail, members of the Cincinnati International Labor Defense and the Cincinnati American Civil Liberties Union urged the NAACP to intervene on his behalf. Though inactive during the time when McPerkins was arrested and convicted, the Covington branch was revived. One of the leaders, Reverend David M. Jordan, pastor of the Ninth Street Methodist Episcopal Church, used his church as a rallying place for the supporters of McPerkins. Members of the local NAACP also worked closely with J. Max Bond of the Kentucky CIC, who had become director of this interracial organization at the death of his father. The crucial turning point in the case occurred when Bond traveled to Kenton County and confirmed information the NAACP had received about the "disreputable character" of the white woman. Bond's information was turned over to Governor Flem Sampson. Though the governor moved very slowly, taking several months to resolve the case, the sixteen-month ordeal of McPerkins ended with his release from prison in July 1931.[6]

Several years later, the national office in New York forwarded the following letter to the president of the Covington branch:

> I am informing you that I am in trouble here in Covington, Kentucky charged with first degree murder and held without bond. And haven't got anyone in the world. But myself and I would like a little help or to have my case investigated please. I am very sorry to have to do this. but I haven't any people in the world to help me in anyway. And I thought that this is the only way I have in receiving help, is by writing to the Advancement of the Association. I have been in jail here four months and the grand jury will not be until October 1934 this year and I have 5 or 6 more months before trial, and I will appreciate anything that you all do in my behalf and I would like to see one of the representatives of the association and I could explain my case in more details, which my case need the support of the association very much. I will be looking for an earliest reply and to see one of your nearest representatives in your local branch.
> I am respectfully yours
> Huston Mosler
>
> P.S. Covington City Jail
> #224 Court St.
> Covington, Kentucky[7]

156 / *A History of Blacks In Kentucky*

Very few details are known about the case of Huston Mosler. In Kentucky the vast majority of blacks charged with the murder of whites received death penalties and eventually died in the electric chair in Eddyville. With the assistance of the NAACP, Mosler avoided execution, though it is possible that he was sentenced to life in prison. But, when considering the fate of most blacks convicted of killing whites, a prison sentence—even one for life—would have been looked upon as a victory of sorts.[8]

The activities of the NAACP in challenging discrimination and the denial of basic human rights to Afro-Americans illustrated clearly that prior to launching an assault on "separate and unequal" public schools, the organization had been involved and successful in Kentucky for almost two decades. Without question, however, making inroads against the state's dual school system presented a great challenge. On one occasion Charles H. Houston, chief legal counsel for the NAACP, received a report from Harry H. Jones, an attorney in Wheeling, West Virginia, about black education in Kentucky. Jones concluded: "I am satisfied from my cursory review of this subject that in Kentucky we have a glaring example of perhaps the rottenest bi-racial school arrangement in this country; that within the several topics outlined above are to be found one or more provisions that violate the 14th Amendment; that Kentucky is not square with its Negro children, and that they cannot have under such a set up equal and necessary facilities."[9] In other words, the officials of the NAACP knew right from the beginning that they would encounter staunch resistance from white Kentuckians when attempting to integrate blacks into the public schools.

From the early 1930s to the mid-1950s, Charles W. Anderson played a leading role throughout the state of Kentucky on behalf of the NAACP. A native of Louisville, Anderson held undergraduate degrees from Kentucky State and Wilberforce (1927) and a law degree from Howard University (1931). After completing law school, he returned to Louisville and opened a law practice. Anderson's arrival coincided with the emergence of several new black leaders and the decline of several older blacks. Newspaper editors I. Willis Cole and William Warley, active with the NAACP since 1914, still championed black rights, but their leadership positions in civil rights agitation passed quickly to Anderson, Lyman Johnson, C. Eubank Tuck-

"From the early 1930s to the mid-1950s, Charles W. Anderson played a leading role throughout the state of Kentucky on behalf of the NAACP." In this 1936 photograph, Anderson, newly elected to the state legislature, is seen with his mother. Photograph by Cusick Studio.
Kentucky Historical Society

er, and Frank Stanley. Tucker, a presiding bishop in the African Methodist Episcopal Zion Church, practiced law. While defending blacks in several small communities, Tucker was physically attacked by white mobs and narrowly escaped being lynched in Elizabethtown. Stanley published the Louisville *Defender*, which soon surpassed Cole's and Warley's newspapers as the leading black paper in the city and in the state as well. Johnson taught at Central High School. He quickly became the most vocal public school teacher in denouncing discrimination and being involved in controversial issues. All of these men were well educated, with Johnson and Stanley having M.A. degrees and Tucker, like Anderson, holding a law degree. All four had something else in common as well: they were outspoken against racism and had little patience with Kentucky's Jim Crow practices.[10]

Shortly after his return to Louisville, Anderson presented Governor Ruby Laffoon and the Department of Education with a proposal to provide professional and post-graduate aid for Afro-Americans. Anderson said that blacks should be admitted to the University of Kentucky and the University of Louisville for graduate training until Kentucky State or some other black institution was placed on an equal footing with the state's white colleges. As an alternative, however, public funds should be used to pay the tuition for blacks who were compelled to leave the state to pursue courses not offered at Kentucky State. This, Anderson added, would be similar to the laws of Missouri and West Virginia. Even though Anderson's proposal was a modest one, when considering that the state was not providing any—much less equal—graduate training for Afro-Americans, and that other southern and border states were being forced to make changes, Kentucky officials completely ignored the request. They eventually realized that paying tuition fees for a few Afro-Americans to attend out-of-state universities was a convenient loophole to forestall desegregation. Indeed, several years later, state officials adopted Anderson's plan, but only because additional pressure to desegregate white colleges had been exerted. For spearheading this movement to provide equal graduate education opportunities for blacks, Anderson was selected as president of the local NAACP branch even though he had been back in Louisville for less than a year.[11]

Two years later, Anderson campaigned for the state legislature from Louisville's predominantly black Fifty-eighth District. Two other men, a white running as an Independent, and Bishop Tucker, the candidate of the Democratic party, also campaigned for the seat. For years Tucker had complained about the refusal of the Republican party to support blacks as candidates for elective office. In 1933 he switched to the Democratic party, and though defeated in the election, Tucker had aided the Democrats in regaining control of city government for the first time in more than a decade. In 1935 the Democrats again backed Tucker, reasoning that the party had very little to lose since the Fifty-eighth District had always voted Republican. This convinced Republican party officials to act, and they reluctantly agreed to back Anderson's candidacy. This marked the first time in the history of Louisville that the Republicans had endorsed a black for elective office.[12]

The campaign turned out to be bitter. Tucker relied on personal appeal to win voters, reminding the black community of his service to the race over the years as the reason he should be elected to office. Throughout the campaign, Anderson proclaimed that his program—repeal of the Kentucky Public Hanging Law; appropriations for black students to attend graduate school outside the state; enactment of legislation allowing female public school teachers marital privileges without losing their jobs; and employment of blacks in public works projects and other departments in local and state government—would benefit Kentucky blacks. The Independent candidate, without party backing, was never a factor in the race. Anderson won overwhelmingly, receiving 2,337 votes to 956 for Tucker. Nevertheless, Tucker, to the dismay of several local black leaders who had refrained from endorsing either candidate, challenged the election results. As Anderson explained in a letter to Charles H. Houston of the NAACP: "Inasmuch as I was the only Republican elected to office here the Democrats are fighting me with heels and toes in an election contest. My opponents being a Negro Democrat and a white Independent. They are alleging fraud, purchase of votes, intimidation of voters, etc. The whole matter will come before an election committee of the Legislature in January. The body has a Democratic majority, but I am depending upon the support of the better class of white citizens for a square deal." Anderson's election was upheld, and on January 7, 1936, he was sworn in as Kentucky's first black legislator. He was only twenty-eight years old.[13]

Over and beyond the symbolic importance of Anderson's being the first Afro-American to serve in the Kentucky legislature, his election proved to be extremely important for the civil rights movement. "As a member of the Legislature I shall endeavor to sponsor legislation long advocated by the NAACP and will from time to time communicate with your office and Mr. Houston relative to suggested bills and information," Anderson wrote to Walter White. During his very first month in office, he introduced a bill to appropriate state funds to "pay the tuition of qualified students who desire courses offered at the University of Kentucky or other state-supported institutions which are denied to Negro students on account of the provisions of the Kentucky Constitution governing separate education." The bill, known as the Anderson-Mayer State Aid Act, passed both the house and senate without a negative vote. Also in 1936, Anderson was influential in the enactment of a law requiring school districts to provide twelve grades of education for blacks. This, of course, was an important piece of legislation designed to improve educational opportunities for blacks living in rural, isolated counties. Two years later the law was amended (in a real sense "watered-down"), allowing counties with only a few black students to pay tuition fees and provide them with transportation to nearby districts. Many counties thereby avoided the staggering cost of establishing separate but equal high schools for a handful of blacks and at the same time evaded desegregating black students into white schools. The new feature of the law also benefited Lincoln Institute. As Professor Dennis Dickerson points out: "Since most Kentucky communities failed to provide high schools for blacks, the new law offered state funds to underwrite transportation costs and tuition for students who wished to attend Lincoln Institute or some other high school within the state."[14]

It can be argued that Anderson advocated moderate proposals, in that the United States Supreme Court had ruled in cases from Missouri and Maryland that blacks were entitled to attend the state universities for graduate training, and, therefore, allocating $175 per black student was actually doing very little. Furthermore, $175 per academic year was probably sufficient to cover tuition fees but fell short of paying all of the related costs involved in relocating to attend universities in other states. Also, the law mandating twelve grades of school for Afro-Americans was simply complying with separate but equal and was an acknowledgement (and a forced one at that) that the County School Law of 1908 had applied to white education only. Most surely, school districts all over Kentucky were not living up to their responsibilities under separate but equal when they were allowed to pay the tuition fees and transport their black residents to nearby districts instead of opening their own black high schools. (This transporting of black students was, of course, an early form of school busing, a phenomenon that elicited no complaints from whites as long as it was done in the name of segregated schools). Nevertheless, the legislation sponsored by Anderson, even though in reality it meant that the state was still doing only the minimum necessary to satisfy temporarily the federal courts, was viewed as a breakthrough by the national office of the NAACP. In a press release from New York, Charles H. Houston stated that the Kentucky tuition bill was similar to scholarship laws already in effect in four other states. Houston added: "The NAACP appreciates the efforts of Rep. Anderson to improve Negro education in Kentucky and commends him for pressing his point immediately upon taking his seat in the Legislature. If the bill is taken as an optional measure giving Negro students their choice to go outside the State of Kentucky or to remain in the state to secure graduate and professional training, the NAACP does not object to it." The press release concluded by stating clearly how the organization viewed what was occurring in Kentucky: "The NAACP appreciates that these acts relieve the situation somewhat but they are only palliatives and do not cure the inequalities which exist."[15] In other words, these partial victories were important, but the NAACP had dedicated itself to ending all forms of discrimination in the Bluegrass State.

Though achieving some success, Anderson found that much of his proposed legislation was rejected by his white colleagues in the general assembly. He was especially frustrated in 1946 when several of his bills, most notably House Bill 224 or the "Anti-Discrimination Bill," which would give black women the right to try on clothes and shoes in white department stores, were defeated. In an outburst of anger, Anderson said that a lack of action on the part of Afro-Americans led to the defeat of his efforts. "Negroes are too often mere talkers at the big gate. They too often fail to turn their words into action. They too frequently have more criticism to offer than support to give. . . . They are too satisfied with being secure in insecurity."[16]

Anderson's harsh criticism of his fellow Kentucky blacks for the defeat of House Bill 224 was totally unjustified and misdirected. In his caustic remarks, he failed to explain how the passive actions of blacks had led to the defeat of his proposed bill. Anderson's mere presence in the state legislature demonstrated that blacks were taking part in the political process; but since Afro-Americans were such a distinct, if not despised, minority in the state, they usually could accomplish very little besides voicing their complaints unless members of the majority group worked as their allies. Anderson, of course, deserved praise from Kentucky blacks for his diligent work in trying to pass bills that ended various forms of racial inequality; nevertheless, his legislation passed only when whites realized, as they had when appropriating funds for blacks to attend graduate programs in other states, that it maintained a form of segregation. The "Anti-Discrimination Bill" brought no benefits to whites, and, furthermore, the federal government was not pressuring states to enact such measures. It was not until the 1960s in most places in Kentucky that this form of humiliation came to an end. In short, Anderson's failure to make progress in this area was not due to his lack of effort nor to blacks' being content with discriminatory practices, but to the strong determination of Kentucky whites to maintain segregation wherever possible in society.

Charles Anderson and the NAACP became involved in a prolonged struggle to equalize the salaries of black teachers with their white counterparts. Practically every school district in Kentucky paid black teachers only a portion of what whites received. In Lexington, for example, the board of education had been guided by "an elaborate salary study" done by the Bureau of School Service of the University of Kentucky, which recommended that white teachers with college degrees but with no teaching experience be paid beginning salaries of $1,000, while black teachers with the same qualifications be paid $850. The report did not say that blacks had received inferior training as a way of justifying this obvious discrimination. Instead, using the wisdom of that day, the report said that "observation alone would suggest to the unbiased observer that the negro teacher will be able to purchase within her society a relatively higher standard of living than the white teacher will be able to secure with the same amount of money."[17]

In early January 1938 the Louisville Association of Colored Teachers formed a committee headed by Victor K. Perry of Central High School to study why the board of education paid black teachers 15 percent less than white teachers. Perry also wrote to Thurgood Marshall of the national office, seeking his advice as to how the black teachers should challenge this form of discrimination. According to Marshall, they needed first to form a committee consisting of representatives from the teachers' association and the local NAACP branch. It was very important, he stressed, that the names of any teachers on the committee remain secret to protect them from retaliation by the school board. Next, the committee needed to raise sufficient funds to pay one year's salary of any teacher who might be discharged for filing a suit against the school board. This procedure, Marshall further explained, had worked successfully in Maryland and had recently been adopted by black teachers in Virginia. The national NAACP showed its strong commitment to ending this form of discrimination by providing counsel without charge or fees of any kind, only requiring that the committee pay the expenses of the counsel and all court costs. Despite Marshall's sound legal advice, the Louisville teachers moved cautiously. They decided to postpone voting on any plan of action until they discussed the salary structure with the superintendent and the Louisville school board.[18]

The black teachers spent almost two years talking and meeting with the Louisville Board of Education. Though refusing to adopt Marshall's plan of action, they grew frustrated with the white board members for doing everything possible to delay action on the matter. However, to the surprise of both the members of the school board and the Association of Colored Teachers, several influential whites voiced approval of the call for equal pay. An editorial in the *Courier-Journal* said: "What indeed would happen to our great Negro population—and they are truly ours—were it not for the loyal host of men and women of their own race, who labor diligently and well to show little dark-skinned children the way to better things. . . . Maybe you don't know it, but every Negro teacher in Louisville draws a salary 15 percent lower than those paid white teachers of identical rating. . . . This is particularly hard in Louisville because Negroes are not admitted to our institutions of higher learning, and, to obtain the education demanded of teachers, they must go outside their native State, at great expense and deprivation." Calling the Louisville Board of Education's two salary scales "unfair," Mayor Joseph D. Scholtz pledged his support to the Afro-American teachers, saying that they had been getting "a run-around" from the school board. "I give you my word when request for the necessary appropriation comes up, it will be made," he assured black leaders. In spite of the support of the influential *Courier-Journal* and the willingness of the mayor to increase the funding of the public schools to offset the pay raises, blacks found that the school board remained firm in its refusal to increase the salaries of black teachers to the level of white teachers.[19]

Black leaders finally ended their talks in December 1939. From New York, attorney Marshall applauded this step. He explained that it was highly unlikely that any progress could be made without a suit, for instead of working to find ways to raise the salaries of black teachers, the Louisville Board of Education had been consulting school districts in other states to learn how best to defend its discriminatory practice. As he informed Anderson: "Here is something which is *confidential* for the present time. The School Board of Louisville and the Attorney for the School Board have both written to the Board of Education of Anne Arundel County and its Attorney seeking full information on the teachers' salary case in Maryland. This makes it quite clear that the School Board is expecting a case."[20]

Surprisingly, despite their futile discussions with the school board and the admonition of Thurgood Marshall that they must file suit, Louisville's Afro-American teachers were still reluctant to take that step. In Anderson's view, the major stumbling block was not the unbending attitude of the board of education but that only a few Negro teachers were truly committed to the movement. "Out of 300 teachers, only 76 contributed to a fund for a purpose which was for their benefit. . . . Likewise, we had lots of promises relative to different ones offering to allow their names as 'plaintiff,' but when the final hour arrived each one who had been a 'parlor' or 'living room' talker, couldn't be found on this side of Finland." Obviously,

Anderson was discouraged, and the conclusion of his letter fully showed his strain: "Therefore, I can offer you little hope at the present time for a test suit here, as it appears as most of the teachers are 'fizzled-headed weazel backs.'" In all fairness to the teachers, they realized the risk involved in being the plaintiff in an unsuccessful suit against the school board. Also, despite Anderson's commitment to black concerns, some of the teachers had expressed doubts about his motives, assuming that he was a mere self-seeker.[21]

Although attempts to reach a settlement continued, they were considered fruitless by black teachers, who were still being paid 15 percent less than whites. The school board probably viewed the meetings as successful since the different pay structure was maintained. In October 1940 the Louisville Board of Education publicly commented on the matter. "While it is true, at the present time, only teachers of colored schools are affected by the provisions under consideration for revision, at the time of the adoption of the schedule the teachers in certain white schools were also affected. These white schools have since been discontinued. . . . It is the opinion of the Board that inequalities in the salary schedule should be corrected when it is possible to do so." The board failed to set a date to equalize the funds, but the statement suggested that salaries would not be equalized in the fiscal year 1941. The board also added a typical response to justify the existence of discrimination: "The interest of all teachers in the system can best be served by making gradual adjustments in the schedule so that the general level of the salaries not be disturbed. Such disturbances might result if such an extraordinary burden were thrown on our budget in any one year." At the bottom of the letter stating the position of the Louisville Board of Education, someone at the national NAACP office (probably Marshall) wrote: "This is an attempted explanation and justification for differences in salary schedule. 'The sense' of the Board has been changed, the justification being that there is not enough money in Louisville to equalize the salaries."[22] In response to the board's position that raising the salaries of black teachers would lead to a severe financial burden on the entire school system, Mayor Scholtz once again offered to increase the city's appropriation to the public schools. But the board rejected his offer, making a vague statement that contractual obligations that could not be broken legally or morally, prevented them from "equalizing the salaries in the immediate future."[23]

The black teachers now agreed with the NAACP that a suit must be filed. On November 7, 1940, Valla Dudley Abbington, a teacher at Jackson Junior High School, petitioned the school board to increase her salary from $1,490 to $1,750, the amount paid white teachers of similar experience. Undoubtedly, very few white teachers in Louisville matched Abbington's educational background: Bachelor of Science from Michigan State, graduate work at the University of Michigan and Columbia University, and a certificate of Public Health from Delmar Institute in New York City.[24] The school board considered Abbington's petition on December 3. Thurgood Marshall attended the meeting, as did a large number of black teachers. The board, however, remained unmoved, with chairman John A. Miller stating that "no monies would be added to the 1941 education budget in order to equalize salaries during 1941." On December 5 the NAACP filed suit, contending that the discriminatory wages paid Abbington and other Afro-American teachers violated "the constitution and laws of the Commonwealth of Kentucky and is a denial of the equal protection of the laws guaranteed by the Fourteenth Amendment to the Constitution of the United States." The NAACP urged the United States District Court to restrain the Louisville Board of Education from operating under its present salary schedule.[25]

Continuing the line of argument endorsed eighteen months earlier, the *Courier-Journal* once again supported the call for equalizing the salaries of white and black teachers. Political cartoons showed the injustices of paying black teachers less. Several editorials appeared, with one of them saying: "It is true that we have made great strides within recent years in our attitude toward Negroes. But what of our failure to pay Negro teachers on an equal footing with white teachers. This shows that the goal of democracy has not been reached." The editorial then made a telling point about the plight of American blacks: "It is a recognized fact that a Negro in competition with a white man must, in order to succeed, have a great deal more ability than the white man. That is not just. It is not democratic and not in keeping with the Constitution, which guarantees all men equal rights. There is no place in the American system for discrimination against any man because of color, race or religion."

Another editorial, "Let's Throw Off Prejudice," said "That Negro teachers in the public school system of Louisville must have recourse to the courts in order to secure justice is everlastingly to be deplored. What they seek is no more than reasonable. The discrimination against which they protest is out of line with the best modern practice, to say nothing of the best modern thought, and if the Board of Education holds back, one wants to know that financial considerations, not a prejudiced reluctance, are the compelling urge." *Courier-Journal* editor Mark Ethridge, a southern liberal on the race issue, encouraged Thurgood Marshall to remain optimistic that the intransigent position of the board would be overturned by the courts. In his reply, Marshall thanked Ethridge for his strong support, concluding it was immeasurably helpful to the struggle.²⁶

The case was set for March 10, 1941. Several weeks prior to that date, the school board notified attorney Prentice Thomas (the law partner of Charles W. Anderson) that the board now planned to equalize the salaries beginning that coming fall term, a move the school board had previously said was impossible. In return the board of education asked the NAACP to drop its suit. Thomas wrote to Marshall, asking what steps to take in light of this new development. Marshall's reply clearly expressed his doubts about the sincerity of the school board when dealing with Louisville's Afro-American teachers:

> The mere statement by them that they are working this out is not sufficient to protect the Negro teachers. Nothing will protect the Negro teachers short of a court decree and that is what the School Board is trying to dodge. Unless they are willing to consent to a decree, I think we should press for a hearing on the merits so that we can get a decree before the end of the school year. It is my opinion that if we push for a hearing on the merits they will yield and agree to a consent decree. I do not trust any School Board, and this is the result of past experience, unless and until I have a court decree filed in the case. In addition, we have the additional factor that the Louisville School Board is even worse than any I have gone up against so far. We have nothing to gain by allowing the case to be

168 / A History of Blacks In Kentucky

pushed off and this would be in the School Board's favor and our loss.

Marshall was correct; the Louisville Board of Education refused Thomas's request for a court decree. In district court on March 10 the case was delayed at the request of the school board until May 27. This gave the board time to reach a settlement acceptable to black leaders. On April 1 the school board formally abolished the 15 percent salary differential effective at the end of the school year. The black teachers proclaimed victory.[27]

But not the national office of the NAACP. At its insistence, the local branch petitioned the United States District Court for a permanent restraining order to keep the school board from returning to its old unequal pay scale. In July Judge Shackleford Miller filed a memorandum on the case, setting trial during the October term of the court. As a press release from the NAACP commented: "The judge's decision to call the case for trial is a victory for the teachers." As a letter from Dr. P.O. Sweeney of the Louisville NAACP to Marshall explained, the court decree was granted in October 1941, bringing "to an end a two year effort [actually a three-year battle] to remove a most flagrant discriminatory practice. Needless to say, we are glad that our fight was successful." Sweeney concluded by praising Marshall's role in the case.[28]

The successful challenge over discriminatory salaries had an immediate monetary benefit for Louisville's black teachers. The Louisville case also aided the cause of the national office of the NAACP. Thurgood Marshall and Charles Houston included Louisville as another place where they had succeeded in equalizing the pay for Afro-American teachers. Within Kentucky other black teachers followed the example from Louisville and demanded equal pay from their local school boards. For black teachers, the victory led to their willingness to challenge school boards over other discriminatory practices.

A much more protracted struggle for the NAACP would be the desegregation of higher education in Kentucky. During the Great Depression the NAACP adopted the strategy of challenging the concept of separate but equal by demanding that states create truly equal institutions for blacks. NAACP strategists knew that duplicating white institutions would prove too costly, thereby leading to desegregation. At the very least, they reasoned, their efforts would compel all states operating dual school systems to upgrade schools for blacks, creating new opportunities at the graduate and professional levels.[29] To be sure, Kentucky, with its tuition plan of sending black students elsewhere, and the other southern and border states found ways to forestall integration. Nevertheless, beginning with Maryland and then Missouri, the NAACP made headway in these cases. Victory in Maryland did not cause Kentucky officials to realize that the courts would eventually strike down their dual systems and that to avoid costly litigation, they should begin to admit blacks. In other words, desegregation in Kentucky required a supreme effort by the NAACP, despite victories in other states.

Several unsuccessful attempts to integrate higher education in Kentucky began in the 1930s. The failures resulted from the opposition of the governors and other state officials who became adept at delaying the issues. Equally important was the position taken by the president of Kentucky State College, Rufus Atwood, who greatly hindered the cause of desegregation in the state. Also, the NAACP and other Afro-American leaders found it extremely trying to raise the needed funds to finance court cases and to remain united when their cases were repeatedly delayed in court.

Albert Benjamin "Happy" Chandler served as governor during the first attempt to desegregate higher education in Kentucky. Historians have not said the last word on Chandler and race relations. He has been applauded for being the commissioner of major-league baseball who broke the color barrier. Yet a recent scholar suggests that Chandler actually had very little to do with the action of the Brooklyn Dodgers in signing Jackie Robinson.[30] Most black "old timers" in Kentucky view Chandler as a friend of the race. During the 1930s, however, he seemed no more willing than other Kentucky politicians to dismantle the state's Jim Crow practices. During his campaign for governor in 1935, Kentucky's Afro-American press criticized Chandler for refusing to speak out against mob rule and lynchings and against the deplorable state of black schools. After the election, Chandler and his associates stated publicly that the black vote had been cast for his opponent, implying that he owed no political debts to blacks. Several years later, when running against Alben Barkley for the United States Senate, Chandler again showed little inclination to address the issues of greatest concern to blacks. Throughout the campaign, no blacks were hired to speak on his behalf in the Afro-American communities, while the Barkley faction formed a Colored Division to tour the state.[31]

In early 1936, shortly after assuming office, Chandler was approached by Charles W. Anderson about the admission of black graduate students to the University of Kentucky. His reply is well-known: "Such will not happen in your time nor mine."[32] A positive interpretation of Chandler's statement means that school integration, though a desirable goal, was unlikely to occur given the desire of white Kentuckians for segregated institutions. In all actuality, however, the governor meant that he did not favor such a radical step. Indeed, when prodded by Anderson, Chandler pointedly refused to endorse desegregation of the state university.

Alfred M. Carroll, a twenty-year-old native of Louisville, applied for admission to the University of Kentucky Law School in January 1939. A graduate of Wilberforce, Carroll was attending Howard University's Law School but desired to return home to complete his legal training. Carroll's application led to action on the part of Governor Chandler. From his Emergency Fund, he allocated an additional $1,600 for black students to attend schools in other states, a measure he had previously refused to consider, even though black leaders had pointed out that the funds available were insufficient to meet the demand. In one of his harsher statements, the governor warned blacks against demanding admission to the University of Kentucky.[33] Chandler also spurred President Rufus Atwood of Kentucky State College into action.

Trained as a chemist at the University of Iowa, Atwood succeeded Green P. Russell as president of Kentucky State in 1929. During his more than three decades at the helm of the school, he was largely responsible for Kentucky State's becoming fully accredited and growing immeasurably. Atwood quickly learned that appropriations for Kentucky State were considered by state officials only after the white schools, and his being outspoken against racial discrimination could greatly harm the school. But unlike Benjamin Mays and other black college presidents who maintained their sense of independence and dignity even though they needed white financial support, Atwood became a pawn of white politicians. Starting with Chandler, governors

President Rufus Atwood in a 1931 photograph with three Kentucky State teachers. Photograph by Cusick Studio.
Kentucky Historical Society

and other state officials used Atwood's testimony to prove that Kentucky State met the needs of blacks, that appropriations were fair, and that blacks had no real cause to seek admission to white schools. For example, Atwood agreed completely with white officials when they called for the introduction of certain accredited programs at Kentucky State or Louisville Municipal College instead of admitting blacks to white institutions. Not surprisingly, white officials named Atwood to a host of interracial boards in the state.[34]

Atwood stated that the decision of Governor Chandler to appropriate additional funds for blacks to attend schools out of state satisfied Carroll, and that he would withdraw his application to the University of Kentucky. When contacted by a black newspaper, Carroll carefully but forcefully explained that Atwood's statement was untrue, that he had never spoken with

Atwood. This led to Atwood's being roundly condemned in the black press. I. Willis Cole, long-time editor of the Louisville *Leader* and civil rights activist, harshly proclaimed: "Negroes classed as leaders of the race who are always willing and ready to barter with . . . whites . . . in a pact which would give the Negro less than that guaranteed him under the Constitution, and supported by the Supreme Court, . . . are not only spineless cowards in the eyes of those whom they serve as puppets, but they are hypocrites and traitors. They are enemies of the race who should be relegated to the past."[35] Within days of being roundly condemned in the black newspaper, Atwood wrote to Governor Chandler about a recent meeting of the legislative committee of the Kentucky Negro Education Association. The tone of the first part of the letter suggested that Atwood was merely informing the governor that members of KNEA wanted to meet with state officials regarding desegregation:

> The Legislative Committee, after considerable discussion, voted that its chairman, Professor A.E. Meyzeek, send a letter to you requesting that you give consideration to the question of equality of educational opportunity for the Negro in Kentucky in light of the Supreme Court decision referred to above; and that at a date, convenient to you, the Committee be given a conference with you, with the State Superintendent of Public Instruction, and such other persons as you may wish to invite. The purpose of this conference would be that you could present to the Committee the state's plans for bringing about equality of educational opportunity for the Negro in Kentucky.

The last paragraph of the letter clearly revealed that Atwood had become a "spy" for the governor, that he provided Chandler with confidential information from the meeting of the black leaders:

> So far as I was able to learn, there is at present no organized Negro effort interested in the Alfred Carroll case. As a matter of fact, Attorney Anderson assured the Committee verbally, that no suit would

be filed at this time. There probably may be other individual applications, but so far as I know, these do not have the endorsement of organized effort.

Five days later, Governor Chandler responded, informing Atwood that he had received Meyzeek's letter. He assured Atwood of his intention to meet with the black organization to "discuss the proper educational opportunities for negroes in this State." Though not referring directly to the information Atwood had given him about the black leadership's lack of support for Carroll's suit, Chandler said: "I appreciate the attitude manifested in your letter of the eighth."[36]

For advice on Carroll's application, Chandler appointed Atwood, Charles Anderson, school principals Albert E. Meyzeek and William H. Fouse, and a host of prominent whites to the Governor's Advisory Committee. At a crucial meeting, Atwood shocked his fellow black members by making a motion to exclude from consideration the admission of Negroes to graduate programs at the white universities, a position that was quickly seconded by the president of the University of Kentucky. In a letter to Lizzie Fouse, Nannie Burroughs, president of the National Association of Colored Women, praised Fouse and other blacks for publicly condemning Atwood. Burroughs then added to the condemnation of Atwood: "What are we going to do to stiffen the backbones and broaden the vision of our people? Sometimes I think even some of those who could perhaps be classified as our enemies see the handwriting on the wall, so far as graduate and professional training are concerned, far more clearly than many of our own people. A little more courage could speed up the process of getting what rightfully is ours if only we could inject some of that courage into some of those who need it."[37]

The presidents of the University of Kentucky agreed even more than Atwood about the necessity of maintaining segregated schools. Neither Frank L. McVey, who retired in 1941, nor Herman L. Donovan, who served from 1941-56, adopted any positive steps to admit Afro-Americans to the state university. McVey authored a book that pointed out the shortcomings of education in Kentucky, the repeated failure of the state to provide adequate support for higher education. Yet at the same time, he failed to note the irony of his own situation of endorsing a dual system of higher education in the state. The title of McVey's book, *The Gates Open Slowly*, was a phrase that black leaders should have used to describe his attitude and that of other university officials toward desegregation.[38] Indeed, by their willingness to explore any possibility to maintain segregation and satisfy the courts, they demonstrated clearly that their primary goal was to keep intact the University of Kentucky as a lily-white college. In a letter to Carroll, Alvin E. Evans, dean of the law school, outlined the position of the university and explained his personal views on race. To make sure that Carroll understood the significance of his application, Evans briefly mentioned that Kentucky had a number of laws prohibiting blacks and whites from attending the same school. Regardless of the law, Carroll should reconsider his desire to enter the university primarily because white students were unaccustomed to being in class with a black, and that would make the black feel uncomfortable, leading, of course, to an interruption of the learning process. Evans added: "Speaking for myself only, I am very strongly in sympathy with adequate preparation of the colored race. Having come from the North, I do not have any prejudice, of which I am conscious, against colored men and their opportunities for equal education. I am not, however, able to ignore this fact that in this community many people do not feel as I do and human nature cannot be made over inside of a few weeks, months, or even years. Since human nature is what it is, it seems to be in the interest of both white and colored not to press such an issue as you are presenting at the present time. My experience with the law leads me to believe that we get much further by other means than by insisting upon abstract and perhaps theoretical rights in particular cases. I believe in adjustment and compromise in order that all may profit by our combined wisdom." Evans then informed Carroll that his application had been denied for two reasons—first, because of Kentucky's laws against school integration, and second, because he had not graduated from an accredited college.[39]

The information Atwood had given Chandler proved accurate; Thurgood Marshall strongly advised Charles Anderson to drop the case. "The Dean of the Law School took the position that since Carroll was a graduate of Wilberforce and since Wilberforce was not an accredited school, then there might be difficulties in admitting him. . . . We are of the opinion that We should not follow this case through because of a technicality that Wilberforce is not an accredited school." Marshall, concerned about the momentum of the NAACP in its college desegregation cases, knew that a defeat in court could greatly set back the entire cause. Surely another candidate could be found to desegregate the University of Kentucky, he concluded.[40]

Two-and-a-half years later, in October 1941, a seventeen-year-old honor student from Louisville Central High School filed suit in Fayette Circuit Court seeking admission to the University of Kentucky School of Engineering. Charles Lamont Eubanks explained that he applied to the state university because none of the black schools offered civil engineering. The assistant attorney general's comments about the Eubanks suit foreshadowed the position that would be adopted by both the university and state officials: "The Attorney General's office believes it is a part of an organized effort to stir up class feelings. The colored people and the white people have been getting along fine in Kentucky and we don't like the idea of stirring things up." Charles W. Anderson and his law partner, Prentice Thomas, were hired as counsel for Eubanks. Throughout the case, they relied on the assistance of Thurgood Marshall.[41]

At the urging of Governor Keen Johnson and University of Kentucky President Donovan, who was described as being "extremely anxious for the State Board of Education to give it consideration," an engineering program was created for Kentucky State College. State officials openly acknowledged that the program was an attempt to provide separate but equal opportunities, to prevent the desegregation of the University of Kentucky. The admission requirements at both the white and black schools were the same. Students enrolling in engineering courses at Kentucky State were to be charged the same fees as those at the white school.[42] After reviewing the engineering program at Kentucky State, several spokesmen for the University of Kentucky proclaimed that Eubanks's suit was now moot, that the state had provided separate but equal facilities for Afro-Americans. The NAACP, however, had a different view of the engineering program: "It was found on inspection that the engineering school at Kentucky State has only one teacher, not an engineer, but a bachelor of science in industrial education. The school is practically without equipment. The curriculum is not an engineering course but an industrial course which includes such subjects as welding." Eubanks refused to attend the school, a position strongly endorsed by Charles W. Anderson. As he told Walter White: "I do not want him enrolled at the make-shift, wholly inadequate department of 'Engineering' at Kentucky State College. This would be inconsistent with our position that the provisions for engineering at Kentucky State are in no sense a substantial equivalent for those offered at the University of Kentucky; and in fact they are not." Expressing a view similar to that of University of Kentucky officials, President Atwood was elated at the introduction of the new program at his college, even though he well understood the motives of the state board of education.[43]

Due to the delaying tactics of the state, it took over three years to resolve Eubanks's suit for admission to the University of Kentucky. In the meanwhile, he resisted several overtures from the state to enroll at Kentucky State or to have his way paid to Ohio to receive the training denied him in Kentucky. On one occasion the NAACP did attempt, without success, to have Eubanks awarded an engineering scholarship to attend Howard University. His attorneys reasoned that if he earned high grades at Howard it would strengthen their case.[44] Finally, on January 6, 1945, the case was resolved when the suit was dismissed due to a lack of prosecution. "No action had been taken in the case during the last two terms of court. A Kentucky rule of court procedure calls for the dismissal of a case which has not been prosecuted during two consecutive terms of court." Commenting on the outcome of the case, Anderson said that the blame for the defeat rested with President Atwood of Kentucky State. Atwood's endorsement of the makeshift school of engineering gave the state and University of Kentucky attorneys a chance to argue that the state provided an equal education for blacks, thereby circumventing the U.S. Supreme Court's ruling in the Gaines case. Anderson added that as long as Atwood allowed the establishment of other makeshift courses, the advancement of black education in the state would be effectively stalemated. Thurgood Marshall called the outcome of the Eubanks case an "awful licking." Eubanks declined to pursue the case further. Having been out of school for more than three years, he now wanted to further his own education, and as soon as possible.[45]

Defeat in the Eubanks case made the NAACP more determined than ever that its next attempt to desegregate the state university would be a solid case, with an applicant of unquestionable credentials. It took three years, but on March 15, 1948, Louisville school teacher Lyman T. Johnson applied for admission to the graduate program in history at the University of Kentucky. A native of Tennessee, Johnson held the A.B. degree from Virginia Union University, the M.A. degree from the University of Michigan, and had taken a number of courses toward the Ph.D. at the University of Wisconsin. (He would often boast that very few, if indeed any, whites in the Louisville school system had attended schools the equal of Michigan and Wisconsin.) Upon arriving in Louisville in the early 1930s, he became involved with the NAACP, and even served as president, a step normally not taken by public school employees. In Johnson, the NAACP had found a person with the right educational background and one who would not quit for any reason.[46]

These two attributes of Johnson turned out to be very important, because despite the fact that blacks were being admitted to white universities in other states during the late 1940s, the University of Kentucky was determined to resist. "Our policy has been pretty well defined. We are prohibited by State law and the State Constitution from accepting the registration of a Negro," the university said when rejecting his application for admission. University officials, as they had in the Eubanks challenge, then went on the offensive, calling for "equal" opportunities for Afro-Americans at Kentucky State. The attitude of Kentucky's white educators and politicans is very significant because it proves that the NAACP had been correct in the early 1930s when adopting the strategy of compelling white schools either to desegregate or equalize. Their actions also reveal that in Kentucky, funds could be made available for black education, but only when integration seemed imminent. The state board of education and the University of Kentucky Board of Trustees passed resolutions calling for introducing at Kentucky State College all courses, even those at the graduate level, that were available to white students within the state. White leaders agreed that no stone should be left unturned in providing for blacks (but only at Kentucky State) all of the training, library, and laboratory facilities offered at the University of Kentucky. The governor did his part, giving Kentucky State $25,000 from his emergency fund to help in the development of new undergraduate and graduate courses.[47]

By July 1948, only a few months after Johnson had applied for admission to the state university, new courses were being offered at Kentucky State. Black teachers who desired to take courses in the summer applied to various departments at the University of Kentucky. The departments, in turn, selected students for admission to summer school at Kentucky State. Professors at the University of Kentucky sent bibliographies to Kentucky State and aided the black school in selecting books for the library. With courses at Kentucky State as an alternative to leaving the state for graduate training, thirty blacks enrolled in the summer of 1948, including Lyman Johnson. In Johnson's case, as well as most of the other black students, white professors from the University of Kentucky drove to Frankfort to teach the course.

Shortly after Johnson sought admission to graduate school, another Afro-American, John Wesley Hatch, applied to the University of Kentucky law school. Starting in September, seven law professors drove to Frankfort to instruct one student in the law. Two months into this costly, time-consuming practice, President Donovan, who had urged President Atwood to accept this "ideal arrangement," announced several changes. Four Frankfort lawyers would teach Hatch, and his classroom work would be shifted to the state capitol to take advantage of the state's law library. Donovan noted: "By having professors who live in Frankfort, the student will be able to have a much better daily schedule for his classes than heretofore, and making the State Law Library available to him in the same building as his classes represents a distinct improvement. In both instances, a closer parallel to the opportunities afforded law students on our Lexington campus is achieved."[48]

Donovan's action led to a rare protest from Atwood, who charged the University of Kentucky president with violating their agreement to teach law courses at the campus of Kentucky State. "Without raising any question of the competency of the new teaching personnel, it must be apparent to all that the new arrangement is even more cumbersome than the former plan and works an additional hardship upon Hatch who must adjust himself to the new teachers in the middle of the semester," Atwood complained.[49] Donovan, in adopting the new plan, was in effect acknowledging that the first plan had proved unworkable and that carrying a few books to Frankfort was not the same as having access to a law library. To be sure, Atwood's criticism of Donovan was self-serving. As his comments showed, he realized all along that his agreement with Donovan was cumbersome and unworkable and far from being truly separate but equal. Atwood protested the change not because of the bad effects on the student but merely because the courses would no longer be taught on his campus.

While Donovan and Atwood tried to maintain segregated institutions, Lyman Johnson and the NAACP pressed his right to attend the white university. The suit stated that Johnson's application had been rejected solely because of his color. At the pretrial conference, the NAACP raised three issues: whether provisions had been made for the education of Negroes in the graduate school at Kentucky State; whether the provisions allegedly made by the defendants for the graduate education of Negroes in Frankfort satisfied the Fourteenth Amendment; and whether any facilities established on the basis of segregation, solely because of race or color, could satisfy the requirements of the Fourteenth Amendment. The University of Kentucky argued that because of the graduate programs at Kentucky State, the willingness of the state to purchase required books for Kentucky State's library, and the arrangement for the professors to travel to Frankfort, equality existed for blacks in education.[50]

As the trial approached, the NAACP took steps to strengthen its case. A number of white students and professors from the University of Kentucky law school agreed to testify on Johnson's behalf, to argue that class interactions were an essential part of graduate training. Experts from a wide range of disciplines were prepared to testify that the books and facilities at Kentucky State were inadequate and could not compare with those at the white school. Dr. George M. Johnson, dean of Howard University's law school, in an interview in the *Courier-Journal* called the arrangement between Kentucky State and the University of Kentucky a "dodge" that would be declared unconstitutional. Since Lyman Johnson had applied for admission to graduate school in history, the NAACP decided to have the nation's foremost black historian, John Hope Franklin of Howard University, testify about the value of the training received by Johnson at Kentucky State. "We would like from you testimony showing the need for an extensive library in order to pursue the subjects which Johnson desires to take; the value in having other students in a class with him, they would be able to interchange ideas, the necessity for having professors available for consultation and assistance after hours; the necessity for having an extensive library within easy access over and above whatever bibliography might be furnished by UK," wrote the NAACP's counsel. Franklin traveled to Lexington for the trial; as it turned out, however, he was not called to testify. Nevertheless, it does show the thoroughness of the preparation of the NAACP for the case.[51]

On March 30, 1949, Judge H. Church Ford of the United States District Court reached a quick decision, a judgment in favor of Lyman Johnson and the NAACP. He said: "How can anyone listen to this evidence without seeing that it is a makeshift plan?" The University of Kentucky was under an obligation to admit qualified black students, Judge Ford forcefully explained, since the state had failed to provide graduate and professional schools for blacks that in any respect equaled the university for whites.[52] Despite the ruling of the court and the reality that most of the other border states had also been ordered to admit black students to graduate and professional programs, some of the members of the University of Kentucky Board of Trustees were unwilling to accept defeat and called for appealing to the United States Supreme Court. In an attempt to ensure that the University of Kentucky remained a "lily-white" institution, at least one board member wanted the state legislature to meet in special session and appropriate the funds necessary to build a black university that would equal the white school in every respect. The decision on how the University of Kentucky chose to respond to the ruling of the United States District Court was resolved at the next board meeting. In the words of Charles G. Talbert, a historian of the university:

> At the next meeting of the board, Donovan presented the issue and recommended that the decision be accepted without appeal to a higher court. After a heated discussion, the board voted 7 to 5 in favor of appealing the case. It was the first time that one of Donovan's recommendations had been turned down by the board. The discussion,

however, did not end with the taking of the vote. At this time Judge [Richard C.] Stoll . . . stated that he had voted against Donovan's recommendation, but would like to reconsider. He also reminded the other members that when the board followed the recommendation of the President, it seldom made a mistake. Another vote was taken, and it stood ten to two against appeal and in favor of the admission of Negroes.[53]

The NAACP moved quickly to have black students enroll at the University of Kentucky for summer courses. Robert L. Carter, Marshall's assistant, wrote to the blacks who had attended graduate courses at Kentucky State: "You, however, being, technically at least, students attending classes sponsored by the University are entitled to immediate admission. I think, therefore, that it is advisable and highly desirable that you immediately apply to the University of Kentucky for the courses of instruction that you are now taking. Your application should not be held up but should be sent on immediately." That summer, Lyman Johnson and thirty other blacks integrated the University of Kentucky. After classes had started, Johnson wrote to Carter about his experiences, saying: "I am now into my 2nd week at the U. of K. Everything goes along smoothly. The only open segregation is in the cafeteria. There we have been asked to sit at three tables with the signs on them: RESERVED. At first they said 'Reserved for Negroes.' I asked the lady in charge, the hostess, if that was necessary. She replied that she had been told to put up the signs. Thereupon she returned to her office and clipped off the bottom line [for Negroes] and came back to my table with 'Reserved' on the cards. In the class-rooms and libraries we experience no noticeable segregation. Professors and students are cordial. Two Deans have called me in for conference. They want the thing to work. But they [the Administration] are afraid of the Federal judge and the Kentucky [Day] law. I have told both that we would not 'put ourselves on the white students' in return if they will not resort to the objectionable signs, 'For Negroes,' 'For Colored,' etc. So far the 'Reserved' is the only indication of open segregation I know about here."[54]

When writing about the desegregation of the University of Kentucky in his memoirs, President Donovan explained that because he wanted integration to succeed, he decided that the school should move "slowly and unostentatiously, the less publicity the better." The decorum he urged Afro-Americans to observe, however, clearly indicated that he desired only a minimal amount of interaction between whites and blacks and that in actuality his proposals amounted to segregation within the supposedly integrated schools. In short, in the view of Donovan, black students should voluntarily segregate themselves to avoid offending whites by their very presence at the white school. Upon being admitted to the university, black students were personally interviewed by the deans of their chosen fields of study, who assured the students of their desire to see this "experiment" of interracial education work. Donovan, in personal conversations with the black students, told them to "sit together in the classroom rather than scatter over the room, that when they entered the cafeteria, they sit at a table with their fellow Negro students instead of each occupying a separate table." In advice that sounded remarkably similar to what slaveowners had said to blacks a century ago, the president advised them to avoid initiating any conversation or interactions with whites, but if whites spoke to them and sat at their table, then the black students "should feel at ease." In fact, Donovan advised the black students to refrain from going to the student union and all social programs. "We told them to find their own living quarters and to work out their own social life with their own people." As Donovan explained in a matter-of-fact manner, several years passed before university officials assigned rooms to blacks in one of the dormitories. But he did note in an obvious defense of his strategy of integration: "After the first year, we leaked out the word to them that it made no difference where they sat in classrooms or cafeteria, and that it was all right for them to go to the Student Union Building." This paternalistic—if not outright racist—attitude of telling blacks to postpone participating in much of what the University of Kentucky offered students was in keeping with how Donovan viewed school desegregation. Prior to the successful court challenge of Lyman Johnson, he had not advised the board to desegregate willingly but had devised the makeshift arrangement with Kentucky State. So, in a real sense, the ruling of the district court that the makeshift arrangement at Kentucky State was a farce had been a public repudiation of both

Donovan and Atwood, two college presidents who desired to maintain segregated institutions.[55]

A number of laudatory comments were published about the integration of the University of Kentucky. The admission of Afro-Americans had occurred without "a riffle at the University and the students took it in stride." In an editorial, the Lexington *Leader* applauded the peaceful desegregation process, noting that the university's experience showed what could happen when agitators, like those farther South who were doing far more harm than good, are not present. "A calmer, more gradual course is better and in the long run more effective." One of the obvious reasons for the "success" was the very small number of Afro-American students involved in the desegregation of the University of Kentucky; by 1956, only eighty-three of the 7,200 students were black. Most were natives of Lexington, coming to the campus for classes only and not participating in extracurricular activities.[56] They were, in other words, no threat to the status quo of the university. But in applauding themselves, whites obviously ignored the long struggle waged by blacks to be admitted to the University of Kentucky.

In fact, scholars, and especially the commentators who have praised whites for accepting college desegregation, have failed to discuss the actions of state officials in formulating yet another plan to prevent desegregation. On February 8, 1948, state leaders signed an agreement with fourteen southern states to establish a regional university. Instead of being forced by the courts to admit blacks to their state universities, southern whites envisioned a large southern university for Afro-Americans (with various departments scattered in strategic locations), offering first-rate programs that were similar in every respect to those for whites. The compact Kentucky officials agreed to called for the "development and maintenance of regional educational services and schools in the Southern States in the professional, technological, scientific, literary, and other fields, so as to provide greater educational advantages and facilities for the citizens in the several States who reside in such region; to declare that the State of Kentucky is a party to said compact, as amended, and that the agreements, covenants and obligations therein are binding upon said State; and appropriating funds for Kentucky's share of the cost of administrative services and operations under said compact." Since they avoided mentioning race and whom the regional university was being designed to serve, the southern states failed to explain why such a university was needed, since every state already had the various programs that were to be created for the new institution. The only hint of the obvious intent was the statement that Meharry Medical College in Nashville, a black institution located near Fisk University, had agreed to serve as the site for the medical, dental, and nursing programs. On March 25, 1950, fully a year after the United States District Court had ordered that Lyman T. Johnson be admitted to the University of Kentucky, the Kentucky house and senate formally approved the compact, though not before adding an additional clause, one that was clearly designed to impress the court that they were no longer discriminating against blacks: "the Commonwealth of Kentucky shall not erect, acquire, develop or maintain in any manner any educational institution within its borders to which Negroes will not be admitted on an equal basis with other races, nor shall any Negro citizen of Kentucky be forced to attend any segregated regional institution to obtain instruction in a particular course of study if there is in operation within the Commonwealth at the time an institution that offers the same course of study to students of other races." In short, Kentucky's white leadership—the very people who had worked diligently to keep blacks from attending the state university—were hoping that Afro-Americans would accept the concept of a regional all-black college as a better alternative than school integration for them.[57]

For scholars fully aware of the determined commitment of blacks and the NAACP to end the farce of "separate but equal," it seems ridiculous that white lawmakers thought that blacks would willingly agree to yet another Jim Crow institution. Yet, when considering how whites in responsible positions had consistently refused to face the possibility of desegregation and initiate programs to make the transition as smooth as possible, it is highly likely that they thought their latest dodge would be acceptable to the courts. When reviewing the irrational racism of whites, one should bear in mind that before the University of Kentucky Board of Trustees agreed not to challenge the court's ruling in admitting Johnson, one member, a judge no less, had recommended "That the Governor be memorialized by this Board to call into extraordinary session the General Assembly of Kentucky to provide by appropriation such funds, and provide such other authority to the State Board of Education, if said Court finds that Board lacks authority, to so provide the Kentucky State College with equal facilities in all respects to those at this University."[58] In their last futile steps to prevent desegregation, these whites openly acknowledged that colleges for blacks were grossly inferior, totally lacking in legal, medical, engineering, and other programs that were commonplace for whites. These southern states were asking for one final chance to right their own wrongs. Though the idea of a regional university won approval from Kentucky's lawmakers, as far as can be determined, nothing came of it. Its importance lies ultimately in demonstrating how few of Kentucky's white leaders willingly acquiesced in desegregation, but rather, as late as a year after the Johnson decision, were still trying to find a way to combat the changing world.

After the successful completion of the Johnson suit, the NAACP called for the admission of blacks to all colleges in Kentucky, but the Day Law remained a barrier. On February 1, 1946, Charles W. Anderson had introduced legislation to admit black nurses to post-graduate or in-service training in white hospitals and institutions, a measure that finally passed in 1948. Two years later, in 1950, the death blow to the Day Law occurred when the state legislature further allowed colleges on both the undergraduate and graduate levels to desegregate at their own choosing. Immediately thereafter, several Catholic colleges in Louisville opened their doors to Afro-Americans. The University of Louisville announced the admission of black students and the closing of Louisville Municipal College for Negroes.[59]

Fully aware of the abolitionist legacy of their school, a number of people associated with Berea College moved quickly to open its doors to black students. In 1947 a group of students, calling themselves the Young People's Socialist League of Berea, had written to the NAACP for assistance in having the Day Law overturned so that black students could again be admitted at Berea. That same year, William R. Schorman, an alumnus of Berea, also urged the NAACP to participate in a movement to end the Day Law. In other words, it is clear that a segment of the school's population desired desegregation. After the Day Law was amended in March 1950, the Berea Board of Trustees voted to accept "qualified Negro students" to the college. The board reaffirmed its commitment to the youth of the Appalachian region, but added that they also expressed their "interest in the efforts of Negro youths of this region to get an education and we hereby empower our administration to admit such Negro students from within this mountain region whom we find thoroughly qualified coming completely within the provisions to the Kentucky law and whom in their judgment it appears we should serve."[60]

In addition to working successfully for the admission of blacks to white colleges and equal salaries for Negro teachers, the NAACP continued to challenge other forms of discrimination. In the early 1940s black citizens of Lynch, Benham, Harlan, Middlesboro, and Barbourville formed the Regional NAACP of Eastern Kentucky, pooling their resources to better attack Jim Crow. In Bell County blacks called for a public library, since there was one in existence for whites. They eventually won a concession: "White library met our committee and consented to give books and shelfs [sic] if we gave place. Will be using portion of a funeral home." Officials from the national office found this arrangement unacceptable, informing the leaders of the Bell County NAACP that as taxpayers they were entitled to a library equal in quality to that of the whites and to continue their protest. This advice was followed, and the local government eventually relented, appropriating funds to construct a building for the black library. The branch in Bell County, encouraged by this action, worked until a paved road and bridge were built to several churches and schools. Members of the branch next planned an even more ambitious campaign: "Our next step is getting jobs for Negroes where they spend their money." Finally, several years later the Regional NAACP raised money to prosecute the case of a black woman who had lost her unborn child as a result of a beating she received at the hands of a white bus driver.[61]

The Paducah branch became active on a number of fronts in the years before World War II. In 1936 Joe Hale, a black man, was sentenced to death for killing a white man. The NAACP argued that because blacks had been excluded from the jury, Hale had not received a fair trial. The organization raised the needed funds to fight the case before the Kentucky Court of Appeals and later before the United States Supreme Court. On

Biracial education returned to Berea in the 1950s.
Berea College Archives

April 11, 1936, the Supreme Court ruled in the case of *Hale* v. *Kentucky* that blacks had been systematically excluded from serving on juries in the state. The court ordered the inclusion of Afro-Americans in the pool of potential jurors. When one considers that except in minor cases, no blacks served on juries in Kentucky, even in Louisville, this was truly a major victory for the association in the Bluegrass State.[62]

The successful litigation in the Hale case gave the Paducah NAACP the momentum to press for additional changes. For years the black residents of Smithland, an area in Livingston County, complained that the school board provided no schooling for blacks beyond the eighth grade and refused to pay the transportation costs for black students to attend high school in Paducah. The Paducah NAACP hired an attorney and helped secure a judgment requiring Livingston County, as part of its obligation to black students, to provide bus service to the high school in Paducah. In the early 1950s the branch successfully sued for the right of Afro-Americans to attend Paducah Junior College. Also, during this time the Paducah NAACP, unlike most branches elsewhere, worked for better employment opportunities. The branch's efforts helped a number of skilled blacks to find employment on the Atomic Energy Project as carpenters and electricians and in a wide range of clerical jobs. Despite these successes, the president of the branch complained that most Paducah blacks, though benefiting from the efforts of the NAACP, did not truly support the organization. "Much more should have been accomplished, and much more would have been accomplished, if only a reasonable percent of Paducah's Negro population had supported it. Only 3% of Paducah's 'pigment' suffering population belongs to the organization, and less than 3% of those who belong attend the meetings or help with the actual work of the Branch. It is difficult to understand why the organization . . . is so poorly supported. One is almost forced to believe that our people must be masochistic and get a big thrill from being punished and humiliated."[63]

Of all the NAACP branches in Kentucky, the Louisville organization, which could draw on the city's large black population and the presence of black attorneys and other professionals, was consistently the most active in the years immediately after World War II. NAACP records clearly show that in addition to working for equal pay for teachers and school desegregation, the Louisville branch had an agenda to end other forms of discrimination. With Lyman Johnson serving as president for most of the years, the branch sent telegrams to the Kentucky delegation whenever Congress considered federal antilynching bills, worked with Charles W. Anderson in an attempt to provide equal accommodations on Jim Crow trains, and investigated police brutality in Louisville, something that had long been a major concern to Afro-Americans. On several occasions the branch picketed local theatrical and stage performances featuring black actors because the management continued the practice of segregating black patrons. One such incident occurred in November 1945 during the showing of *Carmen Jones* at Memorial Auditorium, where the NAACP had a long line of demonstrators outside. When informed of the actions of the NAACP, most black ticket holders demanded refunds. The efforts of the NAACP succeeded to a degree; the cast of *Carmen Jones* vowed not to return to the city as long as Jim Crow existed and promised to inform other black entertainers about race relations in Louisville. Though it took several years to reach a conclusion, the NAACP began campaigns in the late 1940s to end restrictive covenants in housing and park segregation. In both cases members of the organization filed suit in court. NAACP officials were proud of their efforts on behalf of the race. When reviewing accomplishments in 1949, the year the University of Kentucky was desegregated, the branch said: "This year has been a memorable one. One that will go down in the annals of NAACP history."[64]

As a way of bringing unity to their efforts to end racial discrimination, the various Kentucky branches formed a statewide NAACP organization, held annual conferences, and elected officials to lead the movement. By 1948 the Kentucky State Conference of Branches of the NAACP represented twenty-five local branches with over 7,500 members. The organization adopted as "its fundamental purpose the attainment of an equal opportunity to exercise and enjoy full citizenship rights for all citizens of this commonwealth." Like Afro-American leaders throughout the nation, these Kentucky blacks said that now more than ever, since blacks had played a part in World War II, they had a legitimate claim to equal rights. The Kentucky organization then outlined its immediate goals. "We are shocked and outraged at the extent and degree of brutality exhibited by officers of the law and directed against Negro citizens." The organization urged that blacks be appointed to police forces in communities all over the state. In its declaration, the NAACP said that many qualified blacks, for a variety of reasons, have not exercised the important and fundamental privilege of voting. "We call upon all such persons to recognize the importance of the ballot and to register in the party of their choice and participate in all elections for public office held within this commonwealth. We pledge our resources and membership toward the attainments of full registration of qualified Negro citizens of this commonwealth and of their active participation in all future elections for public office." The NAACP called for an end of discrimination in employment: "Since the termination of World War II Negro citizens have been increasingly the victims of unfair hiring and firing employment policies." The organization urged blacks to join labor unions to help secure employment. Of special concern were the black youths, many of whom were veterans of the war, who "are still being grossly discriminated against in the administration of vocational and on the job training programs provided by the state of Kentucky." Private banks and insurance companies, the declaration pointed out, have continually refused to treat Negro veterans applying for government loans and mortgage insurance on a par equal to whites. "In recognition of this flagrant discrimination directed against our honorably discharged veterans, the state conference of branches hereby creates a state veterans committee for the specific purpose of working vigorously towards the elimination of all such discriminatory practices and policies." The statewide organization reaffirmed its determination to end segregation in public facilities and agencies receiving public funds.[65]

During the same years that the NAACP worked aggressively for changes, white civic and government leaders formed interracial committees to make recommendations on issues affecting race relations. Were these organizations a conservative movement on the part of state officials to forestall action on civil rights issues? Or, did the various interracial organizations represent sincere attempts by whites to aid Afro-Americans in their quest for equality? Given the opposition of Governor Chandler toward desegregation of the University of Kentucky, it is not surprising that his advisory committee accomplished little besides bringing together black and white leaders to discuss the merits of Kentucky State College's being made the equal of the white colleges. In 1939, after a group of blacks strongly expressed their disapproval of the continuation of inequality in higher education, Governor Keen Johnson appointed an advisory committee. Composed of black and white educators, the committee made a number of modest recommendations to improve conditions for Afro-Americans within existing segregated institutions. They called for the start of courses in public health work, nurse training, and social service administration at Louisville Municipal College for Negroes. Instead of calling for the admission of blacks to white universities, the report concluded that Kentucky State needed to offer more effective training in agriculture and business administration and to start a graduate program in education. Though avoiding any criticism of the committee's recommendations, an editorial in the *Courier-Journal* declared that a call for upgrading black schools instead of admitting blacks to white institutions was in a real sense postponing the inevitable: "It is obvious that Kentucky, a relatively poor State, cannot provide equal opportunities for Negroes in the highest branches of education unless Negroes are allowed to attend the same classes as white citizens." The editorial ended with a most telling point: "Sooner or later we must all face the fact that the American tradition, of which we boast so glibly, demands far more than we have ever accomplished in the way of equality in rights and opportunities for the Negro. Fortunately, we are not willing to repudiate that tradition; but neither do we seem willing to live up to it."[66]

Another biracial committee, the Kentucky Commission of Negro Affairs, was created by Governor Simeon Willis in September 1944. The commission had subcommittees on education, economics, housing, social welfare, health, and civil affairs. Charles W. Anderson and a number of well-known Afro-Americans served on the commission. On November 1, 1945, after more than a year of investigation, the commission released its findings in a thirty-nine-page report. The report pointed out the obvious wrongs that blacks faced in segregated Kentucky. For instance, blacks received inadequate medical care because they were relegated to inferior hospitals or excluded entirely from health agencies. The committee chaired by Anderson investigated civil affairs, calling for a modification or repeal of the Day Law to allow black students on the graduate level to attend white universities within the state. That adequate funding for Kentucky State would lead to the school's being on par with the University of Kentucky was an overly optimistic conclusion reached in the report. Robert E. Black of the Louisville Urban League chaired the economic committee. After detailing the discrimination blacks faced in industry, Black's committee ended with a plea: "Employers are urged to give opportunities to Negroes from which custom has barred them: i.e., in sales personnel, on telephone switchboards, operators of street cars and buses, etc."[67]

The views expressed by these three committees made them the legitimate heirs to the Commission on Interracial Cooperation, an organization active during the 1920s and 1930s. Black and white members of CIC aided blacks when they called for the creation of black schools and other institutions and when they worked for improved health care in black communities. But, significantly, the CIC, and the predominantly white organizations formed decades later, believed firmly in blacks' staying "in their place." What is most revealing about the moderate approach to black problems as outlined by Governors Chandler's and Johnson's advisory committees and the members of the Kentucky Commission on Negro Affairs is, with the exception of the Anderson subcommittee's call for a modification in the Day Law, the failure of these groups to ask for any massive changes to end segregation. Instead, a group of Kentucky's leading citizens urged the uplifting of blacks within the realm of Jim Crow. In other words, these leaders pointed out the obvious wrongs that Afro-Americans faced but refused to call for the solution needed to wipe out these wrongs. In that regard, one wonders what would have occurred in Kentucky if the NAACP had not been persistent and had merely allowed the "better class of whites" to handle what they called the "Negro problem." Given the white opposition to every step toward desegregation, it is not surprising that the ultimate goal of the NAACP—a color-blind society with equal opportunities for all—was not achieved prior to the 1950s and even continued to face much opposition during that time.

Five

The 1950s to the Present: Change and Continuity

THE United States Supreme Court ruling in the case *Brown v. Board of Education of Topeka* proved to be the stimulus for increased civil rights agitation and eventually led to numerous breakthroughs by Kentucky blacks in the decade following 1954. It is significant, however, that these changes in race relations, though backed by federal law, were hard fought, with many areas of society still remaining closed to Afro-Americans. Looking back at the long, difficult struggle to obtain equal pay for teachers and to desegregate higher education, it probably came as no surprise to Kentucky's civil rights leaders that they encountered numerous overt and covert roadblocks to full implementation of the Brown decision. For instance, board members of school districts throughout the state said they would abide by the court decision, but then explained that, given their already overcrowded schools and lack of funds, it would take time—several years at best—before integration could occur. These school districts formed various committees (often comprised of the area's most conservative blacks) to study the "problems" associated with school desegregation. What is really amazing, however, is not the delay but the public statements of school officials and political leaders arguing that desegregation should not go forward until white approval had been obtained for each step in the process. They reasoned that whites should have time to adjust to the idea of black students before Afro-American teachers were introduced into the classroom. This belief in the necessity of white approval for each phase of school integration rested on the false assumption that the Supreme Court had somehow tied integration to white approval, and, second, that in America and in Kentucky, abiding by the law was somehow negotiable. Also, after realizing what a lengthy struggle was involved in desegregating the public schools in Kentucky, it is easy to understand why changes in other areas, such as housing and employment, have often not occurred at all or have fallen far short of the expectations of Afro-Americans.

In the early 1950s, before the Brown decision, some observers proclaimed that the state's dual school system served both races well. Entitled "Kentucky Gives the Negro Best Education in the South," *Courier-Journal* reporter Allan M. Trout did a long, detailed survey of black education in 1953. Though acknowledging the poverty in Kentucky's schools for whites and blacks alike, Trout brushed over this crucial fact by claiming that the state's policy of not discriminating against blacks in the dispersal of education funds had borne fruit, and that black Kentuckians received a good education. He based this absurd conclusion on the law of 1882 equalizing school funds and the rhetoric of politicians who said that the expenditures were the same for white and black education. Therefore, Trout wrote that the length of the school year was identical in the white and black schools; that all students, regardless of race, used the same textbooks; that black and white students had access to the same health facilities; that teacher qualifications were the same, requiring a B.A. degree to teach in the high school and at least two years of college to teach at the elementary level. Trout ended his article by stating that "Whatever the faults of public education in Kentucky, and they are legion, this state cannot be criticized fairly, along with the rest of the South, for robbing Negro children to educate the white."[1] Trout avoided commenting on the issue of school integration, but his interpretations suggested that segregated schools did not discriminate against Afro-Americans. Also, he failed to understand how the duplication of schools for whites and blacks was an important factor in why schools in Kentucky and the South rated so poorly in every respect when compared with the rest of the nation.

The NAACP quickly responded to Trout's article. In a letter to the editor of the *Courier-Journal*, board members R. Everett Ray and Lyman Johnson pointed out that Trout "has indulged in inaccuracies, has drawn invalid conclusions and has omitted certain pertinent facts in accounting for the showing of Negroes and whites in education." They correctly noted that Trout neglected to mention that many counties throughout the state failed to provide schools for blacks and many school boards paid token amounts for their black pupils to attend school elsewhere. "In those communities it is preposterous to think of affording equal opportunity to the few in a separate school, even if the proper per capita share is spent toward that end. It should be mentioned that, even in the more fortunate communities, quite often Negro students find libraries, recreational facilities and theaters closed to them." In concluding their letter, Ray and Johnson wrote that the positive changes which had occurred in the public schools for blacks had happened within the past few years and not because of the 1882 law as Trout proclaimed.[2]

A very impressionistic statement regarding race relations was made by a writer in a national magazine when he explained: "As a border state, Kentucky's allegiance to segregation was not as firmly rooted as in the Deep South. Moreover, it has a large number of northern-born citizens. And the newspapers of the state, particularly the liberal-minded *Courier-Journal* and Louisville *Times*, have supported the Negroes' fight for economic and education rights." The article applauded the repeal of the Day Law, the integration of several programs for wayward youths, and the cooperation of whites and blacks in the Kentucky division of the Southern Regional Council and other organizations. Governor Lawrence W. Wetherby was equally optimistic that racial problems were ending due to the state's "go slow" approach. He explained away the continuation of segregation in Frankfort by saying that no law, only local custom, prohibited blacks and whites from eating in the same cafeterias in government buildings, that white and black employees found it convenient to eat in separate areas.[3] The governor failed to acknowledge the effectiveness of unwritten local customs in keeping Afro-Americans out of white institutions and places of amusement.

In the early 1950s whites repeatedly cited Louisville as a "progressive" city where numerous changes in race relations were occurring. Blacks were routinely appointed to positions in city government, including the assigning of black firemen to stations in white neighborhoods. A black regularly served on the board of aldermen. Afro-Americans were now being admitted to all of the branches of the public library and to the city's parks, swimming pools, and amphitheaters. Blacks could sit wherever they desired at the Greyhound Bus Terminal. White civic leaders pointed with pride to the closing of Louisville Municipal College for Negroes and the admission of blacks to all departments of the University of Louisville. The University became the first southern white institution of higher education to hire a black faculty member when it retained Dr. Charles H. Parrish of Municipal College. The holder of a Ph.D. from the University of Chicago, perhaps the best sociology department in the nation, Parrish was obviously highly qualified for the job. His hiring by the University of Louisville, however, probably was small consolation to the other Municipal College faculty members who were not retained upon the closing of the black school.[4]

This idyllic white view of the positive changes occurring for blacks in Kentucky carried over to two areas—housing and employment—where blacks clearly were subjected to a continuation of racial discrimination. It was pointed out that blacks were moving into better housing, primarily in subdivisions in Louisville, Lexington, and several other places. However, this view contrasted sharply with that of the Louisville *Defender*, which conducted a survey of black housing conditions in Louisville. The paper noted that, though comprising only one-sixth of the city's population, Afro-Americans lived in fully one-third of the substandard housing. Deplorable conditions characterized many of the city's all-black communities. Just as in the past, nothing was done to rid their neighborhoods of rampant lawlessness in the forms of gambling, bootlegging and prostitution. Unfortunately, what existed for blacks in Louisville was experienced by blacks in other Kentucky cities, the *Defender* noted with dismay. Also, in stark contradiction to white observations about the lessening of racism, blacks still encountered strong opposition when attempting to move into white neighborhoods.[5]

In spite of the reality of racial discrimination, the *Courier-Journal* took as its mission the writing of positive stories on black progress in the early 1950s. Using Louisville as the model of what the state should strive for, the paper noted that "Some industrial plants here make a special point of 'integrating' Negroes—putting them to work side by side with whites in skilled and other tasks." Several large companies, General Electric, International Harvester, and Ford Motor, were determined to hire workers on qualifications and aptitudes, regardless of race. The *Courier-Journal* focused attention on the Dunne Press, a trade-journal publisher. Included among the company's 130 employees were eighteen blacks, one an associate editor and another the private secretary of the owner. Furthermore, throughout Louisville black women were now finding secretarial and stenographic positions open to them instead of being limited to jobs in domestic service. The *Courier-Journal* admitted that while some white labor unions still denied Afro-Americans membership and a few industries remained closed to them, overall positive changes had occurred and the likelihood for additional opportunities for blacks seemed bright.[6] In short, on the eve of the historic Brown decision additional cracks in the once-solid walls of segregation had occurred in higher education, housing, and employment. For many Kentuckians, any change in race relations assured them that conditions had improved dramatically for blacks. Not surprisingly, most whites remained largely unresponsive to black demands for total equality of opportunity in all aspects of society.

The public schools, more than any other area of society, received the most attention concerning desegregation in the early 1950s. Fully aware that blacks had been admitted to white colleges and that numerous cases concerning the public schools were being argued in the federal courts, school officials in many parts of Kentucky had anticipated the court's ruling in the Brown case and had already begun planning for court-ordered desegregation. Upon assuming the position of superintendent of the Louisville schools in the late 1940s, Omer Carmichael instituted several changes, one of which was to have black and white teachers come together in workshops, an idea eventually adopted by other school districts. Immediately following the court decision, practically all of the comments from school boards throughout the state were positive, indicating a willingness to obey the law. The board of education for the Jackson City Schools in Breathitt County met in special session to begin preliminary plans to merge Rosenwald, the black school, with the schools for whites. Governor Wetherby, despite objections from his political advisors, came out strongly in favor of school integration. He immediately appointed an advisory commission of four whites and three blacks to assist the Kentucky Department of Education in setting guidelines for desegregating the public schools. To be sure, farther South, many of the first responses to the Brown decision seemed positive before a reactionary movement developed to protest the idea of school integration. Governor Wetherby, however, remained supportive of school desegregation. As he explained: "At the recent Southern Governor's Conference . . . an attempt was made to band the states in the conference in a fight against enforcement of the Supreme Court's ruling. This was voted down in favor of an attitude allowing the southern states to meet the nonsegregation procedure to the best of their individual abilities. I was among those favoring this attitude."[7]

Because of the logistics involved, the attitude of most whites to "go slow" and, perhaps most important, the Supreme Court decision to postpone for a year its final ruling on how school desegregation was to proceed, the dual school system remained intact for the school year 1954-55. By mid-1955, after the court's ruling in "Brown II" (where the justices were purposely vague, saying that desegregation was to occur "with all deliberate speed"), the first tentative steps toward school integration were taken in the state. The Kentucky Department of Education issued a directive to all public school districts to move rapidly to end school segregation. All districts, at the very least, should begin studying ways to implement the court decision and to work with community leaders.[8]

While applauding the work of the Kentucky Department of Education and the positive comments which were being made by white Kentuckians, the NAACP was determined to push for immediate integration, or at the very least the drawing up of clear desegregation guidelines with deadlines for school integration. As Roy Wilkins of the national office noted: "Kentucky is one of the key states. We expect it to move off in a good fashion, helping to bring pressure on public opinion against those loudly publicized areas which are resisting the Court's opinion." To NAACP officials, successful school integration in Kentucky would be a positive example to the South of peaceful desegregation. To assist in that goal, the NAACP branches throughout the state voted unanimously to press for immediate desegregation of all the public schools by September 1955. At their annual statewide meeting they were advised on implementation by Gloster Current, director of the branches, and

Donald Jones, regional secretary of the NAACP. Plans were also made for the possibility of filing lawsuits against intractable school districts to enforce school integration.[9]

At the NAACP statewide conference Donald Jones agreed to visit fourteen key cities throughout the state to talk with school officials and black leaders about desegregation measures. On Tuesday, July 19, in the company of NAACP state president James A. Crumlin, Jones went to Columbia (located in south-central Kentucky), where a countywide meeting on school integration was being held. As he later informed the national office: "Surprisingly, there were some 300 whites, mostly farmers, and 12 Negroes gathered in the dining room of the high school. In general, the sentiment of the whites was against desegregation, although there was obvious acceptance of the fact that non-segregation was now the law and must be abided by." According to Jones, the whites appeared genuinely astonished that the Afro-Americans unanimously agreed that the schools should be integrated immediately, even at the elementary level. Both Crumlin and Jones gave presentations, and "though the mood of many of the whites was ugly and sullen, they listened respectfully." To the surprise (and relief) of the NAACP officials, attending the meeting were several self-described "liberals" who spoke openly for integration. Jones and Crumlin departed from Columbia, confident that school integration would occur; the Columbia NAACP had filed a petition for immediate desegregation, and several parents expressed a willingness to present their children for admission to the white schools on August 29 and thereafter to serve as plaintiffs if a suit became necessary.[10]

Jones's optimism was severely tested during his visits to several other communities, however. In Shelbyville he and members of the local NAACP branch met with the Shelbyville Board of Education. When pressed for a realistic deadline for school integration, the superintendent "stated that not only were there no plans existing for desegregation, but that their boards had not even seriously discussed the matter." Jones replied that unless the school board began immediate action toward school desegregation, the NAACP would file suit in court. Jones next traveled to Irvington and Owensboro, where black and white leaders had yet to reach any decisions to end school segregation. Even worse was the situation in Henderson. Worried about a confrontation with the school board, the local NAACP president had resigned, leaving the branch in disarray. To fill the void in black leadership, James W. Clancy, whom Jones described as "an earnest and sincere young man whose aggressiveness is resented by the old heads in Henderson," assumed the presidency of the branch, but, unfortunately, he accomplished very little. The Henderson Board of Education appointed several special committees to make recommendations regarding the pace of desegregation. The school board, however, made sure that all of the blacks serving on the advisory committees worked as servants for prominent whites, and these blacks "are reminded of their jobs by the white members on every opportunity." Not surprisingly, the blacks were easily intimidated, agreeing to the recommendation put forward by whites that instead of school integration, their community desired for the races to remain separate and for new schools to be constructed for Afro-American students. Henderson's black citizens responded with anger over this new attempt at "separate but equal." But, as Jones sadly concluded, very little progress could be expected from Henderson in the near future.[11]

Little was being done to end school segregation in Hopkinsville and Madisonville, two of the larger urban centers of black concentration in western Kentucky. Just as in Henderson, blacks in these cities feared economic reprisals for becoming involved in school integration. As Jones explained: "Madisonville has not filed a petition, and it appears . . . that action in this direction is remote at the present." On the other hand, both Jones and Crumlin had praise for attempts by the black citizens to end segregated schools in Paducah: "The Paducah Branch, under the turbulent Mr. Curlee Brown, is the most aggressive and vocal in the state of Kentucky. Petitions, signed by scores of parents, have been filed with both county and city, and parents will be ready to present their children to the 'white' schools on opening day. This is certainly one of the communities in Kentucky in which we would want to file suit in the event the board of education procrastinates." The same optimism which existed in Paducah was found in Princeton, Fulton, and Hazard, small towns where blacks also expressed interest in adopting formal steps to desegregate the schools. As the black leadership of Hazard confidently explained, once pressured by blacks, the school board would have no choice but to relent and admit Afro-American students to white schools.[12]

Jones's final visit was to Lexington, a city described in his reports as "the best opportunity among the larger cities in Kentucky for a major break through on the school segregation front this September." The school board, led by superintendent John M. Ridgway, met several times with local NAACP officials. All of the meetings had been fruitful. The board had adopted a policy statement, though it was not made public, that no resistance would be made to blacks who desired to enroll in previously all-white schools. Officials of the Lexington NAACP expressed to Jones their desire to cooperate with white school officials and stated that "unless the school board chooses to give publicity to its statement we would not do so. Instead [we] would work quietly to see to it that Negro children in considerable numbers presented themselves to a formerly all-white school on opening day. This quiet policy might keep the board from panicking and receding on its policy." With his tour of Kentucky ending on this upbeat note, Jones remained confident that blacks should press unceasingly for the right to attend integrated schools. The United States Supreme Court had outlawed segregated schools, Jones had reminded blacks on every stop of his travels, but "the 'when' the Supreme Court left up to Negroes themselves, and that their communities would remain as they are unless they brought the issue to focus."[13]

After consulting with Jones, NAACP officials said that legal action would be taken against all school districts that failed to announce desegregation plans by September 15, 1955. Specifically, NAACP officials targeted Shelbyville, Madisonville, Columbia, and Paducah as places for court challenges, given the lack of positive steps by the school boards in these areas. Shelbyville school officials remained adamant in saying that, despite their legal obligation to desegregate, nothing could be done until overcrowded conditions at the schools were alleviated. They mentioned the possibility of raising taxes in the future as a solution. School officials in Paducah and Madisonville said essentially the same thing; the overcrowded conditions presented a serious obstacle to school integration. Events from Columbia greatly surprised and disappointed the NAACP. Previously the Columbia Board of Education had agreed to desegregate the high school in September 1955 and the elementary school the following year. This announcement caused such an uproar among whites that the board dropped integration plans indefinitely and made plans to transport black students to an adjacent county for high school classes. In a more uplifting vein, the NAACP noted that at least ten school boards planned to start integration that fall, and sixteen more would do so in 1956.[14]

Realizing that a successful lawsuit would go a long way toward school desegregation in Kentucky, the association carefully investigated all of the school districts and filed suit in federal court on September 1 against the Columbia School District. Attorney James A. Crumlin, state president of the NAACP, argued that the twenty-five blacks of high-school age living in Columbia must be admitted to the white high school. Board members countered by explaining that the high school was already overcrowded, with its 541 white students, and desegregation would create additional problems that had to be resolved before blacks could be admitted to Columbia High. On December 1, Federal District Judge Mac Swinford ruled that the high school in Columbia must open its doors to black students on February 1, and that the elementary school would be desegregated when school started in September 1956. Furthermore, the judge forcefully argued that the education of all young people was so important in American society that the learning process could not be delayed, and that overcrowded conditions simply were not a valid excuse. The *Courier-Journal* applauded the reactions of the citizens of Adair County for agreeing to stop protesting mixed schools. (This was a sign of those times when whites could be lauded for abiding by the law after their attempts to avoid the law had failed). The paper failed to mention the attempts by whites in Columbia to forestall school desegregation that had now been overruled by the court.[15]

The school year 1956-57 witnessed two highly publicized events: the sending of the National Guard to protect black students at Sturgis and the peaceful entrance of blacks into the white public schools in Louisville. Located in western Kentucky, Sturgis was another small Kentucky town where race relations remained amicable as long as Afro-Americans refrained from challenging the white power structure. On Friday, August 31, eight black students enrolled in Sturgis High School. The following Tuesday, the first day of class, the black students were blocked from entering the school by a white crowd estimated at about three hundred. The students, unsure of what steps to take, returned home. Members of the school board and city officials refused to stop the mob, though several white leaders said that the black students were actually not threatened with violence. The very next day, however, Governor Albert B. Chandler (who had been elected for a second term in 1955, after serving in the United States Senate and as commissioner of major-league baseball) ordered the state police and the Kentucky National Guard to Sturgis. Many Kentuckians praised Chandler's actions, saying that he had prevented bloodshed, while others proclaimed just as loudly that it was a grandstand move on his part. In the presence of more than a thousand angry whites, including many outside pro-segregationists who came to Sturgis to lend their support, the black students entered the school on September 6 under the protection of two hundred heavily armed guardsmen. For the next week, blacks attended Sturgis High under these conditions, while more than 50 percent of the white students boycotted the school. Eventually, the state attorney general ruled that since the school board had failed to develop a definite integration plan, the black students were prohibited from further attendance at the school. Acting on this advice, the school board voted to bar the blacks until a satisfactory plan had been formulated. The black students remained determined to attend the school; but on September 19, they were refused admission by the principal, to the delight of the white crowd. Rather than return to the black Dunbar High School, the eight students chose to remain out of school for the entire academic year. The following school year, the Sturgis Board of Education closed the black high school and transferred the students to Sturgis High. No racial incidents occurred in 1957, when blacks were admitted to the school.[16]

Undeterred by the threat of a violent outbreak in Sturgis, the Louisville Board of Education launched its desegregation plan that same September. For more than a year the Louisville NAACP had denounced the school board for delaying the start of school integration. Superintendent Omer Carmichael had ignored black criticism, saying that it was important for everything to be well in place before proceeding. As Carmichael stated: "There were some demands for immediate or overnight desegregation voiced, but they never won majority support. Instead, during the next two years, despite occasional individual impatience, Louisville's articulate Negro leadership showed helpful restraint and moderation in allowing the desegregation process to develop uncomplicated by impetuous or intemperate demands for speed." Carmichael consistently refused all overtures to work with the NAACP, viewing its members as "radical and often pushy." It is clear from all of his actions that Carmichael wanted white approval of school integration. Though his desegregation plan contained several parts, including the redistricting of all the students to the school closest to their homes, his scheme actually relied on "permissiveness," with the school board opposing compulsory segregation and integration. Under Carmichael's plan, "freedom of choice" was all-important. Blacks could, if they desired, attend mixed schools, while whites could attend segregated schools. Because of housing patterns in Louisville, there were many all-white residential areas, and even for the whites living in close proximity to Afro-Americans, the option was made available for them to avoid integration by sending their children to schools in these exclusive white districts. Though the Louisville school system was widely heralded in 1957 for peacefully desegregating its schools, very little integration occurred, with only a few blacks enrolling in white schools and no whites going to the black schools. It seemed, to many observers, that the Afro-Americans attending the white schools had been carefully selected. The black students at Male High School, for example, had high intelligence test scores and were very strong scholastically—which came as a surprise to many whites. Also, a significant number of the first black students at white schools were outstanding athletes, a pattern that became all too common in Louisville. Again, it is a reflection of American society of the 1950s that the moderate plan initiated by Superintendent Carmichael was praised by educators and politicians in Kentucky and all over the nation.[17]

By the mid-1960s, most of Kentucky's black students no longer attended all-black schools, though a few schools in the state remained all-white. In the school year 1964-65, 95.2 percent of the school districts had integrated. Eleven school districts with small black populations continued to operate segregated schools, and they took great pains to reassure state education officials that school integration was "forthcoming." In reality, several mountain school districts simply evaded the law, sending their black students to other school districts instead of admitting them to white schools. The desegregation plans from Glasgow, Mount Sterling, and Montgomery County were extremely vague (maybe on purpose), saying that blacks enjoyed the privilege of attending mixed or segregated schools, though it seems as if the option given Afro-Americans was to remain in all-black schools. And despite the repeated threats of the NAACP, Shelby County, which had a large black population, resisted desegregation until the mid-1960s. Only one county in the entire state—Graves County—had failed to adopt a desegregation plan, though officials from the area, fully aware of the court's mandate of "all deliberate speed," consistently expressed their willingness to begin investigating steps that would lead to interracial schools. That Graves County was the last holdout came as no surprise, given the level of violence and racial discrimination that Afro-Americans had experienced in that western Kentucky community since the end of the Civil War.[18]

Significantly, upon close examination, many school boards, though claiming integration had taken place, had blacks attending only a few schools. Not only was this the case in Louisville but in Lexington as well. As Kentucky's most noted historian, Thomas D. Clark, explained: "Lexington made fewer plans and embarked on desegregation of its schools on a less extensive scale than Louisville. In 1966 the United States Office of Education was critical of what had been accomplished in the Lexington area in the light of the new mandates of the Civil Rights Law of 1965." In an attempt to conform to the law, school officials changed Dunbar into a junior high school for all students and sent black high school students to Henry Clay. This move greatly upset many white parents who opposed sending their children to Dunbar, since it was located in a black neighborhood. Eventually the Lexington Board of Education closed all of the schools in black communities, meaning that whites attended schools in close proximity to their homes while Afro-Americans were compelled to travel great distances to schools.[19]

All over Kentucky the desegregation of the public schools ultimately exacted a high price from Afro-Americans—the elimination of blacks as teachers and school administrators. In 1955 the Kentucky NAACP warned that some school boards "are scheming to eliminate the Negro teachers when they do decide to put the decision into effect." In an otherwise laudatory account of race relations in Kentucky, the New York *Times* noted in 1956 that black teachers were being displaced as a result of school integration. Not surprisingly, in many communities where blacks had the option of remaining in all-black schools, the teachers discouraged their students from entering white schools because they realized the impact that the drastic drop in enrollment or the closing of the black schools would have on their jobs. The Kentucky Negro Education Association conducted surveys that clearly illustrated that a sizable number of black teachers, especially on the high-school level, were graduates of northern white schools, which were superior to the southern schools white teachers had attended. That black teachers probably had more advanced degrees, or credit hours toward advanced degrees, than their white counterparts was another point stressed by KNEA in its effort to prove that black teachers possessed the qualifications to teach white students. Furthermore, throughout the state 3,500 whites without college degrees had been awarded certificates allowing them to teach, while no blacks had received emergency certificates. Nevertheless, these undisputed findings did little to prevent black teachers from being phased out with the closing of black schools.[20]

This phasing out of black teachers from the public schools had been a crucial part of Omer Carmichael's desegregation plan in Louisville. A native of Alabama who had served as superintendent in Virginia before coming to Louisville, Carmichael was at best a paternalistic racist, who believed that black students and teachers were inferior to whites. At the beginning of desegregation discussions, he listed student integration as the first priority and called for a postponement of discussion on the integration of the teaching staffs. Offering no supporting data, he eventually stated publicly that white parents and students would not accept black teachers and that, most surely, white teachers would not accept Negroes as principals and teachers. Again, during the 1950s, reluctant whites constantly cited as a rationale for their unwillingness to integrate completely that they would not approve "radical changes," when in reality most whites had been opposed to *any* changes in the racial status quo. To further prove that whites were justified in not wanting blacks to teach their children, Carmichael boldly stated in his book: "The average Negro teacher is less competent than the average white teacher. I can foresee that some Negro teachers of apparently superior training and experience may be passed over for white teachers seemingly less well-equipped."[21] Local black leaders produced information showing that Carmichael lacked the facts but was merely expressing his racial biases against Afro-American teachers. The Louisville *Defender* published ten articles covering a wide range of issues relating to black teachers, including how they performed in mixed schools in cities throughout the nation, proving that the color of a person's skin was no indicator of his/her performance as a school teacher. When challenged with this material at a board meeting by Lyman Johnson, Carmichael grew angry and shouted: "I've been watching you for a long time . . . you're just too aggressive. . . . I'm through with you." Because of the staunch resistance of the superintendent, it would be the mid-1960s—almost a decade after school desegregation—before black teachers were integrated into the Louisville schools, and their numbers always remained small. Given the fact that the elimination of black teachers occurred in Louisville, a city with a strong black newspaper, aggressive black leaders, and a rather enlightened white public, then it is no surprise that the elimination of black teachers became a fact of life in Kentucky.[22]

In what must have been an overly optimistic mood in 1962, members of the Kentucky Commission on Human Rights proclaimed that teacher integration was successful, noting that blacks served on interracial teaching faculties in seventeen city and county districts throughout the state, and that the number of black teachers in school districts all over the state would increase. By that time, however, Kentucky had over two hundred school districts, and the only way that such a small number of integrated teaching faculties could have been labeled successful was if the goal had been to keep to a minimum the number of blacks teaching in white schools.[23] The paucity of Afro-American teachers in the schools meant that for young blacks (not to mention white youth who rarely saw a black in a position of authority) one of the most important role models in their communities—the public school teacher—was gone. This was especially true of black men who, for whatever reasons, became something of a novelty in the public schools.

When investigating desegregation in the Louisville public

schools a decade later, the Human Rights Commission reluctantly conceded the obvious, that virtually no progress had been made in the hiring of black teachers. Where a decade earlier the commission had readily accepted the word of school officials that they were integrating blacks into the teaching force, the commission in 1972, using Louisville as an example of the rest of Kentucky, carefully examined the employment of black teachers in that city with nine southern cities. In comparison to such supposedly unenlightened areas (when compared to Louisville) as Jackson, Mississippi, Birmingham, Alabama, Little Rock, Arkansas, Columbia, South Carolina, and Jacksonville, Florida, Kentucky's leading city had the worst record in hiring blacks and integrating them into the faculties of the previously all-white schools. It was unfortunate, the commission noted, "that the Louisville Board of Education is following a plan for teacher assignments that is not achieving the goals clearly laid down by the federal courts and by HEW." In spite of the threat of court suits, nothing changed during the 1970s. In a report completed in 1979 (several years after school busing had been ordered for the merged Louisville-Jefferson County schools), the commission concluded that a survey of employment practices clearly revealed the Jefferson County school system had "failed to effectively implement affirmative action and follow the personnel procedures ordered as part of the desegregation plan."[24]

To justify their failure to hire blacks as teachers in present-day Kentucky, school boards and administrators exclaim with dismay that a severe shortage of black teachers exists. The fact that Afro-Americans now enjoy new opportunities in employment, they argue, has led few blacks to the teaching profession. The relatively low salaries paid teachers is repeatedly cited to explain why few black men enter the profession. Undoubtedly, these reasons contribute to the shortage of black teachers in the public schools. Nevertheless, these rationales fail to explain adequately why the very best-paying positions in the public schools—those as principals, department heads, directors of special programs, and especially the upper levels of administration such as superintendents and vice superintendents—have only a token number of blacks. While bemoaning their lack of success in recruiting black teachers, school districts neglect to state that, though now actively seeking black employees, they fail to use the same level of energy, intensity, and ingenuity that once was exerted in excluding blacks from teaching in integrated schools.

In retrospect, the experience of black teachers in the school desegregation process is part of a much larger problem initiated by the Brown decision. In their lengthy court litigation from the 1930s to the 1950s, the NAACP protested the discrimination in funding and the inferior school facilities, including the lack of libraries, science laboratories, and other needed equipment in Afro-American schools. School integration in America (with Lexington serving as an excellent example) resulted in the closing of black schools at the start of the desegregation process. School integration was not a blending of the best programs of the white and black schools but a rejection of the Afro-American schools and the embracing by blacks of the white schools. Also, once in the white schools, blacks were often required to give up an emphasis on Afro-American culture and history, participation in student government, and other non-sport activities. In other words, though few black leaders openly acknowledged some of the deeper meanings of integration (though racist whites readily did so), blacks all but admitted that the entire program of their schools, not just the physical plants, had been inferior to the white schools. Schools, however, are far more than brick and mortar. Schools are places where the young learn, grow, and are encouraged to set high goals and then strive to reach them. Therefore, the most crucial aspect of the entire education experience is the teacher-student encounter in the classroom. With their highly trained and dedicated teachers, who often served as surrogate parents, counselors, and friends, the black schools in the state of Kentucky definitely were the equal to white schools, even though the entire evolution of school integration, with the elimination of Afro-Americans from the teaching ranks, fits nicely with the racist belief that black teachers were inferior.

To be sure, no one in the Afro-American community, even the ones who clearly understood the total impact of school integration, wanted to go back to the "good old days" before 1954. They realized, however, that school integration created a dilemma for them that often resulted in a host of new problems, such as the failure of white teachers to encourage their children to perform to the best of their abilities, and an increase in the number of discipline problems in the schools. That the black suspension rate greatly exceeded that of whites is to cite but one example of a "problem" that existed in the integrated schools. In the Louisville schools, which is the district investigated most by state and federal officials, Afro-Americans accounted for 53 percent of the suspensions even though they comprised less than a quarter of the student population. Not surprisingly, in Louisville and elsewhere the number of blacks who leave school without graduating has increased substantially since desegregation.[25]

Even at the height of the attempt to desegregate the schools in the 1960s, total integration was far from achieved in Kentucky's two largest cities. By contrast, the smaller cities and counties usually had only one high school and at best only a handful of elementary schools, making the desegregation process less complicated. Not so in Lexington and especially Louisville. To remedy the lack of complete integration, the courts ordered school busing. In Lexington, complaints by whites were seldom heard because blacks bore the burden of busing, while white children in most cases attended schools in their neighborhoods. This became possible because over the years school officials had systematically closed all of the black schools while upgrading schools in the white community.

A 1972 report by the Human Rights Commission detailed the lack of integration in the Louisville schools and all but predicted the advent of school busing. According to the report, resegregation of black and white students had occurred in Louisville, a trend different from most of the South and the nation. "As late as 1968, only 55.7 percent of the city's students were in schools with extreme segregation but the level had increased to 73.5 percent in 1971. Meanwhile, the national level dropped from 64.3 per cent in 1968 to 43.3 percent in 1970 and the level in the Southern states dropped from 77.8 percent in 1968 to 33.4 percent in 1970." The Commission stated emphatically that the Louisville school system had "failed—either by design or by lack of effort—to deliver on the promise of full student and faculty desegregation. The myth of 'neighborhood schools' has been put forward to conceal this basic failure."[26] With the school board unwilling to end its voluntary plan for desegregation, members of the Kentucky Civil Liberties Union, the NAACP, and several other groups filed suits against both the Louisville and Jefferson County school systems in 1971 and 1972. State law eventually merged the school systems. In 1975 massive busing started under orders of the United States District Court, resulting in much anger and the city's losing its reputation (which, of course, it never deserved) as a liberal community regarding race relations.[27]

From blue-collar workers at General Electric and Ford Motor Company to a wide range of organizations, whites protested busing in Louisville. Many of them enrolled their children in local Catholic schools or moved to new subdivisions in Oldham and Bullitt counties to avoid having their children assigned to Louisville's inner-city schools. Though many arguments have been put forth against school busing, it is clear that busing is most unattractive when tied to integration. As we have seen, for most of the twentieth century it was common for Afro-Americans to travel far beyond their neighborhoods and most surely past the closest schools to attend classes at all-Negro schools. Without question, during the 1930s and 1940s Kentucky whites often turned to school busing as an effective tool to maintain segregated schools. In short, none of the outspoken opponents of busing in the 1970s denounced the busing that occurred to promote segregation or the paying of tuition fees for blacks to attend schools in other districts, both practices that whites considered to be a part of black public education prior to the drive to desegregate the schools in the 1950s and 1960s.

Integrating the public schools was not the only goal of the civil rights movement that gained momentum after the Brown decision. These same years saw efforts by Afro-Americans in Kentucky to achieve equal access to public accommodations and the enactment of open housing laws to ensure their right to live wherever they could afford. The few breakthroughs achieved by blacks during the late 1950s occurred in Louisville, where Afro-Americans won a few concessions from downtown merchants, most notably the right to be served at lunch counters in drugstores. But for the most part, blacks in that city and Lexington—not to mention the smaller towns in the state— remained as segregated as blacks in the Deep South throughout the 1950s. For instance, in Kentucky's largest cities the various recreational facilities—bowling alleys, skating rinks, and amusement parks—completely excluded blacks. Most hotels refused overnight lodging to blacks or at the very best accepted them as guests on a limited basis, but only if white patrons did

Georgia M. Davis Powers, the first black woman to serve in the Kentucky state senate, 1968-89, was a leader in the civil rights movement in the 1960s.
University of Louisville Photographic Archives

not protest. According to the NAACP, no hotels served blacks in public dining rooms, a practice that existed in most restaurants and cafeterias as well.[28]

The 1960s witnessed spectacular changes in access to public accommodations in Kentucky's largest cities and some breakthroughs in smaller communities. The successes, both large and small, resulted from the efforts of many different groups and organizations. The NAACP remained active though the organization's strategy of working through the courts was often challenged by individuals and groups calling for immediate direct action against all forms of discrimination. Black high school and college students played a key role, often providing the "footsoldiers" for demonstrations and sit-ins. All over the state, the black churches proved crucial by providing meeting places for the movement's strategy sessions. Moreover, most of the leaders and, just as important, the people taking part in the demonstrations were recruited in the churches. The black struggle in the 1960s also benefited from the assistance of the white liberals who challenged Jim Crow practices in restaurants, hotels, and movie houses. The Kentucky Human Rights Commission was formed and quickly became involved in negotiations with city officials to end racial discrimination and published reports on the status of the movement throughout the state. Local mayors and officials created committees of prominent whites and blacks to give advice on how best to proceed. In Paducah, for example, the Non-Partisan League was formed in the early 1960s. This interracial organization's efforts led to the removal of Jim Crow signs in the downtown area and the admission of Afro-Americans to the local theater. Also, the Non-Partisan League worked in other areas of concern to blacks, always hoping that its actions could lead to changes without much fanfare by blacks or whites.[29]

The Congress of Racial Equality (CORE) was perhaps the most controversial group involved in the protest for equal access to public accommodations in Kentucky during the civil rights movement. From its founding at the University of Chicago in the early 1940s, CORE's membership consisted primarily of black and white college students and a handful of white intellectuals. At an early date, CORE held demonstrations and sit-ins, tactics that other groups came to rely on greatly during the 1960s. Despite CORE's long commitment to racial justice, the organization was viewed with suspicion by both the white power structure and the established black leaders, and this often led to tension between CORE and the NAACP and an unwillingness to cooperate on issues that all agreed were important for black progress.

Led by William O. Reichert, a professor of political science at the University of Kentucky, a CORE branch was formed in Lexington in 1959. The holder of a B.A. from Transylvania College and the M.A. from the University of Kentucky, Reichert had firsthand knowledge of race relations in Lexington. After completing his Ph.D. degree at the University of Minnesota, he returned to Lexington to teach in 1956. Though finding the "racial situation in Lexington absolutely unacceptable," Reichert took no action until 1959, when one of his black students informed him "that he could not find any place to eat Sunday evenings when the campus cafeterias were closed except by walking several miles across town to the black area where there were ethnic restaurants." Several evenings later at a meeting of the American Civil Liberties Union, Reichert heard a prominent black woman recount the discrimination she and other Afro-Americans encountered when shopping in the downtown area, of not being allowed to use the restrooms except for the toilet in the "colored" waiting room in the train station. Reichert and a number of whites, primarily members of the American Civil Liberties Union and university professors, and a group of black professionals and college students, formed a CORE organization. Reichert agreed to head the organization. As he explained: "CORE's purpose was to do something immediately about the racial discrimination that exists in this city. . . . None of the variety stores on Main Street will serve Negroes at their lunch counters despite the fact that these same Negroes are welcome to spend their money at other counters in the stores."[30]

For over a year CORE tried without much success to negotiate with the business community to eliminate all discriminatory practices. In the words of Reichert:

> At one of our first meetings we decided to concentrate our efforts on the four dime stores in town which would not serve black people sitting down at their lunch counters but would if they stood to eat; although we did include several private restaurants that bordered on the campus. Using nonviolent means, we arranged visits by teams to each of the stores, one black person and two whites, all of the same sex, of course. The team would enter and sit down waiting to be served. The white persons were always served but the black person refused invariably. For several months we kept this up hoping to change the management's attitude. On one occasion when we sent in a large group on

a Saturday, the manager called the police, claiming a riot under way and of course the squad cars came from all directions with sirens shrieking, the manager hoping that we would become frightened and appear to be breaking the peace so that we could be arrested and brought to court. Although we were successful in getting a lot of people, both black and white to participate, this effort took a great deal of energy and caused considerable tension within the group.[31]

Though failing to achieve its goals, CORE would not, Reichert explained, deviate from its dedication to "nonviolent social action as illustrated by the lives of Christ and Gandhi." Yet, in response to this view, he and other CORE members came in for verbal abuse and were threatened with violence. Reichert received a steady stream of letters addressed "Wm. Reichert, Nigger Lover." On occasion, both the Lexington *Herald* and *Leader* refused to print letters from CORE members who were trying to inform the public of their positions and tactics. After being condemned by Reichert for taking such a stance, Herman Phelps, managing editor of the *Herald*, responded: "We refused to publish these letters because we felt that they might have a tendency to intensify racial discord." In an editorial, the *Leader* denounced CORE, stating that CORE's rhetoric had led to a student riot at Kentucky State College: "CORE's activities contributed to the student demonstrations, which were followed by the setting of small fires in dormitories and finally the burning of the gymnasium-auditorium." Continuing its criticism of CORE, the *Leader* noted: "In the attempts in Lexington to open lunch counters to Negroes, CORE has gone beyond its avowed dedications to 'nonviolent social action,' and has interfered with the peaceful conduct of private business." As a way of ending CORE's unnecessary involvement in Lexington affairs, the newspaper called on University of Kentucky officials to silence the leader of the organization: "Dr. Reichert should realize, also, that he is on the faculty of an institution of public education which depends upon the good will of the people of Kentucky. . . . As the university stated a few years ago, employees should avoid public activities which adversely affect that institution."[32]

Reichert left the University of Kentucky in the early 1960s, citing the pressures of being involved in CORE and a mild heart attack as his reasons. Whether or not he was actually forced out of the University is unclear, even to Reichert. At the close of his first year of involvement in CORE, he was given a very low salary increase, much below his previous pay raises. At a meeting with President Frank Dickey, Reichert was told in very blunt words "that there were many faculty who were most unhappy with our civil liberties actions and that we should know that we had enemies." He concluded: "Whether or not that would have affected me adversely when I came up for tenure in several years I do not know for certain but it was certainly a concern." Reichert, once considered a "rising star" in the University of Kentucky's Department of Political Science, resigned, taking a one-year appointment at the University of Nebraska, even though that institution made no promise of extending his employment beyond the first year.[33]

As scholars August Meier and Elliott Rudwick explain, CORE encountered problems in Louisville because Carl and Anne Braden and Bishop C. Eubank Tucker were closely associated with the organization. For decades, Tucker had been a critic of the NAACP and other black leaders. In turn, they viewed Tucker as a person involved in civil rights only for personal gain. As attorney Crumlin of the NAACP said, Tucker "has always been anxious to lead. He is trying to draft his preachers and church members into his Civil Rights Commission. But it has no firm status." *Courier-Journal* reporter Hank Messick was equally critical of Tucker: "It might be said that he literally sees issues as black or white. There are no intermediate colors in his spectrum." The Bradens, a white couple, were labeled as Communists because of their "liberal views." During the 1950s and 1960s, it was common—and effective—to accuse civil rights activists of being Communists in an attempt to dismiss their complaints about American society and to bring negative and often hostile attention to bear on them. Instead of embracing the Bradens as allies, Louisville's established black leaders listened to the charges of white officials—who often opposed black progress—against the couple and refused to work with them. Eventually the Bradens, for the good of the overall movement, disassociated themselves from CORE. In 1960 Len Holt, a CORE representative from Norfolk, Virginia, came to

In 1990, Louisville native Muhammad Ali was recognized in *Life* magazine as one of the "100 most important Americans of the 20th century."
Gift of Muhammad Ali, Kentucky Historical Society

the city and held sit-in workshops. This greatly angered local black leaders, for they had assured city officials that there would be no demonstrations during their negotiations. CORE, however, distrustful of the city's business leaders, resumed demonstrations, an act that led to much bickering within the civil rights organizations. From that point on, CORE and the other groups refused to work together in Louisville, often going so far as to hold separate demonstrations. NAACP president Lyman Johnson said that he and other members of the NAACP doubted the sincerity of CORE, viewing the organization as a "band of white radicals" and economically affluent blacks. "What did they have in common with us [the black masses]?"[34]

Regardless of what its critics have contended, CORE made a positive contribution to the civil rights movement in Kentucky. The NAACP and church groups often started a protest only to see their efforts end because of delaying tactics by white officials. CORE's small band of followers was far more committed to demonstrating and picketing and continued to do so even when the likelihood for positive results seemed remote. By being clear on their goals, CORE members were often more effective than other blacks in dealing with white officials; they were less likely to "sell out" than established black leaders, who often had developed warm relationships with city fathers. Also, the presence of CORE undoubtedly led mayors and city councilmen to be more willing to negotiate with established black leaders in an attempt to avoid what they viewed as the disruptive tactics of CORE from taking place. It is significant that after the early goal of the civil rights movement was reached—equal access to public accommodations—CORE more than other organizations continued to press for jobs and other changes. For example, in Lexington, CORE's agitation and calls for boycotts led to the hiring of Afro-Americans as bus drivers and as cashiers in supermarkets. Likewise, in Louisville the organization led a boycott of several businesses (ice cream and soft drinks) which relied heavily on black patronage while refusing to hire blacks. Eventually, these demonstrations bore fruit and blacks were hired in new positions.[35]

For CORE, the NAACP, religious groups, and others, fully desegregating the downtown areas in Kentucky's cities proved to be a difficult struggle. In Louisville, which prided itself on being "liberal," it took well over three and one-half years of negotiating and demonstrating, including a boycott of white merchants during the Easter season of 1961 and exertion of political power by blacks to desegregate all of the businesses. Lexington experienced similar demonstrations before conditions changed in 1963. By that time, with desegregation occurring in most of the state's larger cities, black leaders realized that discrimination would not cease in smaller cities without intervention by the state legislature. Accordingly, they urged Governor Bert Combs, who had consistently expressed sympathy for the goals of the civil rights movement, to throw the weight of his office behind a measure to end all vestiges of Jim Crow in Kentucky. Governor Combs called upon the general assembly to act, but was informed by leaders of the house and senate that an anti-discrimination law stood no chance of passing. On June 26, 1963, the governor responded by issuing an executive order ending racial discrimination in all establishments and by all professions licensed by the state. This broad ordinance covered virtually every area of secular activity in Kentucky, "outside the private homes of citizens."[36]

The struggle to achieve access to public accommodations foreshadowed the strong opposition Afro-Americans encountered when protesting discrimination in employment and housing. In a real sense, the "victory" in this phase was a moderate one: Afro-Americans were asking for the right to spend their money in white establishments. Too often, however, whites relented only after considerable pressure had been exerted by blacks. Not surprisingly, therefore, many whites viewed the call by blacks for equal employment opportunity as a real threat to them and their livelihood. Many whites who had been sympathetic to the movement to end public accommodation discrimination assumed that employment opportunities were based on education and merit, not race, and that once blacks had acquired the right skills they would face no problems in this area. Some whites, of course, were opposed on racial grounds to having blacks live in their neighborhoods. Others were unconvinced that discrimination excluded blacks from white communities. They believed, despite any evidence of discrimination uncovered by blacks, that it was in the economic best interest of realtors to sell homes to anyone willing to pay the price to move into certain neighborhoods.

Although it sounds like a cliché, Afro-Americans desired to

live in white neighborhoods not because they received an ego boost in living close to whites but because of certain tangible advantages, from the increase in the value of their property, to living close to good public schools, to living in areas that received adequate city services. Also, just like so many other goals of the civil rights movement, blacks wanted the option to choose where they could live instead of being relegated to a certain part of town. Undoubtedly, having a free choice in where to live would result in more affordable housing for blacks. As long as housing was segregated and blacks were restricted from living in a certain area, the law of supply and demand forced up the prices of the homes available to Afro-Americans.

A very dramatic account of a black family's attempting to move into a white neighborhood is told in Anne Braden's *The Wall Between*. Andrew Wade, a successful businessman, found it impossible to purchase a decent house in Louisville in the early 1950s. There were two problems: Louisville was a town of "unspoken restrictive covenants," effectively keeping blacks out of white neighborhoods. Second, no new housing for blacks had been constructed since before World War II. Wade, an associate of Carl and Anne Braden in a radical organization, had the couple purchase a home for him in the suburb of Shively in 1954. Immediately after it became known that Wade, not the Bradens, lived in the house, there were demands that he vacate the area. The builder, James Rone, and the bank which held the mortgage, hoping to void the sale, tried to prove the Bradens had violated the contract in transferring the house to Wade. The Bradens were accused of being Communist agents. Wade, an electrician in business with his father, saw the company suffer as economic pressure was applied to force him to move from Shively. On Saturday night, May 15, ten shots were fired into the house, but the Wades still refused to move. Meanwhile, the Bradens continued to be the targets of white abuse, even from the usually reasoned and moderate voice of the *Courier-Journal*, which blamed them for the May 15 violence. The drama reached a peak on the night of June 27, when Wade's house was substantially damaged by a bomb. All of the white residents on the street had been warned of the impending bombing and had left their homes. Failing to apprehend the bombers, the police blamed the Bradens for the violence, saying that it had been a ploy on their part to win support for the Communist cause. Carl Braden was arrested, convicted, and sent to prison for violating a state sedition law. Sentenced to fifteen years in prison and fined $5,000, he was freed in April 1956, when the United States Supreme Court overturned Kentucky's sedition laws. Wade and his family never returned to the house; in August 1957 he put up a "for sale" sign and eventually sold the property.[37]

Far more common than the violence experienced by the Wade family were countless incidents in which blacks were denied the right to purchase a house or rent an apartment, and where little or nothing was done about the discrimination they experienced. To end this injustice, black leaders in all parts of the state called for an open housing law. By 1966 in Louisville (and to a lesser degree in other cities) blacks were conducting demonstrations in white neighborhoods to highlight the existence of discrimination in housing. The Rev. Martin Luther King, Jr., participated in several of these open housing marches. The presence of King, however, failed to prevent a number of hostile acts by whites from occurring, with white girls who marched in support of open housing becoming the special target of the hecklers. Louisville's black leadership also contemplated an economic boycott and demonstrations during the week of the Kentucky Derby to aid their cause. White opponents of an ordinance to prohibit discrimination in housing received encouragement from the actions of the president of the Louisville Board of Realtors and a number of white Republican politicians who campaigned against open housing legislation.[38]

Despite much controversy and strong opposition, both the federal government and the state of Kentucky enacted laws to end racial discrimination in housing in 1968. A far-reaching piece of legislation, Title VIII of the 1968 Civil Rights Act, was designed to end virtually every type of discrimination in housing.[39] The major problem with Title VIII, like so much of the legislation passed during the civil rights movement, became the enforcement of the law. Likewise, proponents of black civil rights hailed the Kentucky Fair Housing Law of 1968. Yet, shortly after the law went into effect, an official for the Housing Information Service in Louisville noted: "Ordinance or no ordinance, finding homes for Negroes is hard." As numerous surveys of housing discrimination attest, this remained the case through the next decade and down to the present. On several occasions the Kentucky Commission on Human Rights reported that in both government housing projects and other dwellings, discrimination still limited where Afro-Americans could live. "In fact, the evidence is that most of our cities are as segregated or more segregated than they were ten years ago," the commission reported in 1975. The commission noted that in many instances discrimination was less overt and blatant, but nevertheless just as effective. "Housing discrimination has become so sophisticated that many persons are not even sure when they are being discriminated against." Consistently in cities all over the state, black professionals encountered problems when attempting to purchase houses in white neighborhoods. After school busing started in Louisville, a number of black leaders tried to convince whites that an end to housing discrimination would eliminate the need for school busing. These blacks arranged a meeting with anti-busing leaders, but the session ended quickly with the anti-busing group walking out, proclaiming they would not actively seek integrated housing.[40]

It is perhaps more difficult to assess fully the changes that have occurred in housing than in education, employment, or other areas of major concern to the civil rights movement. Any number of national and state reports document the percentage of blacks living in substandard housing, the number of blacks owning homes, the black percentage living in integrated or all-black neighborhoods, and the number of blacks residing in subsidized or government housing. The data can often be confusing and conflicting, though there seems to be several points of agreement. First, the quality, cost, and location of where they live have ramifications for the total well-being of blacks. Second, because blacks live primarily in segregated communities, their property as a rule does not increase in value as substantially as the property owned by whites. Third, despite state and federal law and actions by Afro-Americans, residential segregation has not declined; rather, segregation in the 1980s has increased when compared with the 1960s. Some studies suggest that given the reality of increased racial separation in housing, the real question is whether or not Afro-Americans are moving toward "equal but separate housing." Finally, as several scholars noted: "Whites, in general, seem to be open to the idea of residential integration. . . . Yet, it is very significant that a majority of whites still oppose federal laws forbidding discrimination in housing against blacks. In other words, while whites are more frequently willing to agree in principle to the goal of equal opportunity in housing, they continue to resist what they see as infringements on their property rights and what they see as threats to their property values."[41]

Throughout the civil rights movement, Afro-American leaders called for increased employment opportunities for the race. To be sure, the mid-1960s witnessed breakthroughs regarding employment; but were these changes substantial, and did all blacks benefit from the fact that many companies began to hire black workers for the first time? Without a doubt, some blacks—teachers and school administrators—were hurt by integration. Yet, when looking over Kentucky, it is remarkable to see the many changes that have occurred for blacks. Practically every city during the late 1960s and early 1970s employed blacks for the first time in certain jobs. This was most apparent in government jobs on the local and state levels. However, employment breakthroughs for blacks can be easily overstated, for, in reality, many of the changes have been token or have affected only the very small percentage of blacks holding college and advanced degrees. In practically every year of the 1970s, the Kentucky Commission on Human Rights published data on black employment in the public and private sector. These well-researched reports paint a dismal picture, indicating in great detail that in most areas of private employment blacks are completely excluded from managerial positions. Furthermore, the employment gains made by the race have gone largely to men, while Afro-American women remain underemployed in the work force. Also, though institutions of higher learning have declared a strong desire to find and secure the services of "qualified" blacks as professors and administrators, for whatever reasons, very few have been hired in Kentucky's colleges and universities, and of that number even fewer have received tenure. Another revealing look at black employment in many Kentucky cities can be gleaned from local histories, like the one on Henderson, which have been published in the last decade. In Henderson and elsewhere very few blacks have been hired as policemen, firemen, or as administrators and secretaries at city hall. By 1980 some communities still had no black workers, while others had only one in each department of the government. A journey through any Kentucky city indicates that even fewer changes have occurred in the private sector, especially above entry-level positions. In the final analysis, while black progress in employment has occurred, it has fallen far short of the expectations of the civil rights movement. Furthermore, many of the gains have been short-lived as Afro-Americans were the first to experience layoffs and unemployment when the economy worsened in the state and nation during the late 1970s and early 1980s.[42]

Statistical data further documents that both change and continuity have characterized black employment in Kentucky since the civil rights movement. In a trend that seems rather consistent with the past, fully three-fourths of all blacks worked as servants, laborers, or at lower-level jobs in industry in 1970. By comparison, whites had taken advantage of innovations in technology and only one-third of them worked in jobs at the very lowest rung of the work force ladder. At the opposite end of the employment scale are the highly sought after "white collar jobs"—professionals, such as lawyers, doctors, college professors, and trained clergymen, managers of large corporations and businesses, and upper-level technical and sales personnel. For whites, fully 40 percent of them found jobs in these high-paying occupations, while blacks comprised less than 20 percent in these fields. Furthermore, the figures fail to show the exact number of Afro-Americans employed in white collar jobs who actually worked for black-owned companies, or at one of the virtually all-black colleges like Kentucky State, or at black-operated hospitals or clinics—people, in other words, who had positions in part because of the continued presence of segregation. Though affirmative action programs would lead eventually to increased numbers of black professionals, it is possible that the actual number of blacks in white collar jobs failed to increase because of the closing of black businesses and other enterprises, a phenomenon that has been one of the by-products of the civil rights movement. Likewise, it is commonly believed that the civil rights movement witnessed a narrowing of the economic gap between whites and blacks. Just how much this gap has narrowed can be debated; the fact that whites still enjoy a much higher income than Afro-Americans is a point on which all observers agree. In rural Kentucky by 1970, blacks earned only 70 percent of the median income of whites. In a

Dr. Henry E. Cheaney, a pioneer in the study of Kentucky blacks, served for many years as professor of history at Kentucky State University. *Courtesy of Dr. Cheaney*

trend consistent for much of this century, far more Afro-Americans by 1970 lived in urban areas, where presumably they found a greater diversity of jobs and opportunities. Significantly, however, a much higher disparity in the average income of whites and blacks existed in Kentucky cities when compared with rural areas. In the state's urban areas, the median family income for blacks was less than 60 percent of that for whites. Overall, when considering both rural and urban Kentucky, the data showed that median income for a black family in 1970 was

$5,128, or $2,500 less than the average white family. According to most reports, this gap had widened by the mid-1970s.[43]

In 1966, editor Frank Stanley wrote an article, "The Negro In Kentucky: Is His Progress More Apparent Than Real?" assessing the status of blacks. According to Stanley, on the surface blacks were making tremendous progress in the state, but the facts showed this to be far from true. It had been, he noted, thirty years since Charles W. Anderson first served in the state legislature, and the number of blacks serving in the state legislature had not increased. Blacks remained relegated to low-paying jobs and lived in segregated neighborhoods and slums. "Negroes generally—the masses—have not benefited greatly from local, state and federal civil-rights laws. The barometer is the widening of the economic gap between Negroes and whites both on a per capita and a per family average." In a very strongly worded passage, Stanley explained: "Frankly, the average Caucasian Kentuckian is mostly unaware of the important goals yet to be achieved, or more specifically, of the amount of nonprogress that has been made. Certainly most are totally incapable of realizing the tortures of hellish racial prejudice and what it does to the souls and minds of people who are forced to suffer it." He further noted that civil rights laws were not enough, that Kentucky needed to do much more: "The plain truth is, regardless of how many civil rights laws we pass, Negroes cannot win complete equality or total integration without broad crash programs for full employment, abolition of slums, the reconstruction of our education system and new definitions of work and leisure."[44]

Stanley's assessment of the lack of real progress being made by Afro-Americans in 1966 proved prophetic in the 1980s. The civil rights movement has led to two black Americas. One group of blacks has received the very best education and has what seems to be unlimited employment possibilities. This group can live practically anywhere it desires, except, of course, in a handful of residential areas in Kentucky where whites make no pretense of allowing any Afro-Americans to purchase homes. On the other hand, many blacks seem to have been missed entirely by the civil rights movement and exist in a world that has changed little since 1950. In other words, just like blacks throughout the nation, Kentucky blacks have experienced both meaningful change and unceasing continuity.

NOTES

1. Black Life from the 1890s to the Great Depression

1. See the various United States censuses from 1860 to 1900 for information on Kentucky's total population. Three sources are invaluable for specific data on the black population: Bureau of the Census, *Negro Population in the United States, 1790-1915* (Washington, D.C., 1918), 43-44; idem, *Bulletin 8, Negroes in the United States* (Washington, D.C., 1904), 19-21, 102-6; idem, *Negro Population in the United States, 1920-1932* (Washington, D.C., 1935), 6-9.

2. Bureau of the Census, *Negro Population in the U.S., 1920-1932*, 15.

3. Bureau of the Census, *Fifteenth Census of the United States*, Vol. 3, Part 1: *Population* (Washington, D.C., 1932), 893; and Vol. 2, Part 17: *Characteristics of the Population*, 26.

4. Bureau of the Census, *Negro Population, 1790-1915*, 588, 607-9; idem, *United States Census of Agriculture: 1959*, Vol. 1, Part 30 (Washington, D.C., 1959), 6-7.

5. Louisville *Courier-Journal*, August 2, October 6-8, 1908, February 9, 12, 1909; see *Browder v. Commonwealth*, 136 Kentucky Reports 45-54 (1909).

6. Louisville *Courier-Journal*, August 2, 1908; New York *Times*, August 2, 1908; Paducah *News-Democrat*, August 6, 1908; Boston *Guardian*, August 8, 1908; Christopher Waldrep's article, "Planters and the Planters' Protective Association in Kentucky and Tennessee," *Journal of Southern History* 52 (1986): 565-88, speaks about the shortage of black workers, as many of them were leaving western Kentucky during the early years of this century.

7. Hambleton Tapp and James C. Klotter, *Kentucky: Decades of Discord, 1865-1900* (Frankfort, 1977), 378-79; the General Records of the Bureau of Refugees, Freedmen, and Abandoned Lands, Record Group 105, National Archives, Washington, D.C., are very useful in documenting numerous attempts by whites to force

blacks off their lands after the Civil War. See, for example, A. W. Lawwill to John Ely, February 12, 1867; Benjamin P. Runkle to Sidney Burbank, March 13, 1868; J. J. Landrum to Freedmen's Bureau office in Covington, August 3, 1866; Landrum to Ely, August 13, 1866; R. E. Johnson to Ely, August 31, 1867, all in *ibid.*; Cincinnati *Commercial*, August 8, 1877; New York *Times*, April 26, 1872, August 12, 1877.

8. See two sources on the Tobacco War: Marie Taylor, "Night Riders in the Black Patch" (M.A. thesis, University of Kentucky, 1934), and William Cunningham, *On Bended Knees: The Night Rider Story* (Nashville, 1983); for data on the forcing of blacks off their land in Birmingham, see the Louisville *Courier-Journal*, March 1908, especially March 11, 24, 28; additional information on the running off of black farmers can be found in the Tuskegee Institute Newspaper Clippings, Reel 221, Frame 277 (microfilm, Harvard University Library).

9. Indianapolis *Freeman*, August 16, 1890. Because of the paucity of Kentucky Afro-American newspapers, it is extremely important for scholars to consult the *Freeman* and other newspapers which had correspondents in Kentucky. For additional information on black employment, see John E. L. Robertson, *Paducah, 1830-1980: A Sesquicentennial History* (Paducah, 1980); *Henderson, Home of Audubon* (New York, 1941).

10. Terry Birdwhistell and George Wright interview with Hugh D. Palmer, August 21, 1985, Oral History Collection, Special Collections, University of Kentucky, Lexington (hereafter cited Oral History Collection, UK).

11. Arthur Krock, *Myself When Young* (Boston, 1973), 73-77.

12. Terry L. Birdwhistell and George Wright interview with Arlene S. Martin, July 9, 1986, Oral History Collection, UK; *The Report of the Kentucky Commission on Negro Affairs, November 1, 1945* (Frankfort, Ky., 1945), 19. For specific references to black domestic servants in Kentucky, see David Katzman, *Seven Days a Week: Women and Domestic Service in Industrializing America* (New York, 1978).

13. For information on waiters, see Indianapolis *Freeman*, July 7, 1900, October 3, December 12, 1903, January 27, 1906, May 4, July 6, 1912; Louisville *Courier-Journal*, June 8, 1924; Alexander Walters, *My Life and Work* (New York, 1917), 30-32; Krock, *Myself When Young*, 203-5, discusses blacks' working as waiters at the Pendennis Club in Louisville; C. H. Wade to NAACP, December 12, 1937, NAACP Papers, Manuscript Division, Library of Congress, Washington, D.C.

14. Indianapolis *Freeman*, August 16, 1890, December 29, 1900, February 9, 1901.

15. *Ibid.*, January 27, 1906, May 4, 1912; Louisville *Courier-*

Journal, June 8, 1924; Charles M. Meacham, *A History of Christian County Kentucky, from Oxcart to Airplane* (Nashville, 1930), 203; *Prather's Directory of the City of Lexington, Kentucky* (Lexington, 1895), 292. Additional information on black barbers can be found in George C. Wright, *Life Behind A Veil: Blacks in Louisville, Kentucky, 1865-1930* (Baton Rouge, 1985), 82-84.

16. See Wright, *Life Behind A Veil*, 92-93, for whites' protesting the employment of blacks at the post office in Louisville.

17. Indianapolis *Freeman*, July 19, 1890, February 7, 1891.

18. Thomas L. Dabney, "Bowling Green, Kentucky, A Summary of Industrial Conditions, Organized Labor and Negro Labor," June 5, 1928, National Urban League Papers, Manuscript Division, Library of Congress, Washington, D.C.

19. *Colored American Magazine* 1 (1900): 330.

20. Wright, *Life Behind A Veil*, 93-94.

21. An article in the bicentennial edition of the Lexington *Herald-Leader*, July 4, 1976, has some information on blacks employed in the horse industry; Indianapolis *Freeman*, January 22, 1910.

22. Lexington *Morning Herald*, February 12, 1896; Lexington *Herald*, April 30, May 5, 1967; Louisville *Courier-Journal*, June 21, 1976. The career of another black jockey took a very tragic turn. John Hathaway accumulated a fortune, lost it, and in 1903 murdered his estranged girlfriend. For this crime he was executed January 3, 1905. See the Lexington *Herald*, January 4, 1905.

23. *Crisis* 4 (February 1913): 169; *Louisville Industrial Foundation, 1928* (Louisville, 1928), 32-33.

24. Paducah *Weekly News-Democrat*, October 25, 1906; *Crisis* 9 (January 1915): 132 and 14 (June 1917): 92.

25. Corbin (Ky.) *Times*, October 31, November 7, 1919; information on black workers' leaving Ravenna can be found in the Maysville *Bulletin*, April 8, 1920; Harrodsburg *Herald*, November 14, 21, 1924.

26. *Report of the Commission to Investigate the Conditions of Working Women in Kentucky* (n.p., 1911); *Crisis* 17 (December 1918): 86; Wright, *Life Behind A Veil*, 84-85.

27. "Summary and Report of the Louisville Urban League, 1939" and J. A. Thomas, "The Negro Wage Earner in Kentucky," unpublished papers, Louisville Urban League, March 1942, both in National Urban League Papers; J. Harvey Kerns, *A Survey of the Economic and Cultural Conditions of the Negro Population of Louisville, Kentucky, and a Review of the Program and Activities of the Louisville Urban League* (New York, 1948).

28. Dabney, "Bowling Green, Kentucky, A Summary of Industrial Conditions, Organized Labor and Negro Labor," National Urban League Papers.

29. G. F. Richings, *Evidences of Progress Among Colored People* (Philadelphia, 1899), 511-13; Huntsville (Ala.) *Gazette*, September 21, 1889; Indianapolis *Freeman*, December 6, 1890, July 25, 1891, July 21, 1900, July 6, 1901; *Henderson, Home of Audubon*, 42-43, 58-59.

30. Kansas City *Kansas Blackman*, June 22, 1894. Several oral interviews were conducted by Terry Birdwhistell and George Wright with long-time residents of Henderson's black community: Lorenzo D. Jones, November 17, 1983; Thelma B. Johnson, August 20, 1985; and Austin Bell, August 20, 1985, all in Oral History Collection, UK.

31. Lawrence Harris, *The Negro Population of Lexington in the Professions, Business, Education, and Religion* (Lexington, 1907). Additional information on black businesses in Lexington can be found in the following: *Prather's Directory of the City of Lexington, Kentucky* (Lexington, 1895); Richings, *Evidences of Progress*, 512-13; W. D. Johnson, *Biographical Sketches of Prominent Negro Men and Women of Kentucky* (Lexington, 1897); and Lexington *Herald-Leader*, July 4, 1976.

32. Wright, *Life Behind A Veil*, 99-100; also see the various Louisville city directories from 1890-1915, for instance, C. K. Caron, *Directory of Louisville for 1908* (Louisville, 1908). For additional information on Steward and his newspaper, see George C. Wright, "William Henry Steward: Moderate Approach to Black Leadership," in *Black Leaders of the Nineteenth Century*, ed. Leon Litwack and August Meier (Urbana, Ill., 1988), 275-89; and Richings, *Evidences of Progress*, 508-10.

33. Richings, *Evidences of Progress*, 507-8.

34. Cary B. Lewis, "Louisville and Its Afro-American Citizens," *Colored American Magazine* 10 (April 1906): 259-64.

35. Wright, *Life Behind A Veil*, 220-28; Louisville *Leader*, April 4, 1925, December 27, 1930; Associates of Louisville Municipal College, *Study of Negro Business in Louisville* (Louisville, 1944), 40-41.

36. Booker T. Washington, "The National Business League," *World's Work* (October 1902): 2671-74; Johnson, *Biographical Sketches of Prominent Negro Men and Women*, 22; Wright, *Life Behind A Veil*, 98-99.

37. Ronald L. Lewis, *Black Coal Miners in America: Race, Class and Community Conflict, 1780-1980* (Lexington, 1987), 121-42, 191-93, quotation p. 134. The population figures relating to coal miners must be used with caution, since miners were very mobile, often moving between West Virginia and eastern Kentucky looking for work. This would distort the figures for both states.

38. Lewis, *Black Coal Miners In America*, 136-42; Sterling D. Spero and Abraham L. Harris, *The Black Worker* (New York, 1931),

223; Edward Owens interview with Rev. D. Washington of Drakesboro, Ky., December 12, 1978, Oral History Collection, UK.

39. *Crisis* 12 (June 1916): 63; Washington interview. See two very important sources that discuss coal miners in general and also make several comments on blacks: Harry M. Caudill, *Night Comes to the Cumberlands: A Biography of A Depressed Area* (Boston, 1962) and Ronald D Eller, *Miners, Millhands, and Mountaineers: Industrialization of the Appalachian South, 1880-1930* (Knoxville, 1982).

40. Wendell P. Dabney, *Cincinnati's Colored Citizens: Historical, Sociological and Biographical* (Cincinnati, 1926), 213-355; for information on McLeod, see p. 308.

41. Secretarial letter from Benham, Kentucky, September 1914, Jesse E. Moorland Papers, Moorland-Spingarn Research Center, Howard University, Washington, D.C.; W. K. Bradley, "Negroes in the Kentucky Mountains," *Crisis* 22 (June 1921): 69-71. Lexington *Herald-Leader*, February 24, 1985, did a feature on Appalachian blacks, touching on their community life; James H. Lyons to Robert W. Bagnall, December 8, 1928, folder of the Harlan NAACP, NAACP Papers.

42. Indianapolis *Freeman*, May 10, June 28, 1890.

43. See the following sources on black community activities: J. H. Battle and W. H. Perrin, eds., *Counties of Todd and Christian, Kentucky* (Chicago, 1884); Willard Rouse Jillson, *Frankfort: Capital City of Kentucky* (Frankfort, 1927), 16-20; Leslie S. Smith, *Around Muhlenberg County, Kentucky: A Black History* (Evansville, 1979); Lottie O. Robinson, *The Bond-Washington Story: The Education of Black People, Elizabethtown, Kentucky* (n.p., 1983). See *Crisis* 22 (August 1921) for a trip to Hopkinsville by W.E.B. DuBois. On Lexington, see *The Blue Grass Country* (Lexington, 1938), 6-7; on Louisville, see Wright, *Life Behind A Veil*, chapter five.

44. Lexington *Morning Herald*, January 4, 1899; *The Fiftieth Anniversary of the Emancipation Proclamation* (Lexington, 1914), Fouse Family Papers, Special Collections, University of Kentucky; Louisville *Leader*, January 12, 1935.

45. Indianapolis *Freeman*, August 17, 1895, October 7, 1899; Paducah *Weekly News-Democrat*, August 9, 1906; Louisville *Leader*, August 24, 1935; Robertson, *Paducah*, 123.

46. For information on the early years of the Lexington Fair, see Johnson, *Biographical Sketches of Prominent Negro Men and Women*, 79-85; *Crisis* 14 (October 1917): 313; Indianapolis *Freeman*, September 27, 1890, September 26, 1891; Lexington *Morning Herald*, September 14, 1899, September 12, 1900; Richmond *Planet*, September 30, 1899.

47. Indianapolis *Freeman*, October 8, 1892.

48. New York *Times*, September 17, 1904; Louisville *Leader*,

August 12, 1922, August 15, 1925, July 13, 1929.

49. Louisville *Leader*, August 8, 1931.

50. See the Mary Church Terrell Papers, Manuscript Division, Library of Congress, for numerous references to Kentucky club women. A list of the many different organizations formed by Afro-American women in Kentucky can be found in Mary V. Parrish, ed., *Fourth Statistical Report of the National Association of Colored Women* (Louisville, 1914). An excellent source of information on the yearly activities of the clubs is their newspaper, *The Kentucky Club Woman*, which started in 1916 and was in existence for almost forty years. A few copies of the newspaper can be found in the Lizzie Fouse Papers at the University of Kentucky. See the newspaper for October 1934, page one, for the state song of the Kentucky clubs.

51. Additional data on these organizations can be found in the following: *Crisis* 9 (December 1914): 63; *Kentucky Federation of Colored Women's Clubs, 1916-17* (Louisville, 1919); *Kentucky Federation of Colored Women's Clubs, 1918-1919-1920-1921* (Louisville, 1924); *Kentucky Club Woman*, October 1934.

52. *Kentucky Federation of Colored Women's Clubs, 1916-17* and *1918-21* (Louisville, 1917, 1921).

53. Lucy H. Smith, ed., *Pictorial Directory of the Kentucky Association of Colored Women* (Louisville, 1945); State Association of Women's Clubs Scholarship Loan Fund (Paris, Ky., 1935) in Mary Church Terrell Papers.

54. Charles H. Parrish, ed., *Golden Jubilee, General Association of Colored Baptists in Kentucky* (Louisville, 1915); *Diamond Jubilee: The Story of Seventy-five Years of the Association* (Louisville, 1943); on Pleasant Green, see *150 Anniversary Pleasant Green Baptist Church, October 5-26, 1940;* on First Baptist, see *Souvenir Sesqui-Centennial Celebration First Baptist Church, Lexington, Ky., November 24 to December 2, 1940 (Lexington, 1940).*

55. Paducah *News-Democrat*, March 17, April 14, November 2, 1918.

56. A long, detailed account of the formation of this black organization can be found in the Lexington *Herald*, January 23, 1905.

57. *Report of the Vice Commission of Lexington, Kentucky* (Lexington, 1915), 32, 48.

58. *Ibid.*, 61.

59. *Wentworth's Souvenir Sporting Guide* (New York, 1895); Louisville *Courier-Journal*, July 15, 1907, October 5, 1913, July 7-15, 1927; *Report of the Vice Commission of Louisville, 1915* (Louisville, 1915); Thomas Jackson Woofter et al., *Negro Problems in Cities* (New York, 1928). Additional information on vice and activities in the city's black community can be found in Louisville Goodwill Indus-

tries, "Report of the Social Survey of Adjacent Neighborhood" (1937), Louisville Free Public Library.

2. Race Relations

1. *Hale v. Kentucky,* 303 United States 613 (1938); Paducah *Weekly News-Democrat,* June 7, August 9, 1906. Two very important reports have been issued by the state penal system: "Changing Faces: History of Corrections in Kentucky," and "Men Electrocuted in Kentucky since the Electric Chair was Installed at the Kentucky State Penitentiary at Eddyville, Kentucky in 1911," unpublished report, Kentucky Corrections Cabinet, Office of Corrections Training, Louisville. See also Robert Gunn Crawford, "A History of the Kentucky Penitentiary System, 1865-1937" (Ph.D. diss., University of Kentucky, 1955).

2. James H. Letcher, "The Treatment of Some Diseases by the 'Old Time' Negro," *Railway Surgical Journal* (December 1910), 1-16; Krock, *Myself When Young,* 34.

3. New York *Times,* November 26, 1904.

4. *Kentucky Statutes, 1903* (Louisville, 1903), 842-45.

5. Paducah *News-Democrat,* July 26, August 2, 1906.

6. Pardons and Rejected Petitions, Kentucky's Governors' Papers, 1792-1926, Augustus Willson Papers, Box 790, Kentucky Department for Libraries and Archives, Frankfort.

7. "Mr. Watterson's Friendship for the Blacks," Chicago *Tribune,* January 5, 1889; Louisville *Courier-Journal,* June 8, 1894, March 9, 29, 1898, August 25, 1901; Tuskegee Newspaper Clippings, Reel 221, Frame 287.

8. The poem can be found in the Mayfield *Monitor,* March 2, 1898. Examples of derogatory references to blacks can be found in newspapers from all over the state of Kentucky. See, for example, the early 1900s editions of the following: Madisonville *Daily Messenger,* Winchester *Sun,* Hopkinsville *Kentuckian,* Maysville *Bulletin,* Paducah *News-Democrat,* and various newspapers from Lexington and Louisville; for example, Louisville *Leader,* November 9, 1935.

9. Paducah *News-Democrat,* August 9, 10, 1916.

10. See, for example, the Louisville *Commercial,* November 4, 1897.

11. The Lexington *Herald,* November 17, 1914.

12. James C. Klotter, *The Breckinridges of Kentucky, 1760-1981* (Lexington, 1986), 178-81, 218-21; Lexington *Morning Herald,* July 7, 1897; *Crisis* 9 (January 1915): 125-26; Lexington *Herald,* March 5, 6, 1926. For an example of Desha Breckinridge's supporting a black

for political appointment, see Lexington *Herald*, April 22, 1913.

13. A copy of the letter from William Hart to W.C.P. Breckinridge, March 21, 1894, Breckinridge Family Papers, vol. 468, Manuscript Division, Library of Congress, was shared with the author by James Klotter. See also Lexington *Herald*, June 8, 1911, August 9, 1912.

14. James C. Klotter, "Slavery and Race: A Family Perspective," *Southern Studies* 17 (1978): 375-97.

15. Krock, *Myself When Young*, 58-59.

16. *Ibid.*, 77-79.

17. Robertson, *Paducah*, 129; Indianapolis *Freeman*, May 2, 1891; Louisville *Courier-Journal*, October 21, 1901.

18. Letter to American Library Association, March 22, 1917; Henderson Library to James Bertram, secretary of the Carnegie Corporation, both in the Henderson Public Library; Maralea Arnett, *The Annals and Scandals of Henderson County, Kentucky, 1775-1975* (Corydon, Kentucky, 1976), 100.

19. *Crisis* 15 (April 1918): 293; Louisville *Leader*, July 13, 1930.

20. Kentucky *Acts* (1916), 431-34; *Crisis* 1 (January 1911): 6; Lexington *Press-Transcript*, March 20, 1895; "The Colored Orphan Industrial Home of Lexington, Kentucky, Second Annual Report," January 1, 1896, Special Collections, University of Kentucky.

21. P.H. Kennedy et al. to the "Committee of Ladies Having Charge of Barret Park," September 7, 1903, Henderson Public Library.

22. Meacham, *History of Christian County*, 360-61. The *Crisis* is an excellent source for information on park segregation in Kentucky cities. See, for instance, 8 (October 1914): 273; 10 (May 1915): 8. See also Wright, *Life Behind A Veil*, 274-80.

23. Krock, *Myself When Young*, 8; Woofter, *Negro Problems in Cities*, 103-4.

24. Henderson County Deed Book 50, pp. 12, 28, Henderson City Hall.

25. For a discussion of residential segregation ordinances, see *Crisis* 3 (November 1911): 27-30; and 15 (December 1917): 69.

26. On Lexington, see Peter Craig Smith, "Negro Hamlets and Gentlemen Farms: A Dichotomous Rural Settlement Pattern in Kentucky's Bluegrass Region" (Ph.D. diss., University of Kentucky, 1972), and Herbert A. Thomas, Jr., "Victims of Circumstance: Negroes in a Southern Town, 1865-1880," *Register of the Kentucky Historical Society* 71 (1973): 253-71.

27. Buchanan v. Warley, 245 United States 60; George C. Wright, "The NAACP and Residential Segregation in Louisville, Kentucky, 1914-1917," *Register of the Kentucky Historical Society* 78 (1980): 39-54.

28. Indianapolis *Freeman*, April 17, August 14, 28, September 4, 11, 1909; Meacham, *A History of Christian County*, 360; Lexington *Herald*, January 15, 1912. For Bond's comment on Lexington, see the Commission on Interracial Cooperation Papers, Woodruff Library, Atlanta University, Atlanta, Ga.

29. *Crisis* 13 (January 1913): 147; Woofter, *Negro Problems in Cities*, 263-64.

30. Louisville *Leader*, January 17, May 9, 1925, May 14, 1927.

31. *Ibid.*, August 30, 1924, September 23, 1933, May 11, 1935.

32. Bradley, "Negroes in the Kentucky Mountains," 69-71.

33. Eller, *Miners, Millhands, and Mountaineers*, 170-71; Lewis, *Black Coal Miners in America*, 148; Spero and Harris, *The Black Worker*, 236-38.

34. Joseph Williams, secretary of Bell County Branch, to William Pickens of the National Office, January 15, 1940; J. Johnson Williams, of the Bell County Branch, to the National Association, July 17, 1942, both in NAACP Papers.

35. Biographical information on Underwood can be found in Johnson, *Biographical Sketches of Prominent Negro Men and Women*, 61-62; Clement Richardson, ed., *The National Cyclopedia of the Colored Race* (Montgomery, Ala., 1919), 76.

36. *Ibid.*; Washington (D.C.) *Colored American*, October 13, 1900.

37. "The Record of Albert Ernest Meyzeek," *Negro History Bulletin* 10 (1947): 186-87; Ben Horton, "Life and Achievements of Albert Ernest Meyzeek," *Kentucky Negro Journal* 1 (1958): 25-27; Louisville *Courier-Journal*, July 26, 1962.

38. Wright, "William Henry Steward," 275-89; William J. Simmons, *Men of Mark: Eminent, Progressive, and Rising* (Cleveland, 1887), 603-4.

39. Charles A. Lofgren, *The Plessy Case: A Legal Historical Interpretation* (New York, 1987), 20-24. For a chronology of the efforts of blacks to prevent the law from passing, see S.E. Smith, ed., *History of the Anti-Separate Coach Movement of Kentucky* (Evansville, Ind., n.d.).

40. Lexington *Morning Transcript*, March 30, 1886, December 22, 1891, April 5, June 24, 1892, October 12, 1893; Johnson, *Biographical Sketches of Prominent Negro Men and Women*, 20-21; John D. Wright, *Lexington: Heart of the Bluegrass* (Lexington, 1982), 155-56.

41. Kentucky *Acts* (1893), 63-64. See *The Kentucky Statutes Containing All General Laws, with Full Notes of Decisions of the Court of Appeals to June 1903* (Louisville, 1903), chapters 795 to 801. An editorial in the Frankfort *Capitol*, March 25, 1892, stated that every white newspaper in the state, except the pro-Republican Louisville *Commercial*, favored the Separate Coach Law. See also the March

29, 1892, edition of the paper which reprinted an editorial from a Paducah newspaper stating that all of the white people in the state favored the law.

42. Smith, ed., *Anti-Separate Coach Movement;* letter from the Headquarters of the Anti-Separate Coach Movement's State Central and Executive Committee, January 15, 1895, William H. Steward Scrapbook, privately owned; Ida B. Wells, *Southern Horrors: Lynch Law In All Its Phases* (New York, 1892), 22-23.

43. W.H. Anderson v. *Louisville and Nashville Railroad Company,* 62 Federal Reporter 46-51 (1894); Louisville *Courier-Journal,* June 4, 8, 1894.

44. *Ibid.;* Richmond *Planet,* February 9, 1895; New York *Times,* February 5, 1895.

45. Anti-Separate Coach State Central and Executive Committees to Concerned Citizens, January 15, 1895, Steward Papers.

46. Richmond *Planet,* March 9, 1895; *Louisville & Nashville Railroad v. Commonwealth of Kentucky,* 37 Southwestern Reporter 79 (1896).

47. *Bailey v. Louisville & Nashville Railroad,* 44 Southwestern Reporter 105-7 (1898).

48. *Ohio Valley Railroad v. Lander,* 47 Southwestern Reporter 344-47 (1898).

49 *Ibid.*

50. *Chesapeake and Ohio Railway Company v. Kentucky,* 179 United States 388 (1900); Louisville *Courier-Journal,* December 4, 1900; Indianapolis *Freeman,* December 15, 1900. One problem left unresolved related to interurban railway travel between Cincinnati and several Kentucky suburbs and between Louisville and several nearby towns in Indiana. In 1920 the United States Supreme Court said that the Kentucky Separate Coach Law was valid in requiring separate coaches while operating between points in Kentucky. See *South Covington and Cincinnati Street Railway v. Commonwealth of Kentucky,* 252 United States 399 (1920); Louisville *Courier-Journal,* April 20, 1920; New York *Times,* April 20, 1920.

51. Newsclip, March 1908, Augustus E. Willson Papers, Filson Club, Louisville.

52. Indianapolis *Freeman,* May 12, 1900; Paducah *Weekly News-Democrat,* April 5, June 28, November 1, 1906.

53. Booker T. Washington to Milton Smith, February 1, 1912, Booker T. Washington Papers, Manuscript Division, Library of Congress; *Crisis* 8 (May 1914): 11, 178; (June 1914): 59; (September 1914): 219; 9 (December 1914): 64.

54. *Crisis* 18 (August 1919): 207; Louisville *Leader,* June 3, 1939.

55. Information on the number of people killed at the hands

of lynch mobs has been obtained from a number of sources: (1) two national newspapers, the Chicago *Tribune* and *New York Times*, which contain details on many Kentucky lynchings that occurred between 1882 and 1918; (2) local newspapers and county histories, which give accounts (though often racially biased) of why whites felt compelled to lynch blacks; (3) the Louisville *Courier-Journal* and Lexington newspapers, which often sent their best reporters to cover potential lynchings; and (4) the records of the NAACP and Tuskegee Institute, which contains statistical data on the number of lynchings occurring in each state, including Kentucky. For a much larger study on racial violence in Kentucky, the author has investigated every lynching cited by these various sources. I then took a conservative approach, deciding not to count as a lynching many of the deaths these sources have concluded were lynchings. For instance, every instance that suggested blacks had weapons and defended themselves, even if greatly outnumbered, have not been counted as lynchings. Second, at least fifteen murders in the early 1900s that were attributed to the Night Riders of western Kentucky have not been counted as lynchings. For example, the NAACP lists the lynching of a white man on April 1, 1910, and the lynching of twelve men on the night of November 13, 1914, but with no other sources substantiating these killings, I chose not to include them in my count of 353 lynchings in Kentucky.

56. An excellent account of this incident can be found in Ida B. Wells, *A Red Record* (Chicago, 1895), 36-42. For a racist version of the incident, see the Mayfield *Monitor*, July 12, 1893, May 12, 1897.

57. The Louisville *Courier-Journal*, December 30, 1896, reprinted accounts of what out-of-state journals said about the violence in Kentucky.

58. New York *World*, December 7, 1899; Louisville *Courier-Journal*, December 7, 1899; New York *Times*, December 8, 1899; Lexington *Kentucky Standard*, December 12, 1899. Perhaps the best coverage of the lynchings can be found in the Cincinnati *Enquirer* from December 7 to the end of the month. See also an article, "Inability of the Governor of Kentucky to Bring Lynchers to Justice," *American Law Review* 34 (1900): 238-39.

59. The quote comes from Bradley's "Message to the General Assembly, March 13, 1897," in *Public Documents of Governor William O. Bradley* (Louisville, 1899), 55; Kentucky Acts (1897), 29-33; and (1902), 55-60; James E. Cutler, "Proposed Remedies for Lynchings," *Yale Review* 13 (1904): 194-212.

60. The most detailed discussion of this incident can be found in the "Minutes of the Executive Committee of the National Association for the Advancement of Colored People," beginning on

May 2, 1911, NAACP Papers.

61. Kentucky *Acts* (1920), 187-90; Edward E. Underwood to John R. Shillady, April 9, 1920, NAACP Papers; Louisville *Leader*, March 19, 1921; "Legal Punishment of Lynchers, 1899-1930," Commission on Interracial Cooperation Papers, Atlanta University.

62. Wright, *Life Behind A Veil*, 70-76, 253-56; Memphis *Commercial-Appeal*, August 14, 1906; Paducah *Weekly News-Democrat*, August 16, 1906; Madisonville *Hustler*, February 21, 1908; Lexington *Herald*, April 1-5, 1925; Louisville *Leader*, April 23, 1938. For an example of a Lexington black's being abused on public transportation, see the Lizzie Fouse Papers for a number of letters that were written in October-November 1931. Also, in an oral interview Hugh D. Palmer mentioned the corporal punishments that blacks often received at the hands of white employers.

63. Louisville *News*, March 3, 1923; *Kentucky Irish-American*, June 25, July 9, August 13, 20, 1927. See also a series of letters between Robert W. Bingham, editor of the *Courier-Journal* and *Times*, and Henry R. Luce, denouncing the Ku Klux Klan and lawlessness in Kentucky during the 1920s. Robert W. Bingham Papers, Manuscript Division, Library of Congress; see the Madisonville *Daily Messenger*, April 1926, *passim*.

64. Wright, *Racial Violence in Kentucky*, 12, 226-27. Starting around 1882, the Chicago *Tribune* listed the number of people put to death by the state. Local newspapers, because they covered executions in such great detail, are an excellent source for data on blacks who were executed by the state. Another useful source is "Men Electrocuted in Kentucky since the Electric Chair was installed at the Kentucky State Penitentiary at Eddyville, Kentucky in 1911."

65. New York *Sun*, October 8, 1905.

66. Louisville *Leader*, February 19, March 26, April 2, May 14, 1927, January 7, 1928.

67. Information on this case can be found in the Lexington newspaper from March through April 17, 1926; the Louisville *Leader* also covered the story in great detail.

68. *Kansas Blackman*, May 4, 1894.

69. *Crisis* 9 (January 1915): 114.

70. Paducah *News-Democrat*, July 16, 1916.

71. Louisville *Leader*, March 26, 1938.

72. Louisville *Courier-Journal*, October 16, 1885; Wright, *Racial Violence in Kentucky*, 248.

73. *John Taylor* v. *Commonwealth*, 90 Southwestern Reporter 581-84 (1906); *Smith* v. *Commonwealth*, 91 Southwestern Reporter 742 (1906); *McDaniel* v. *Commonwealth*, 181 Kentucky Reports 766-81 (1918).

74. *Hale* v. *Kentucky*, 303 United States 613-15 (1938).

75. Lexington *Standard*, September 6, 1895; Lexington *Daily Leader*, January 4, 1898; Louisville *Courier-Journal*, October 20, 1899; see also W.O. Bradley, *Stories and Speeches of William O. Bradley; with Biographical Sketch by M.H. Thatcher* (Lexington, 1916).

76. Bradley was quoted in the *Public Documents of Governor William O. Bradley*, 55; see also Adalaide Abel Barker, "William O'Connell Bardley" (M.A. thesis, University of Kentucky, 1927), 29; Springfield (Ohio) *Republican*, January 18, 1898. Examples of Bradley's speeches denouncing lynchings can be found in the William O. Bradley Scrapbooks, Special Collections, University of Kentucky; Wright, *Racial Violence in Kentucky*, 177-78.

77. Louisville *Courier-Journal*, November 26, 1910. For information relating to the eleven black men and their requests for pardons, see Pardons and Rejected Petitions, Willson Papers. This collection includes a three-page letter dated November 23, 1910, which is the governor's official statement on the pardon.

78. For Morrow's comments and actions against mob violence, see the following: Commission on Interracial Cooperation Papers, Atlanta University; Edwin P. Morrow Papers, Special Collections, University of Kentucky, which includes *Biennial Message of Governor Edwin P. Morrow Before the General Assembly of Kentucky* (January 3, 1922); and George Madden Martin, "Race Cooperation," *McClure's* (October 1922), 9-20. For data on the incident in Lexington, see the NAACP Papers, Group 1, Series C; *Crisis* 19 (April 1920): 298; J. Winston Coleman, Jr., *Death at the Court House* (Lexington, 1952), and the Lexington newspapers for February 1920.

79. Indianapolis *Freeman*, April 28, 1900; Paducah *Weekly News-Democrat*, January 25, 1906, October 17, 1907.

80. Louisville *Courier-Journal*, April 17, October 2, 1909.

81. Louisville *Times*, September 7, 1899; Louisville *Courier-Journal*, September 9, 1899.

82. Louisville *Courier-Journal*, July 12, 13, 14, September 12, 17, 19, 1899.

83. Tapp and Klotter, *Kentucky: Decades of Discord*, 435.

84. Thomas Randolph, "The Governor and the Mob," *The Independent* (February 26, 1917): 347-48; Paducah *News-Democrat*, November 3, 1918; Louisville *Leader*, October 4, 1924.

85. Louisville *Commercial*, July 20, 1895.

86. Louisville *Courier-Journal*, July 15, 19, 25, 1895; Lebanon *Enterprise*, August 2, 1895.

87. Information on Democratic racist campaigns in Louisville can be found in Wright, *Life Behind A Veil*, 186-92. For information on Laura Clay and her view of blacks, see, for example, Clay to Ida H. Harper, April 3, 1902, saying that black women were register-

ing to vote in greater numbers, Laura Clay Papers, Special Collections, University of Kentucky. See also Lexington *Leader*, October 19, 1910.

88. The 1911 pamphlet is entitled, *To The Voters of Lexington and Fayette County*, Laura Clay Papers.

89. Hopkinsville *Kentuckian*, October 26, 1911; Mayfield *Messenger*, October 4, 1920; James Bond, director of the Commission on Interracial Cooperation, to Lewis Humphrey, editor of the Louisville *Post*, October 26, 1923, Box 5, Bingham Papers; Robert F. Sexton, "Kentucky Politics and Society: 1919-1932" (Ph.D. diss., University of Washington, 1970), 77.

90. Wright, *Life Behind A Veil*, 249-54; on Lexington, see *Crisis* 5 (December 1912): 59; and 14 (July 1917): 145.

91. Hopkinsville *Kentuckian*, November 5, 1897; Meacham, *A History of Christian County*, 228; Louisville *Leader*, May 14, 1921, October 11, 1924, August 10, 1929.

92. Louisville *Leader*, September 7, 1929, September 16, 1939; Georgetown *Times*, August 8, November 7, 1929.

93. Winchester *Sun*, November 5, 1913.

94. *Ibid.*, December 2-6, 1913. In the paper, Colerane was always referred to without the title of "Mr." while all the whites mentioned were given this courtesy.

95. Louisville *Courier-Journal*, December 7, 1913; *Crisis* 7 (February 1914): 171.

3. *An Education: Providing the "Proper Kind of Training: for Blacks"*

1. Lexington *Leader*, January 4, 1898.

2. Thomas Jesse Jones, *Negro Education: A Study of the Private and Higher Schools for Colored People in the United States*, 2 vols. (Washington, D.C., 1917), 1:7.

3. James D. Anderson, *The Education of Blacks in the South, 1860-1935* (Chapel Hill, 1988); George Colvin to Robert W. Bingham, August 23, 1923, Robert W. Bingham Papers.

4. *Commonwealth of Kentucky* v. *Jesse Ellis*, 11 Kentucky Law Report 402 (1882); *Edward Claybrook* v. *City of Owensboro*, 16 Federal Reporter 297-305 (1883); Louisville *Courier-Journal*, April 4, 1882, April 3, 1883.

5. *Crosby* v. *City of Mayfield*, 117 Southwestern Reporter 316 (1909); *Moss* v. *City of Mayfield*, 186 Kentucky Reports 330-434 (1919).

6. Indianapolis *Freeman*, October 25, 1890.

7. Louisville *Courier-Journal*, January 27, 1909.

8. "Report of the Meeting of the Executive Committee of In-

terRacial Commission in the Auditorium of the YMCA, January 21, 1925," Papers of the Commission on Interracial Cooperation, Louisville Free Public Library.

9. Bureau of the Census, *Negro Population in the United States, 1790-1915*, 145, 203; Bureau of the Census, *Negro Population in the United States, 1920-1932*, 238.

10. Bureau of the Census, *Twelfth Census of the United States, 1900*, 1: cv, and 2: ciii.

11. Emma C. Boyd to W.E.B. DuBois, December 10, 1923, NAACP Papers.

12. *Superintendent of Public Instruction Report . . . 1891* in *Kentucky Documents* (1891-92), 153-221.

13. *Ibid. . . . 1901*, 179.

14. Smith, *Around Muhlenberg County, Kentucky*, 73-76.

15. William Foster Hayes. *Sixty Years of Owensboro, 1883-1943* (Owensboro, n.d.), 247-48.

16. Claude Meals, "The Struggle of the Negro for Citizenship in Kentucky Since 1865" (M.A. thesis, Howard University, 1940), 59, 67-70; *Announcement of the Central Colored High School and Colored Normal School of Louisville, Kentucky, 1907-1908* (Louisville, 1908); George D. Wilson, "A Century of Negro Education in Louisville" (manuscript prepared by the project workers of the WPA, n.d.), 76, 93, copy in Louisville Free Public Library.

17. August Meier, "The Vogue of Industrial Education," *Mid-West Journal* 7 (1955): 241-66; Simmons, *Men of Mark: Eminent, Progressive, and Rising*, 47-50; Simmons, "What the Colored People Are Doing in Kentucky," *American Baptist Home Mission Society*, jubilee volume (1883): 85-90; Wright, *Life Behind A Veil*, 160-61; Salisbury (N.C.) *AME Star of Zion*, April 18, 1889, November 20, 1890; the quote on the object of the school comes from *AME Zion Church Quarterly* 3 (July 1893): 554.

18. Charles H. Parrish, "Industrial Education," *AME Zion Church Quarterly* 3 (April 1893): 374-81. For biographical data on Parrish, see *ibid.* 3 (July 1893): 552-55; and Wright, *Life Behind A Veil*, 161-63.

19. Lexington *Morning Herald*, October 7, 9, 12, 1900; William H. Fouse, "Educational History of the Negroes of Lexington, Kentucky" (M.A. thesis, University of Cincinnati, 1937). Fouse was principal at the black high school in Lexington for over twenty years.

20. Information on the County School Law of 1908 and Afro-Americans can be found in Meals, "The Struggle of the Negro for Citizenship in Kentucky," 68-69; Jones, *Negro Education*, 2:259-81.

21. Anderson, *Education of Blacks in the South*, 156-73, 184-85; interview with Lorenzo D. Jones. Jones's father, Hence Jones, was

the first principal of Frederick Douglass High School in Henderson. See also Frieda J. Dannheiser and Donald L. Hazelwood, eds., *The History of Henderson County, Kentucky* (Evansville, Ind., 1980), 245-47.

22. Jones, *Negro Education*, 2:259-81.

23. James T. Haley, *Afro-American Encyclopaedia; or the Thoughts, Doings, and Sayings of the Race* (Nashville, 1895), 446. The various quotes come from a long article headlined "Atkinson College: Its Motto is Thoroughness in All its Branches," in the *AME Star of Zion*, October 11, 1900.

24. Richings, *Evidence of Progress*, 134.

25. R. R. Wright, Jr., *Self-Help in Negro Education* (Cheyney, Pa., 1909), 8-9; Jones, *Negro Education*, 2:269, 271, 276-81. See also Fouse, "Educational History of the Negroes of Lexington," 58-59.

26. Lexington *Leader*, August 4, 1915; Fouse, "Educational History of the Negroes of Lexington," 122.

27. Meals, "The Struggle of the Negro for Citizenship in Kentucky," 91.

28. Lena Beatrice Morton, *My First Sixty Years: Passion for Wisdom* (New York, 1965), 13; Dabney, *Cincinnati's Colored Citizens*, 248-355.

29. L. N. Taylor, "Negro Education Within the Century," *Kentucky School Journal* 16 (April 1938): 30-31; "Report By Bond, 1924," Commission on Interracial Cooperation Papers, Box 167, Atlanta University.

30. *Report of the Kentucky Commission on Negro Affairs*, November 1, 1945.

31. On the founding and early years of Kentucky State, see *Superintendent of Public Instruction Report . . . 1891*, 231-34, and *ibid. . . . 1893*, 3:68, in *Kentucky Documents* (1893), No. 27; United States Bureau of Education, *Circular of Information No. 3* (1899); Alvin F. Lewis, *History of Higher Education in Kentucky* (Washington, D.C., 1899), 294-99; Oscar F. Galloway, "Higher Education for Negroes in Kentucky," *Bulletin of the Bureau of School Service* 5 (September 1932): 13.

32. A copy of the "Dedication Poem" was obtained from the Schomberg Library in New York City. Blank spaces indicate words that are illegible. Information on Perry can be found in Wright, *Life Behind A Veil*, 135, 141-42.

33. Lewis, *History of Higher Education*, 299. For information on Kentucky State's becoming an accredited college, see James Bond to Will W. Alexander, May 22, 1922, Folder 158, Box 167, Commission on Interracial Cooperation Papers, Atlanta University.

34. John Taylor Williams, "A Comparative Study of the Administration of Higher Education In Selected Kentucky Negro and

Notes to Pages 128-37 / 243

White State-Supported Schools" (M.A. thesis, University of Cincinnati, 1932), 63. See also Louisville *Leader*, April 9, 1921; Folder 13, Box 89, Interracial Cooperation Papers, Atlanta Universtiy.
    35. *Superintendent of Public Instruction Report* . . . *1909*, 67-71; Galloway, "Higher Education for Negroes In Kentucky," 81.
    36. John A. Hardin, "A Critical Analysis of Black Higher Education in Kentucky, 1904-1954," 24-25. I wish to thank Professor Hardin for making available this unpublished material.
    37. Clarence L. Timberlake, *Politics and the Schools: An Argument for a State Wide Board of Regents for the Kentucky Normal Institute for Colored Persons, Frankfort, Ky.* (n.p., n.d.).
    38. Louisville *Courier-Journal*, October 20, 1914; *Crisis* 9 (December 1914): 62; the best account of the controversy at Kentucky State can be found in the black Frankfort *Star*, October 24, 31, 1914.
    39. Gerald L. Smith, " 'Mr. Kentucky State': A Biography of Rufus Ballard Atwood" (Ph.D. diss., University of Kentucky, 1988), 74-77.
    40. Hardin, "Black Higher Education in Kentucky," 36-37; Williams, "A Comparative Study," 48; Louisville *Leader*, March 1, 17, 1924, March 2, 1929.
    41. Information on the entire history of Simmons University can be found in the Archives and Records Center, University of Louisville; for example, see *State University Catalogue 1883-84* (Louisville, 1883); *28th Annual Announcement of State University and 20th Announcement of Louisville Medical College* (Louisville, 1908).
    42. Department of the Interior, Bureau of Education, Bulletin No. 7, *Survey of Negro Colleges and Universities* (Washington, D.C., 1929), 345-54.
    43. Galloway, "Higher Education for Negroes in Kentucky," *passim*. See also the Louisville Municipal College Papers, Archives and Records Center, University of Louisville; and Wright, *Life Behind A Veil*, 270-73.
    44. *Kentucky Acts* (1919), 55; Paducah *Sun*, August 7, 1981.
    45. Galloway, "Higher Education For Negroes In Kentucky," 130-31; Williams, "A Comparative Study," 19-20.
    46. *Superintendent of Public Instruction Report* . . . *1939*, 31-32, 52-53; Atwood S. Wilson, "Historical Sketch of Negro Education In Kentucky," *Kentucky School Journal* 16 (February 1938): 16-18.
    47. "Report by Bond, 1924"; Meals, "The Struggle of the Negro for Citizenship," 70.
    48. Frost was quoted in the Louisville *Courier-Journal*, December 5, 1908, and February 2, 1909.
    49. A complete list of all of the donors can be found in Lincoln Institute Donation Vouchers #1, Box 10, Kentucky Department

for Libraries and Archives, Frankfort.

50. Shelbyville *News,* May 27, 1909; Shelbyville *Record,* June 8, 11, 1909.

51. Dr. A. E. Thomson kept a diary on the founding of Lincoln Institute. The author saw a copy of his diary at the home of Dr. Whitney Young (who was one of the school's first students and later the first black named to direct the school) in Louisville, Ky. From the very beginning of the idea of the new school, prominent black leader William H. Steward had endorsed the creation of Lincoln Institute: "This new school will give Kentucky a better standing in the educational world and will place a new emphasis upon industrial training as a means of solving the race problem." *American Baptist,* January 31, 1908.

52. Lexington *Kentucky Standard,* February 14, 1909.

53. Department of Interior, *Survey of Negro Colleges and Universities,* 354-60; copies of the *Lincoln Log,* a magazine published by Lincoln Institute, may be found at the Lincoln Foundation at the Brown Education Center in Louisville; Louisville *Leader,* September 7, 1935; Louisville *Defender,* April 30, 1949; George C. Wright, "The Faith Plan: A Black Institution Grows During the Depression," *Filson Club History Quarterly* 51 (1977): 336-49.

54. *The Nation* 89 (November 17, 1904): 389; Richard Allen Heckman and Betty Jean Hall, "Berea College and the Day Law," *Register of the Kentucky Historical Society* 66 (1968): 35-52; Isabella Black, "Berea College," *Phylon* 17 (1957): 267-76. An excellent source of information on Berea College is the Hampton University Newspaper Clipping File on Berea College (previously called the Peabody Collection), Hampton University, Hampton, Va. Included in this collection are a number of stories from the New York *Tribune,* the Brooklyn *Eagle,* and other white northeastern newspapers favorable to the program of Berea.

55. Indianapolis *Freeman,* May 4, 1899, December 29, 1900. A very important discussion of race relations at Berea can be found in James McPherson, *The Abolitionist Legacy: From Reconstruction to the NAACP* (Princeton, 1975), chapter fourteen.

56. New York *Freeman,* July 25, 1885; Louisville *Courier-Journal,* March 3, 1890.

57. McPherson, *Abolitionist Legacy,* 246-47.

58. Newsclip, the *New South,* November 24, 1894, Negro Collection, Hutchins Library, Berea College.

59. McPherson, *Abolitionist Legacy,* 247. For an excellent article detailing Frost's desire to limit enrollment and of the black response to his actions, see Jacqueline G. Burnside, "Suspicion Versus Faith: Negro Criticisms of Berea College in the Nineteenth Century," *Register of the Kentucky Historical Society* 83 (1985): 237-66.

60. New York *Tribune*, February 9, 1903; Booker T. Washington to William G. Frost, February 11, 1903, Container 258, Booker T. Washington Papers.

61. E. G. Dodge to Frost, April 11, 1925, William G. Frost Papers, Hutchins Library, Berea College; Burnside, "Suspicion Versus Faith," 249.

62. See the Day Law File, Hutchins Library, Berea College; Berea *Citizen*, March 17, 24, 1904; quotation is from *The Southern Problem* in William G. Frost Papers, Hutchins Library, Berea College.

63. Frost to Washington, January 18, 1904, Washington to Frost, January 22, 1904, William H. Steward to Booker T. Washington, February 3, 1904, Container 288, Booker T. Washington Papers. *The Nation* 79 (November 17, 1904): 389, said that Kentucky legislators were bulldozed into supporting the measure: "This explains why thousands of high-minded Southern white people who are opposed to attacks upon the negro are silent in the presence of the ignorant, blatant, and violent portion of the community. In the case of Berea, the evidence accumulates that the attack upon it was due to instructions received from politicians further South."

64. *Berea College* v. *Commonwealth*, 94 Southwestern Reporter 623 (1906).

65. *Berea College* v. *Commonwealth of Kentucky*, 211 United States 45 (1908); Louisville *Courier-Journal*, November 10, 1908, expressed its delight with the ruling of the Supreme Court. Henry Watterson, the self-proclaimed "friend of the Negro," wrote: "Undoubtedly in the South—where the negro has always found his best friends . . . and where he lives more happily than anywhere else—the legal victory of the Legislature will be popular. Southerners, after many years of practical experience, thought, and observation—after many years of co-operation with the negro—have found that the separation of the races works the better results in the long run. The leaders of thought in the negro race have reached the same conclusions. These latter will probably be found praising the outcome of the litigation over Berea College—especially since it means . . . the early establishment of a college for the exclusive use of members of the negro race."

66. New York *Age*, February 16, July 20, 1905; *The Outlook* 85 (April 17, 1907): 921-23; Booker T. Washington to Olivia Egleston Phelps Stokes, June 16, 1908, Booker T. Washington Papers; Carter G. Woodson to the Associated Harvard Clubs, April 13, 1923, Carter G. Woodson Papers, Manuscript Division, Library of Congress; McPherson, *Abolitionist Legacy*, 257-58. The New York *Age* of March 7, 1907, had a sharp attack on Frost and a reply by Frost.

67. Wright, *Self-Help in Negro Education*, 29.
68. Harvey C. Russell, *Kentucky Negro Education Association 1877-1946* (Norfolk, Va., 1946), 60; Louisville *Leader*, April 23, 1921, April 15, 1922; Lexington *Herald-Leader*, April 21, 1940. Several of the various programs of the KNEA can be found in the Fouse Family Papers, University of Kentucky. See, for example, "The Kentucky Negro Educational Association, Thirty-Sixth Annual Session, Louisville, April 21-24, 1915." Fouse, principal of Lexington's Dunbar High School for several decades, served as president of the KNEA in 1938-39.

4. The NAACP and the Quest for Equality

1. *Buchanan v. Warley*, 245 United States 60 (1917); Albert E. Meyzeek to John Shillady, secretary of the National Association, May 2, 1918; Walter White of the National Office to Wilson Lovett, May 7, 1918, both in NAACP Papers.
2. Information on the smaller Kentucky communities that formed NAACP branches can be found in the NAACP Papers, Series 2, Box L-44; for example, see Walter White to James Weldon Johnson, January 25, 1919; Mrs. Maggie Patton, secretary of the Maysville branch, to the National Office, November 24, 1919; J. W. Bell of the Earlington Branch to Johnson, February 10, 1919. See also *Crisis* 17 (April 1919): 284-85.
3. For the activities of the Frankfort branch in Richmond, see Edward E. Underwood to the National Office, June 6, July 23, 1923; National Office to Underwood, June 13, 18, 1923; Underwood to Walter White, November 28, 1924; White to Underwood, December 6, 1924; B.F. Spencer, secretary of the Frankfort NAACP, to William Pickens of the National Office, September 5, 1933, all in NAACP Papers.
4. Details regarding the entire incident can be found in a letter from Oscar M. Smith, lawyer for Samuel Smith, to W.T. Andrews of the legal department of the National Association, August 1929, NAACP Administration Files, Box C-285, NAACP Papers.
5. Ethel B. Winn of Covington to R.W. Bagnall, June 9, September 8, October 28, 1930; Bagnall to Winn, June 10, 1930; National Office to O.E. Jones of the Covington branch, November 24, 1931, all in NAACP Papers.
6. Numerous letters and news clippings concerning this case can be found in Group 1, Series G, Boxes 1-55, NAACP Papers; information on the trial can be found in the Cincinnati *Enquirer*, May 30, 31, 1930; *McPerkins v. Commonwealth*, 33 Southwestern Reporter, 2nd Series, 622-25 (1930).

7. Huston Mosler to the National Office of the NAACP, July 14, 1934, NAACP Papers.

8. Research in the Cincinnati *Enquirer* for the entire year of 1934 failed to uncover any information on this case.

9. See report entitled "Kentucky Legislation on Separate Schools," from Harry H. Jones to Charles H. Houston, December 2, 1937, NAACP Papers.

10. Biographical information on Anderson can be found in the Louisville *Leader*, November 9, 1935, while biographical data on Louisville's black leaders is in Charles H. Parrish, Jr., "Politics," typescript, 1938, Parrish Papers. Information on Lyman Johnson was obtained by the author in an interview, March 16, 1978. See Louisville *Leader*, May 2, 9, 1931, for stories about Tucker's being assaulted in Elizabethtown.

11. Louisville *Leader*, April 8, 1933; "Louisville NAACP, 1927-1937," Box G-77, and Charles W. Anderson to Walter White, June 9, 1933, both in NAACP Papers.

12. The entire story of the Democrats' backing of Tucker can be found in Ralph J. Bunche, *The Political Status of the Negro in the Age of FDR* (Chicago, 1973), 468-69. See also Ernest M. Collins, "The Political Behavior of the Negroes in Cincinnati, Ohio, and Louisville, Kentucky" (Ph.D. diss., University of Kentucky, 1950), 161-62.

13. Charles W. Anderson to Charles H. Houston of the legal department of the National Association, November 24, 1935, NAACP Papers; J.A. Thomas, "Introducing Kentucky's Legislator," *Opportunity* 18 (March 1940): 76-77.

14. Walter White to Charles W. Anderson, November 7, 1935; Anderson to White, November 24, 1935; Charles W. Anderson to Whitney M. Young, April 7, 1937, all in NAACP Papers. For information on the education bills passed in 1936 to 1938, see Rufus B. Atwood, "Financing Schools for Negro Children from State School Funds in Kentucky," *Journal of Negro Education* 8 (1939): 659-65. Dennis Dickerson, who is completing a biography of Whitney M. Young, Jr., made this comment in the section of his study that discusses the early life of Young.

15. Press release, "Kentucky Legislature Passes Scholarship Bill," February 7, 1936, Kentucky materials, NAACP Papers.

16. Louisville *Leader*, March 30, 1946.

17. "A Salary Study for the Lexington Public Schools," *Bulletin of the Bureau of School Service* 7 (March 1935): no. 3; Roy H. Owsley to Will W. Alexander of the Commission on Interracial Cooperation, March 23, 1935, Association of Southern Women for the Prevention of Lynching Collection, Atlanta University.

18. Victor K. Perry to Thurgood Marshall, January 21, Febru-

ary 23, 1938; Marshall to Perry, January 24, 1938, all in Group 2, Box L-37, NAACP Papers.

19. Louisville *Times*, April 3, 1939; Louisville *Courier-Journal*, April 15, 18, May 12, 1939.

20. Anderson to Marshall, June 10, 24, 1939; Marshall to Anderson, June 14, December 13, 1939, all in NAACP Papers.

21. Anderson to Marshall, December 18, 22, 1939; Marshall to Anderson, December 21, 1939; Marshall to Dr. P. O. Sweeney of the Louisville NAACP, December 26, 1939; Marshall to Yolanda Barnett of the Teachers Association, December 26, 1939; Atwood Wilson, president of the KNEA, to Walter White, September 10, 1940, all in NAACP Papers.

22. A copy of the statement of the Louisville Board of Education can be found in Group 2, Box 185, NAACP Papers.

23. Prentice Thomas to Thurgood Marshall [December 13, 1940], NAACP Papers.

24. See press releases from NAACP, November 8, 15, 1940, NAACP Papers.

25. Louisville *Courier-Journal*, December 4, 1940; NAACP press release, December 6, 1940, NAACP Papers.

26. Louisville *Courier-Journal*, December 6, 9, 1940; Mark Ethridge to Thurgood Marshall, December 9, 1940; Marshall to Ethridge, December 12, 1940, all in NAACP Papers.

27. Thurgood Marshall to Prentice Thomas, February 24, 1941, NAACP Papers; Louisville *Courier-Journal*, April 2, 1941; *Crisis* 48 (February 1941): 54.

28. NAACP press release, August 1, 1941, NAACP Papers; *Valla Dudley Abbington v. Board of Education of Louisville*, United States District Court, Civil Docket No. 243, filed July 2, 1941. A copy of the brief filed by Abbington can be found in the NAACP Papers. See also P. O. Sweeney, president of the Louisville branch, to Thurgood Marshall, October 6, 1941, NAACP Papers. Mark V. Tushnet, *The NAACP's Legal Strategy against Segregated Education, 1925-1950* (Chapel Hill, 1987), 90, has a different interpretation of the final outcome of the case. As he explains, "The NAACP wanted to obtain a consent decree as a protection against repudiation of the promise to equalize, but once the new contracts went into effect, it accepted a dismissal of the suit."

29. Richard Klueger, *Simple Justice: The History of Brown v. Board of Education and Black America's Struggle for Equality* (New York, 1975), 132-38.

30. Jules Tygiel, *Baseball's Great Experiment: Jackie Robinson And His Legacy* (New York, 1983), 80-86.

31. Louisville *Leader*, October 5, November 30, 1935, June 25, 1938.

32. Quoted in Kentucky Commission on Human Rights, *Kentucky's Black Heritage* (Frankfort, 1971), 99.

33. Louisville *Courier-Journal*, January 28, March 12, 1939; Louisville *Leader*, February 4, 1939; Charles W. Anderson to Charles H. Houston, February 8, 1939, NAACP Papers.

34. Atwood outlined his position on school desegregation in a long letter to Walter White, March 14, 1939, NAACP Papers.

35. Louisville *Leader*, February 4, 11, 1939.

36. Rufus B. Atwood to Governor A. B. Chandler, February 8, 1939; Chandler to Atwood, February 13, 1939; Richard Stoll, a Lexington attorney, to Chandler, March 9, 1939, all in NAACP Papers.

37. "Minutes of the Advisory Committee," November 24, 1939; Nannie Burroughs to Lizzie B. Fouse, December 4, 1939, both in NAACP Papers.

38. Frank L. McVey, *The Gates Open Slowly: A History of Education in Kentucky* (Lexington, 1949), 150-59.

39. Alvin E. Evans to Alfred M. Carroll, February 9, 1939 (copy), NAACP Papers.

40. Marshall to Anderson, April 5, 1939, NAACP Papers.

41. Louisville *Courier-Journal*, October 14, 23, 1941; Charles Gano Talbert, *The University of Kentucky: The Maturing Years* (Lexington, 1965), 174-75.

42. A copy of the proposed engineering program at Kentucky State can be found in "College Desegregation Suits, 1941," NAACP Papers.

43. NAACP press release, April 9, 1943; Charles W. Anderson to Walter White, September 22, 1943, both in NAACP Papers; Lexington *Herald-Leader*, January 24, 1943; Smith, "Mr. Kentucky State," 205-10.

44. Prentice Thomas to S.A. Burnley, president of the Louisville branch, April 19, 1943; Prentice Thomas to Lewis King Downing of Howard University, August 20, 1943; Charles W. Anderson to Walter White, September 22, 1943, all in NAACP Papers.

45. Thurgood Marshall to Houston, January 16, 1945; Houston to Marshall, February 2, 1945; Marshall to Charles W. Anderson, January 28, 1945; affidavit of Charles L. Eubanks, January 18, 1945, all in NAACP Papers; Tushnet, *The NAACP's Legal Strategy against Segregated Education*, 86-87; Louisville *Defender*, January 13, 1945.

46. Johnson Interview.

47. The NAACP Papers contain a number of memoranda concerning the Lyman Johnson case. For example, see NAACP Folders on Lyman T. Johnson, Group 2, Boxes B-90 and B-150; also, memoranda from Robert L. Carter, one of Marshall's assistants, to Thurgood Marshall, February 23, March 1, 1949; Marshall to James Crumlin, president of the Louisville branch, April 5, 1948.

48. Lexington *Herald*, November 15, 1948; Talbert, *The University of Kentucky*, 175.
49. Lexington *Herald*, November 15, 1948.
50. Especially see the memorandum of Carter to Marshall, March 1, 1949.
51. Louisville *Courier-Journal*, February 17, 1949; Robert L. Carter, assistant special counsel of the NAACP, to John Hope Franklin, March 23, 1949, NAACP Papers.
52. NAACP press release, March 31, 1949, NAACP Papers.
53. Lexington *Herald*, March 31, 1949; Minutes of the Board of Trustees, April 5, 1949, "Consideration of Decision in the Lyman T. Johnson Case," 2-3, Archives, University of Kentucky; Talbert, *The University of Kentucky*, 174-77; Herman L. Donovan, *Keeping the University Free and Growing* (Lexington, 1956), 97-98.
54. Robert L. Carter to Graduate Students at Kentucky State College, April 5, 1949; Lyman T. Johnson to Robert L. Carter, June 29, 1949, both in NAACP Papers; New York *Times*, June 22, 1949.
55. Donovan, *Keeping the University Free and Growing*, 96-101.
56. Louisville *Leader*, October 13, 1954, May 21, 1956.
57. Kentucky *Acts* (1950), 841-45, 850-51.
58. Minutes of UK Board of Trustees, April 5, 1949, 5, Special Collections, University of Kentucky.
59. House Bill No. 225, February 1, 1946; Kentucky *Acts* (1948), 298; Hardin, "A Critical Analysis of Black Higher Education in Kentucky," 70-93; Louisville *Courier-Journal*, March 8, April 6, 1950.
60. William R. Schorman to NAACP, March 18, 1947; Young People's Socialist League to National Office of NAACP, April 24, 1947, both in NAACP Papers; Savannah (Ga.) *Tribune*, April 27, 1950.
61. Bell County NAACP to William Pickens, October 1940; J. Johnson Williams, secretary of the Bell County NAACP, to Pickens, April 22, 1941; Sarah H. Gregory, secretary of the regional NAACP to the National Office, September 1945, all in NAACP Papers.
62. *Hale v. Commonwealth of Kentucky*, 269 Kentucky Reports 743-52 (1937); *Hale v. Kentucky*, 303 United States 613 (1938); *Crisis* 45 (May 1938): 150; C. M. Bolen, president of the Paducah branch, to the National Office, June 24, 1939, NAACP Papers.
63. Information on Smithland can be found in Group 2, Box A331, NAACP Papers. See also "Annual Report of the Paducah NAACP for 1951," NAACP Papers.
64. Louisville NAACP, "Report for 1938" and "Report for 1949," both in NAACP Papers; Louisville *Defender*, January 29, 1944, November 23, 1946.

65. "Resolutions to the Kentucky Branches of NAACP in Conference At Hopkinsville April 24, 1948," NAACP Papers.
66. Louisville *Courier-Journal*, March 8, 9, 1940.
67. "The Report of the Kentucky Commission on Negro Affairs," November 1, 1945.

5. The 1950s to the Present: Change and Continuity

1. Louisville *Courier-Journal*, May 24, 1953.
2. *Ibid.*, June 6, 1953.
3. O.C. Dawkins, "Kentucky Outgrows Segregation," *The Survey* 86 (1950): 357-60; John E. Kleber, ed., *The Public Papers of Governor Lawrence W. Wetherby, 1950-55* (Lexington, 1983), 256.
4. Omer Carmichael, *The Louisville Story* (New York, 1957), 19-37.
5. Louisville *Defender*, January 27, 1951.
6. Louisville *Courier-Journal*, June 12, 1952.
7. Kleber, *Public Papers of Governor Wetherby*, 262-63; Carmichael, *The Louisville Story*, 41-42. For reaction to the Brown decision in several Kentucky communities, see Jackson *Times*, May 20, 1954; Smith, *Around Muhlenberg*, 79-80.
8. "Kentucky," memo, NAACP Papers.
9. NAACP press release, Kentucky State Conference of Branches, Louisville, July 16, 1955; Roy Wilkins to Donald Jones of the Cincinnati NAACP, July 21, 1955, both in NAACP Papers. Much of the material relating to school desegregation attempts by the NAACP in Kentucky can be found in Group 2, Box A232, NAACP Papers.
10. Donald Jones to Gloster Current, July 24, 1955, NAACP Papers.
11. *Ibid.*, July 30, August 3, 1955. For a thorough discussion of the situation in the Henderson area, see James W. Clancy, chairman of the Henderson Legal Committee, to Gloster Current, December 17, 1955, NAACP Papers.
12. Donald Jones to Gloster Current, July 30, August 3, 1955, NAACP Papers.
13. Regarding the school desegregation process in Lexington, see a copy of the "Lexington Board of Education Policy" and W.H. Powell, president of the branch, to John M. Ridgway, August 3, 1955, NAACP Papers.
14. James A. Crumlin to Gloster Current, August 13, 1955; Jones to Crumlin, August 24, 1955, both in NAACP Papers. Also see the typed memo "Kentucky."
15. *Fred Willis et al. v. Harbert Walker, Superintendent of Public*

Schools, 136 Federal Supplement 177-85 (1956); Louisville *Courier-Journal,* December 2, 5, 1955.

16. For an excellent, unpublished, discussion of the Sturgis incident, see Roscoe Griffin, "A Tentative Discussion and Analysis of the School Desegregation Crisis in Sturgis, Kentucky, August 31-September 19, 1956"; see also Griffin to Chandler, December 28, 1956, and Chandler to Griffin, February 8, 1957, all in Albert B. Chandler Papers, Special Collections, University of Kentucky.

17. Though it is self-serving and must be read with caution, it is important to see Carmichael, *The Louisville Story.* Much more revealing of what happened—or did not happen—is Darlene Walker, "Preparation for the Desegregation of the Louisville School System" (M.A. thesis, University of Louisville, 1974).

18. Lexington *Herald,* January 29, 1961; Louisville *Courier-Journal,* May 1, 1962, August 23, 1964.

19. Thomas D. Clark, *Kentucky: Land of Contrast* (New York, 1968), 118; John D. Wright, *Lexington, Heart of the Bluegrass,* 199-200; George H. Yater, *Two Hundred Years at the Falls of the Ohio: A History of Louisville and Jefferson County* (Louisville, 1979), 225.

20. Osceola A. Dawson, secretary of the Kentucky Conference of NAACP branches, to Gloster B. Current, May 4, 1955, NAACP Papers.

21. Carmichael, *The Louisville Story,* 63-64.

22. The ten articles by the Louisville *Defender* were published between July 3 and October 2, 1958; Lexington *Herald-Leader,* March 4, 1962.

23. Lexington *Herald-Leader,* March 4, 1962.

24. Kentucky Commission on Human Rights, *Southern Cities—Except Louisville—Desegregate Schools* (Louisville, 1972), 1, 12. The commission was quoted in the report of United States Commission on Civil Rights, *Desegregation of the Nation's Public Schools: A Status Report* (Washington, D.C., 1979), 47.

25. U.S. Commission on Civil Rights, *Desegregation of the Nation's Public Schools,* 47.

26. Kentucky Commission on Human Rights, *Louisville School System Retreats to Segregation: A Report on Public Schools in Louisville, Kentucky, 1956-1971* (Louisville, 1972), 6, 16.

27. For information on school busing in Louisville, see the following sources: Louisville *Courier-Journal, passim,* fall 1975; U.S. Commission on Civil Rights, *Desegregation of the Nation's Public Schools,* 46-47; J. David Woodward, "Busing Plans, Media Agendas and Patterns of White Flight: Nashville, Tennessee and Louisville, Kentucky" (Ph.D. diss., Vanderbilt University, 1978); Roger M. Williams, "What Louisville Has Taught Us About Busing," *Saturday Review* (April 30, 1977): 6-10, 51.

28. Charles Steele, "Status of Desegregation in Places of Public Accommodation" (report prepared for Mayor's Advisory Committee on Human Rights, February 4, 1959), Archives and Records Center, University of Louisville; Kentucky Commission on Human Rights, *Kentucky's Black Heritage*, 112-23.

29. Robertson, *Paducah*, 130-32. Since its inception, the Kentucky Commission on Human Rights has published dozens of reports on virtually every area of black life in the state. In addition to being essential to concerned citizens and government officials involved in public policy, these documents are an excellent source for scholars trying to assess the successes and shortcomings of the civil rights movement in Kentucky.

30. Invaluable information on Reichert and the founding of the Lexington CORE is obtained in a five-page, single-spaced letter written by Reichert to the author, March 11, 1988 (copy), Special Collections, University of Kentucky; Lexington *Leader*, May 19, 1960.

31. Reicher to Wright, March 11, 1988.

32. *Ibid*. Phelps was quoted in Lexington *Kentucky Kernel* (student newspaper at the University of Kentucky), March 9, 1960; Lexington *Leader*, May 19, 1960; August Meier and Elliott Rudwick, *CORE: A Study in the Civil Rights Movement, 1942-1968* (New York, 1973), 120.

33. Reichert to Wright, March 11, 1988.

34. Meier and Rudwick, *CORE*, 120. For information on the different personalities and tactics of the civil rights activists in Louisville, see the Louisville *Courier-Journal*, September 14, July 26, 1960; Johnson interview.

35. Meier and Rudwick, *CORE*, 120, 191.

36. Louisville *Courier-Journal*, June 27, 1963; George C. Wright, "Desegregation of Public Accommodations in Louisville: A Long and Difficult Struggle in a 'Liberal' Border City," in *Southern Businessmen and Desegregation*, ed. Elizabeth Jacoway and David R. Colburn (Baton Rouge, 1982), 191-210.

37. Ann Braden, *The Wall Between* (New York, 1958).

38. Louisville *Courier-Journal*, January 8, 1966, January 6, March 8, 12, 30, 31, May 4, 18, December 2, 1967.

39. *United States Code Annotated* (St. Paul, 1977), 3601-31.

40. Louisville *Times*, August 18, September 9, 1971, September 23, 1975, August 2, September 20, 1974, November 7, 1975; Louisville *Courier-Journal*, February 4, 1968, November 7, 1974, September 28, 1975; Kentucky Commission on Human Rights, *More Housing Segregation Than Ever . . . In Louisville and Jefferson County* (Louisville, 1973); idem, *Louisville Still Among Most Segregated Cities* (Louisville, 1974); idem, *Fair Housing: A Better Answer*

Than Busing, A Plan for Louisville and Jefferson County (Louisville, 1975); League of Women Voters of Lexington, *Fair Housing: Laws and Social Reality* (Lexington, 1980).

41. Most of the points made in this paragraph come from an important study on blacks and housing, Sar A. Levitan, William B. Johnson, and Robert Taggart, *Still A Dream: The Changing Status of Blacks Since 1960* (Cambridge, 1975), 143-62.

42. Dannheiser and Hazelwood, *History of Henderson County*, 61-81; Kentucky Commission on Human Rights, *Status of Women in Kentucky State Agencies, An Analysis of Employment and Job Level* (Louisville, 1972); idem, *Black Employment in Kentucky State Agencies, An Analysis of Job Levels, Salaries and Hiring Patterns* (Louisville, 1974); idem, *State University Faculties Stuck on Tokensim in Kentucky* (Louisville, 1979); idem, *No Blacks Are Near The Top of Louisville Hotel Employment* (Louisville, 1979).

43. A very important source is A. Lee Coleman and Dong I. Kim, *The Negro Population of Kentucky: Status and Trends, 1970* (Lexington, 1974), 26-33.

44. Louisville *Courier-Journal*, February 6, 1966.

BIBLIOGRAPHY

Manuscripts
Association of Southern Women for the Prevention of Lynching Collection. Special Collections and Archives, Woodruff Library, Atlanta University, Atlanta, Ga.
Bingham, Robert W. Papers. Manuscript Division, Library of Congress, Washington, D.C.
Bradley, William O. Scrapbooks. Special Collections, King Library, University of Kentucky, Lexington.
Breckinridge Family Papers. Manuscript Division, Library of Congress, Washington, D.C.
Bureau of Refugees, Freedmen, and Abandoned Lands. Record Group 105, National Archives, Washington, D.C.
Chandler, Albert B. Papers. Special Collections, King Library, University of Kentucky, Lexington.
Clay, Laura. Papers. Special Collections, King Library, University of Kentucky, Lexington.
Commission on Interracial Cooperation. Papers. Special Collections and Archives, Woodruff Library, Atlanta University, Atlanta, Ga., and Louisville Free Public Library, Louisville, Ky.
Day Law File. Hutchins Library, Berea College, Berea, Ky.
Fouse Family Papers. Special Collections, King Library, University of Kentucky, Lexington.
Kentucky's Governors' Papers, 1792-1926. Pardons and Rejected Petitions. Kentucky Department for Libraries and Archives, Frankfort.
Letters. Henderson Public Library, Henderson, Ky.
Lincoln Institute. Papers. Brown Education Center, Louisville, Ky., and Kentucky Department for Libraries and Archives, Frankfort.
Louisville Municipal College. Papers. Archives and Records Center, Ekstrom Library, University of Louisville,

Louisville, Ky.
Moorland, Jesse E. Papers. Moorland-Spingarn Research Center, Howard University, Washington, D.C.
Morrow, Edwin P. Papers. Special Collections, King Library, University of Kentucky, Lexington.
National Association for the Advancement of Colored People. Papers. Manuscript Division, Library of Congress, Washington, D.C.
National Urban League. Papers. Manuscript Division, Library of Congress, Washington, D.C.
Negro Collection. Hutchins Library, Berea College, Berea, Ky.
Parrish, Charles H. Papers. Archives and Records Center, Ekstrom Library, University of Louisville, Louisville, Ky.
Recorded Deeds of Henderson. City Hall, Henderson, Ky.
Simmons University Papers. Archives and Records Center, Ekstrom Library, University of Louisville, Louisville, Ky.
Steward, William H. Scrapbook. Formerly in possession of the late Carolyn Steward Blanton, Louisville, Ky.
Terrell, Mary Church. Papers. Manuscript Division, Library of Congress, Washington, D.C.
University of Kentucky. Minutes of the Board of Trustees. Special Collections, King Library, University of Kentucky, Lexington.
Washington, Booker T. Papers. Manuscript Division, Library of Congress, Washington, D.C.
Willson, Augustus. Papers. Filson Club, Louisville, Ky.
Woodson, Carter G. Papers. Manuscript Division, Library of Congress, Washington, D.C.

Legal Cases
Abbington, Valla Dudley v. Board of Education of Louisville. United States District Court, Civil Docket No. 243 (1941).
Anderson, W. H. v. Louisville and Nashville Railroad Company. 62 Federal Reporter 46 (1894).
Bailey v. Louisville and Nashville Railroad Company. 44 Southwestern Reporter 105 (1898).
Berea College v. Commonwealth of Kentucky. 94 Southwestern Reporter 623 (1906).
Berea College v. Commonwealth of Kentucky. 211 United States 45 (1908).
Browder v. Commonwealth of Kentucky. 136 Kentucky Reports 45 (1909).
Buchanan v. Warley. 245 United States 60 (1917).
Chesapeake and Ohio Railway Company v. Kentucky. 179 United States 388 (1900).

Bibliography / 257

Claybrook, Edward v. City of Owensboro. 16 Federal Reporter 297 (1883).
Commonwealth of Kentucky v. Jessie Ellis. 11 Kentucky Law Report 402 (1882).
Crosby v. City of Mayfield. 117 Southwestern Reporter 316 (1909).
Hale v. Commonwealth of Kentucky. 269 Kentucky Reports 743-52 (1937).
Hale v. Kentucky. 303 United States 613 (1938).
Louisville and Nashville Railroad Company v. Commonwealth of Kentucky. 37 Southwestern Reporter 79 (1896).
McDaniel v. Commonwealth of Kentucky. 181 Kentucky Reports 766 (1918).
McPerkins v. Commonwealth of Kentucky. 33 Southwestern Reporter, 2d Series, 622 (1930).
Moss v. City of Mayfield. 186 Kentucky Reports 330 (1919).
Ohio Valley Railroad v. Lander. 47 Southwestern Reporter 344 (1898).
Smith v. Commonwealth of Kentucky. 91 Southwestern Reporter 742 (1906).
The South Covington and Cincinnati Street Railway Company v. Commonwealth of Kentucky. 252 United States 399 (1920).
Taylor, John v. Commonwealth of Kentucky. 90 Southwestern Reporter 581 (1906).
Willis, Fred et al. v. Harbert Walker, Superintendent of Public Schools. 136 Federal Supplement 177 (1956).

Public Documents
Biennial Message of Governor Edwin P. Morrow Before the General Assembly of Kentucky. Frankfort, 1922.
Bulletin of the Bureau of the School Service. Lexington, 1932, 1935.
Henderson County Deed Book 50.
Kentucky Acts, 1893, 1897, 1902, 1916, 1920, 1948, 1950.
Kentucky Documents, 1891-1892, 1893, 1901.
Kentucky Senate Bill No. 143 (1920).
Kentucky Statutes, 1903.
Kentucky Statutes Containing All General Laws, with Full Notes of Decisions of the Court of Appeals to June 1903. Louisville, 1903.
Public Documents of Governor William O. Bradley. Louisville, 1899.
Report of the Commission to Investigate the Conditions of Working Women in Kentucky. N.p., 1911.
Report of the Kentucky Commission On Negro Affairs, November 1, 1945. Frankfort, 1945.
Superintendent of Public Instruction Report . . . 1891, 1893, 1899-1901, 1909, 1939. Kentucky Documents.

U.S. Bureau of Education. *Circular of Information No. 3 (1899).*
U.S. Bureau of the Census. *Bulletin 8, Negroes in the United States.* Washington, D.C., 1904.
———. *Fifteenth Census of the United States.* Washington, D.C., 1932.
———. *Negro Population in the United States, 1790-1915.* Washington, D.C., 1918.
———. *Negro Population in the United States, 1920-1932.* Washington, D.C. 1935.
———. *Twelfth Census of the United States.* Washington, D.C., 1901.
———. *United States Census of Agriculture: 1959.* Washington, D.C., 1959.
United States Code Annotated. St. Paul, Minn., 1977.
U.S. Department of the Interior. Bureau of Education. Bulletin No. 7. *Survey of Negro Colleges and Universities.* Washington, D.C., 1929.

Interviews
Bell, Austin. Henderson, Ky., August 20, 1985.
Johnson, Lyman. Louisville, March 16, 1978.
Johnson, Thelma B. Henderson, Ky., August 20, 1985.
Jones, Lorenzo D. Henderson, Ky., November 17, 1983.
Martin, Arlene S. Shelbyville, Ky., July 9, 1986.
Palmer, Hugh D. Trigg County, Ky., August 21, 1985.
Washington, D. Drakesboro, Ky., December 12, 1978.

Newspapers and Periodicals
AME Zion Church Quarterly.
Boston *Guardian.*
Brooklyn (N.Y.) *Eagle.*
Chicago *Tribune.*
Cincinnati *Commercial.*
Cincinnati *Enquirer.*
Colored American Magazine.
Corbin (Ky.) *Times.*
Crisis.
Frankfort (Ky.) *Capitol.*
Frankfort (Ky.) *Star.*
Hampton University Newspaper Clippings.
Harrodsburg (Ky.) *Herald.*
Hopkinsville (Ky.) *Kentuckian.*
Huntsville (Ala.) *Gazette.*

Bibliography / 259

The Independent.
Indianapolis Freeman.
Jackson (Ky.) Times.
Kansas City Kansas Blackman.
The Kentucky Club Woman.
Lebanon (Ky.) Enterprise.
Lexington (Ky.) Daily Leader.
Lexington (Ky.) Herald.
Lexington (Ky.) Herald-Leader.
Lexington Kentucky Kernal.
Lexington Kentucky Standard.
Lexington (Ky.) Morning Herald.
Lexington (Ky.) Morning Transcript.
Lexington (Ky.) Press-Transcript.
Lexington (Ky.) Standard.
Louisville Commercial.
Louisville Courier-Journal.
Louisville Defender.
Louisville Kentucky Irish-American.
Louisville Leader.
Louisville News.
Louisville Post.
Louisville Times.
Madisonville (Ky.) Daily Messenger.
Madisonville (Ky.) Hustler.
Mayfield (Ky.) Messenger.
Mayfield (Ky.) Monitor.
Maysville (Ky.) Bulletin.
Memphis Commercial-Appeal.
The Nation.
New York Age.
New York Freeman.
New York Sun.
New York Times.
New York Tribune.
New York World.
The Outlook.
Paducah (Ky.) News-Democrat.
Paducah (Ky.) Weekly News-Democrat.
Richmond (Ky.) Planet.
Salisbury (N.C.) AME Star of Zion.
Savannah (Ga.) Tribune.
Shelbyville (Ky.) Record.
Shelbyville (Ky.) Shelby News.
Springfield (Ohio) Republican.

Star.
Tuskegee Newspaper Clippings.
Winchester (Ky.) *Sun*.

Books and Pamphlets

Anderson, James D. *The Education of Blacks in the South, 1860-1935*. Chapel Hill, N.C., 1988.
Announcement of the Central Colored High School and Colored Normal School of Louisville, Kentucky, 1907-1908. Louisville, 1908.
Arnett, Maralea. *The Annals and Scandals of Henderson County, Kentucky, 1775-1975*. Corydon, Ky., 1976.
Associates of Louisville Municipal College. *Study of Negro Business in Louisville*. Louisville, 1944.
Battle, J. H., and W. H. Perrin, eds. *Counties of Todd and Christian, Kentucky*. Chicago, 1884.
The Blue Grass Country. Lexington, 1938.
Braden, Ann. *The Wall Between*. New York, 1958.
Bradley, W. O. *Stories and Speeches of William O. Bradley; with Biographical Sketch by M. H. Thatcher*. Lexington, 1916.
Bunche, Ralph J. *The Political Status of the Negro in the Age of FDR*. Chicago, 1973.
Carmichael, Omer. *The Louisville Story*. New York, 1957.
Caron, C. K. *Directory of Louisville for 1908*. Louisville, 1908.
Caudill, Harry M. *Night Comes to the Cumberlands: A Biography of A Depressed Area*. Boston, 1962.
Circular of Information for the Twenty-first Annual Session of Eckstein Norton Institute. Cane Spring, Ky., 1911.
Clark, Thomas D. *Kentucky: Land of Contrast*. New York, 1968.
Coleman, A. Lee, and Dong I. Kim. *The Negro Population of Kentucky: Status and Trends, 1970*. Lexington, 1974.
Coleman, J. Winston, Jr. *Death at the Court House*. Lexington, 1952.
Cunningham, William. *On Bended Knees: The Night Rider Story*. Nashville, 1983.
Dabney, Wendell P. *Cincinnati's Colored Citizens: Historical, Sociological and Biographical*. Cincinnati, 1926.
Dannheiser, Frieda J., and Donald L. Hazelwood, eds. *The History of Henderson County Kentucky*. Evansville, Ind., 1980.
Diamond Jubilee: The Story of Seventy-five Years of the Association. Louisville, 1943.
Donovan, Herman L. *Keeping the University Free and Growing*. Lexington, 1956.
Eller, Ronald D. *Miners, Millhands, and Mountaineers: Industrialization of the Appalachian South, 1880-1930*. Knoxville, 1982.

Haley, James T. *AfroAmerican Encyclopaedia; or the Thoughts, Doings, and Sayings of the Race.* Nashville, 1895.
Harris, Lawrence. *The Negro Population of Lexington in the Professions, Business, Education, and Religion.* Lexington, 1907.
Hayes, William Foster. *Sixty Years of Owensboro, 1883-1943.* Owensboro, n.d.
Henderson, *Home of Audubon.* New York, 1941.
Jillson, Willard Rouse. *Frankfort: Capital City of Kentucky.* Frankfort, 1927.
Johnson, W. D. *Biographical Sketches of Prominent Negro Men and Women of Kentucky.* Lexington, 1897.
Jones, Thomas Jesse. *Negro Education: A Study of the Private and Higher Schools for Colored People in the United States.* 2 vols. Washington, D.C., 1917.
Katzman, David. *Seven Days a Week: Women and Domestic Service in Industrializing America.* New York, 1978.
Kentucky Commission on Human Rights. *Black Employment in Kentucky State Agencies, An Analysis of Employment and Job Levels, Salaries, Hiring Patterns.* Louisville, 1974.
―――. *Fair Housing: A Better Answer Than Busing, A Plan for Louisville and Jefferson County.* Louisville, 1975.
―――. *Kentucky's Black Heritage.* Frankfort, 1971.
―――. *Louisville School System Retreats to Segregation: A Report on Public Schools in Louisville, Kentucky, 1956-1971.* Louisville, 1972.
―――. *Louisville Still Among Most Segregated Cities.* Louisville, 1974.
―――. *More Housing Segregation Than Ever . . . In Louisville and Jefferson County.* Louisville, 1973.
―――. *No Blacks Are Near the Top of Louisville Hotel Employment.* Louisville, 1979.
―――. *Southern Cities—Except Louisville—Desegregate Schools.* Louisville, 1979.
―――. *State University Faculties Stuck on Tokenism in Kentucky.* Louisville, 1979.
―――. *Status of Women in Kentucky State Agencies, An Analysis of Employment and Job Level.* Louisville, 1972.
Kentucky Federation of Colored Women's Clubs 1916-17, 1918-1919-1920-1921. Louisville, 1919, 1924.
Kerns, J. Harvey. *A Survey of the Economic and Cultural Conditions of the Negro Population of Louisville, Kentucky, and a Review of the Program and Activities of the Louisville Urban League.* New York, 1948.
Kleber, John E., ed. *The Public Papers of Governor Lawrence W. Wetherby, 1950-55.* Lexington, 1983.
Klotter, James C. *The Breckinridges of Kentucky, 1760-1981.*

Lexington, 1986.
Klueger, Richard. *Simple Justice: The History of Brown v. Board of Education and Black America's Struggle for Equality.* New York, 1975.
Krock, Arthur. *Myself When Young.* Boston, 1973.
League of Women Voters of Lexington. *Fair Housing: Laws and Social Reality.* Lexington, 1980.
Levitan, Sar A., William B. Johnston, and Robert Taggart. *Still A Dream: The Changing Status of Blacks Since 1960.* Cambridge, 1975.
Lewis, Alvin F. *History of Higher Education in Kentucky.* Washington, D.C., 1899.
Lewis, Ronald L. *Black Coal Miners In America: Race, Class and Community Conflict 1780-1980.* Lexington, Ky., 1987.
Lofgren, Charles A. *The Plessy Case: A Legal Historical Interpretation.* New York, 1987.
Louisville Industrial Foundation, 1928. Louisville, 1928.
McPherson, James. *The Abolitionist Legacy: From Reconstruction to the NAACP.* Princeton, 1975.
McVey, Frank L. *The Gates Open Slowly: A History of Higher Education in Kentucky.* Lexington, 1949.
Meacham, Charles M. *A History of Christian County Kentucky, from Oxcart to Airplane.* Nashville, 1930.
Meier, August, and Elliott Rudwick. *CORE: A Study in the Civil Rights Movement, 1942-1968.* New York, 1973.
Morton, Lena Beatrice. *My First Sixty Years: Passion for Wisdom.* New York, 1965.
150 Anniversary Pleasant Green Baptist Church, October 5-26, 1940. N.p., 1940.
Parrish, Charles H., ed. *Golden Jubilee, General Association of Colored Baptists in Kentucky.* Louisville, 1915.
Parrish, Mary V., ed. *Fourth Statistical Report of the National Association of Colored Women.* Louisville, 1914.
Prather's Directory of the City of Lexington, Kentucky. Lexington, 1895.
Report of the Vice Commission of Lexington, Kentucky. Lexington, 1915.
Report of the Vice Commission of Louisville, 1915. Louisville, 1915.
Richardson, Clement, ed. *The National Cyclopedia of the Colored Race.* Montgomery, Ala., 1919.
Richings, G.F. *Evidence of Progress Among Colored People.* Philadelphia, 1899.
Robertson, John E. L. *Paducah, 1830-1980: A Sesquicentennial History.* Paducah, 1980.
Robinson, Lottie O. *The Bond-Washington Story: The Education of Black People, Elizabethtown, Kentucky.* N.p., 1983.

Russell, Harvey C. *Kentucky Negro Education Association 1877-1946.* Norfolk, Va., 1946.
Simmons, William J. *Men of Mark: Eminent, Progressive, and Rising.* Cleveland, 1887.
Smith, Leslie S. *Around Muhlenberg County, Kentucky: A Black History.* Evansville, Ind., 1979.
Smith, Lucy H., ed. *Pictorial Directory of the Kentucky Association of Colored Women.* Louisville, 1945.
Smith, S. E., ed. *History of the Anti-Separate Coach Movement of Kentucky.* Evansville, Ind., n.d.
Souvenir Sesqui-Centennial Celebration First Baptist Church, Lexington, Ky., November 24 to December 2, 1940. Lexington, 1940.
Spero, Sterling D., and Abraham L. Harris. *The Black Worker.* New York, 1931.
State Association of Women's Clubs Scholarship Loan Fund. Paris, Ky., 1935.
State University Catalogue 1883-84. Louisville, 1883.
Talbert, Charles Gano. *The University of Kentucky: The Maturing Years.* Lexington, 1965.
Tapp, Hambleton, and James C. Klotter. *Kentucky: Decades of Discord, 1865-1900.* Frankfort, Ky., 1977.
Timberlake, Clarence L. *Politics and the Schools: An Argument for a State Wide Board of Regents for Kentucky Normal Institute for Colored Persons, Frankfort, Ky.* N.p., n.d.
To the Voters of Lexington and Fayette County. Lexington, 1911.
Tushnet, Mark V. *The NAACP's Legal Strategy against Segregated Education 1925-1950.* Chapel Hill, 1987.
28th Annual Announcement of the State University and 20th Announcement of Louisville Medical College. Louisville, 1908.
Tygiel, Jules. *Baseball's Great Experiment: Jackie Robinson and His Legacy.* New York, 1983.
United States Commission on Civil Rights. *Desegregation of the Nation's Public Schools: A Status Report.* Washington, D.C., 1979.
Walters, Alexander. *My Life and Work.* New York, 1917.
Wells, Ida B. *A Red Record.* Chicago, 1895.
———. *Southern Horrors: Lynch Law In All Its Phases.* New York, 1892.
Wentworth's Souvenir Sporting Guide. New York 1895.
Woofter, Thomas Jackson et al. *Negro Problems in Cities.* New York, 1928.
Wright, George C. *Life Behind A Veil: Blacks in Louisville, Kentucky, 1865-1930.* Baton Rouge, 1985.
———. *Racial Violence in Kentucky, 1865-1940: Lynchings, Mob*

Rule, and "Legal Lynchings." Baton Rouge, 1990.
Wright, John D. *Lexington: Heart of the Bluegrass.* Lexington, Ky., 1982.
Wright, R.R., Jr. *Self-Help in Negro Education.* Cheyney, Pa., 1909.
Yater, George H. *Two Hundred Years at the Falls of the Ohio: A History of Louisville and Jefferson County.* Louisville, 1979.

Articles
Atwood, Rufus B. "Financing Schools for Negro Children from State School Funds in Kentucky." *Journal of Negro Education* 8 (1939): 659-65.
Black, Isabella. "Berea College." *Phylon* 17 (1957): 267-76.
Bradley, W. K. "Negroes in the Kentucky Mountains." *Crisis* 22 (June 1921): 69-71.
Burnside, Jacqueline G. "Suspicion Versus Faith: Negro Criticisms of Berea College in the Nineteenth Century." *Register of the Kentucky Historical Society* 83 (1985): 237-66.
Cutler, James E. "Proposed Remedies for Lynchings." *Yale Review* 13 (1904): 194-212.
Dawkins, O. C. "Kentucky Outgrows Segregation." *The Survey* 86 (1950): 357-60.
Galloway, Oscar F. "Higher Education for Negroes in Kentucky." *Bulletin of the Bureau of School Service* 5 (1932): 13.
Heckman, Richard Allen, and Betty Jean Hall. "Berea College and the Day Law." *Register of the Kentucky Historical Society* 66 (1968): 35-52.
Horton, Ben. "Life and Achievements of Albert Ernest Meyzeek." *Kentucky Negro Journal* 1 (1958): 25-27.
"Inability of the Governor of Kentucky to Bring Lynchers to Justice." *American Law Review* 34 (1900): 238-39.
Klotter, James C. "Slavery and Race: A Family Perspective." *Southern Studies* 17 (1978): 375-97.
Letcher, James H. "The Treatment of Some Diseases by the 'Old Time' Negro." *Railway Surgical Journal* (1910): 1-16.
Lewis, Cary B. "Louisville and Its Afro-American Citizens." *Colored American Magazine* 16 (1906): 259-64.
Martin, George Madden. "Race Cooperation." *McClure's* 54 (1922): 9-20.
Meier, August. "The Vogue of Industrial Education." *Mid-West Journal* 7 (1955): 241-66.
Parrish, Charles H. "Industrial Education." *AME Zion Church Quarterly* 3 (1893): 374-81.
Randolph, Thomas. "The Governor and the Mob." *The Independent* (February 26, 1917): 347-48.

"The Record of Albert Ernest Meyzeek." *Negro History Bulletin* 10 (1947): 186-87.
Simmons, William J. "What the Colored People are Doing in Kentucky." *American Baptist Home Mission Society* jubilee volume (1883): 85-90.
Taylor, L. N. "Negro Education Within the Century." *Kentucky School Journal* 16 (1938): 30-31.
Thomas, Herbert A. "Victims of Circumstance: Negroes in a Southern Town, 1865-1880." *Register of the Kentucky Historical Society* 71 (1973): 253-71.
Thomas, J. A. "Introducing Kentucky's Legislator." *Opportunity* 18 (1940): 76-77.
Waldrep, Christopher. "Planters and the Planters' Protective Association in Kentucky and Tennessee." *Journal of Southern History* 52 (1986): 565-88.
Washington, Booker T. "The National Business League." *World's Work* (1902): 2671-74.
Williams, Roger M. "What Louisville Has Taught Us About Busing." *Saturday Review* (April 30, 1977): 6-10, 51.
Wilson, Atwood S. "Historical Sketch of Negro Education in Kentucky." *Kentucky School Journal* 16 (1938): 16-18.
Wright, George C. "Desegregation of Public Accommodations in Louisville: A Long and Difficult Struggle in a 'Liberal' Border City." In *Southern Businessmen and Desegregation*, edited by Elizabeth Jacoway and David R. Colburn, 191-210. Baton Rouge, 1982.
_____. "The Faith Plan: A Black Institution Grows During The Depression." *Filson Club History Quarterly* 51 (1977): 336-49.
_____. "The NAACP and Residential Segregation in Louisville, Kentucky, 1914-1917." *Register of the Kentucky Historical Society* 78 (1980): 39-54.
_____. "William Henry Steward: Moderate, Approach to Black Leadership." In *Black Leaders of the Nineteenth Century*, edited by Leon Litwack and August Meier, 275-89. Urbana, Ill., 1988.

Dissertations, Theses, and Unpublished Works
Barker, Adalaide Abel. "William O'Connell Bradley." M. A. thesis, University of Kentucky, 1927.
"Changing Faces: History of Corrections in Kentucky." Unpublished report, Kentucky Corrections Cabinet, Office of Corrections Training, Louisville.
Collins, Ernest M. "The Political Behavior of the Negroes in Cincinnati, Ohio, and Louisville, Kentucky." Ph.D. diss.,

University of Kentucky, 1950.
"The Colored Orphan Industrial Home of Lexington, Kentucky, Second Annual Report." Unpublished report, Special Collections, King Library, University of Kentucky, Lexington.
Crawford, Robert Gunn. "A History of the Kentucky Penitentiary System 1865-1937." Ph.D. diss., University of Kentucky, 1955.
Fouse, William H. "Educational History of the Negroes of Lexington, Kentucky." M. A. thesis, University of Cincinnati, 1937.
Hardin, John A. "A Critical Analysis of Black Higher Education in Kentucky, 1904-1954." Unpublished manuscript in possession of author.
Louisville Goodwill Industries. "Report of the Social Survey of Adjacent Neighborhood." Unpublished report, 1937, Louisville Free Public Library.
Meals, Claude. "The Struggle of the Negro for Citizenship in Kentucky Since 1865." M. A. thesis, Howard University, 1940.
"Men Electrocuted in Kentucky since the Electric Chair was Installed at the Kentucky State Penitentiary at Eddyville, Kentucky in 1911." Unpublished report, Kentucky Corrections Cabinet, Office of Corrections Training, Louisville.
Sexton, Robert F. "Kentucky Politics and Society: 1919-1932." Ph.D. diss., University of Washington, 1970.
Smith, Gerald L. "Mr. Kentucky State: A Biography of Rufus Ballard Atwood." Ph.D. diss., University of Kentucky, 1988.
Smith, Peter Craig. "Negro Hamlets and Gentlemen Farms: A Dichotomous Rural Settlement Pattern In Kentucky's Bluegrass Region." Ph.D. diss., University of Kentucky, 1972.
Taylor, Marie. "Night Riders in the Black Patch." M. A. thesis, University of Kentucky, 1934.
Thomas, J.A. "The Negro Wage Earner in Kentucky." Unpublished report, Louisville Urban League, March 1942.
Walker, Darlene. "Preparation for the Desegregation of the Louisville School System." M. A. thesis, University of Louisville, 1974.
Williams, John Taylor. "A Comparative Study of the Administration of Higher Education in Selected Kentucky Negro and White State-Supported Schools." M. A. thesis, University of Cincinnati, 1932.
Wilson, George D. "A Century of Negro Education in Louisville." WPA manuscript, n.d., Louisville Free Public

Library.
Woodward, J. David. "Busing Plans, Media Agendas and Patterns of White Flight: Nashville, Tennessee, and Louisville, Kentucky." Ph.D. diss., Vanderbilt University, 1978.

INDEX

Abbington, Valla Dudley, 166
Adair County, Ky., 202
Adler, Louis, 11
African Methodist Episcopal Zion Church, 117-18, 158
Alabama, 90
Alexander, Edward, 99
Ali, Muhammad, 217
Allensville, Ky., 153
Allensworth, James L., 99
Alpha Zeta Literary Society, 135
American Baptist 20, 69
American Civil Liberties Union, 154, 214
American Missionary Association, 119
American Mutual Savings Bank, 23
AME Zion Church Quarterly, 112
Amos and Sweatley Restaurant, 17
Anchorage, Ky., 137
Anderson, Charles W.: as president of Louisville NAACP, 158; as state legislator, 159-62, 167; appeals to governor to desegregate the University of Kentucky graduate school, 170, 172-73; advised by Thurgood Marshall to withdraw lawsuit, 174-75, 185; calls for equal treatment on railroads, 188, 191; mentioned, 35, 79, 156-57, 164-65, 176, 192, 226
Anderson, Dennis Henry, 133
Anderson, James D., 104, 115
Anderson, W.H., 71-72, 75
Anderson-Mayer State Aid Act, 160
Anne Arundel County, Maryland, 164
Anti-Discrimination bill, 161, 162
Antilynching laws: of 1897, 81-83; of 1920, 83-84, 92, 153
Anti-Mob and Lynch Law Association, 91
Anti-Separate Coach Movement, 71-72, 101, 153
Appalachia, 186
Arnette, E.G., 73
Ashland, Ky., 103
Atkinson, J.B., 118
Atkinson Literary and Industrial College, Madisonville, 117-18
Atwood, Rufus, 169-74, 176, 178-79, 183

Bailey, Cornelia, 74-75
Barbourville, Ky., 186
Bardstown, Ky., 88-89
Bardwell, Ky., 80
Barkley, Alben, 169-70
Barnes, Pike, 12
Barr, John W., 72, 105
Barren County, Ky., 74, 108
Bath County, Ky., 122
Baxter, _____, 99
Bell County, Ky.: NAACP in, 64-66; mentioned, 186
Benham, Ky., 27, 186
Benjamin, Robert, 93
Berea College: Day Law controversy in, 136, 144-48; helps establish Lincoln Institute, 137-38; blacks as students in, 141-43; desegregation at after repeal of Day Law, 185-86; mentioned 43, 122, 128-29, 132, 135
Berea College Reporter, 143
Berea Hall (Lincoln Institute), 138
Bingham, Robert Worth, 104

Birmingham, Alabama, 208
Birmingham (Trigg County), Ky., 5
Black, Robert E., 191
Black employment: as farmers, 2; as common laborers, 6; as personal servants, 6-8, 10; as postal workers, 10-11; in the horse industry, 12-13; in industry, 14-15; in their own businesses, 17-24; in the coal industry, 24-26
Blacks: illiteracy, 106-7; leisure activities, 27-28; migration, 2; population, 1
Blue Diamond Company, 25
Bond, J. Max, 155
Bond, James, 62, 106, 122-23, 134, 138
Boone County, Ky., 108
Bowling Green, Ky.: black workers in, 16; black high school in, 117-18; mentioned, 11, 127
Bowling Green Academy, 117-18
Boyd, Emma, 107
Boyle County, Ky., 2
Braden, Anne, 216, 220
Braden, Carl, 216, 220-21
Bradley, W.K., 63
Bradley, William O., 44, 67, 81-82, 90-93, 96
Breathitt County, Ky., 144, 197
Breckinridge, Desha, 50-52
Breckinridge, William Campbell Preston, 51-52, 113-14
Breckinridge County, Ky., 46-47
Broadway Temple African Methodist Episcopal Zion Church, Louisville, 36
Brooklyn Dodgers, 169
Browder, Rufus, 3-4
Brown, Curlee, 200
Brown, John Y., 69-70
Browne, M.S., 100
Bugg, J.R., 86
Bullitt County, Ky., 211
Burdette, Jeff, 88
Burnam, A.R., 76
Burroughs, Nannie, 173

Cadentown (Lexington, Ky.), 59
Cairo, Illinois, 78
Caldwell County, Ky., 109
Calloway County, Ky., 70
Campbell County, Ky., 107
Campbellsville, Ky., 74
Carlisle, John G., 145-46
Carmichael, Omer, 197, 203-4, 206-7
Carnegie, Andrew, 54, 136
Carroll, Alfred M., 170-74

Carrollton, Ky., 6, 10
Carter, Robert L., 181
Caulder, J.B., 12
Central City, Ky., 110
Central High School, Louisville: opening of, 110; course offerings of, 111, 113; favorable assessment of, 116-17; blacks seek new building for, 121; mentioned, 106, 158, 163, 175
Cerulean (Trigg County), Ky., 6
Chandler, Albert Benjamin "Happy," 169-74, 190, 192, 203
Chandler Normal School, Lexington, 119
Charleston, South Carolina, 111
Cheaney, Henry E., 225
Chesapeake and Ohio Railway Company v. Kentucky, 77
Chicago, Illinois, 26, 30, 32, 46
Chicago *Tribune*, 82-83
Christian County, Ky.: blacks elected to office in, 99; circuit court in rules on railroad segregation, 75, 78-79
Cincinnati, Ohio: Kentucky blacks migrate to, 26-27, 73, 122; mentioned, 154
Cincinnati International Labor Defense, 154
Cincinnati Veterinary College, 26
Civil Rights Acts: of 1965, 205; of 1968, 221
Civil Rights Commission, 216
Civil War, 4, 86, 111, 114, 205
Clancy, James W., 200
Clark, Thomas D., 205
Clark County, Ky., 2
Clay, Cassius M., 141
Clay, Laura, 96
Claybrook, Edward, 105
Clayter, Henry, 46-47
Clinton, Ky., 86
Cole, I. Willis, 30, 63, 89, 94, 130, 156, 158, 172
Coleman, Richard, 81
Colerane, Horace, 100-101
Colored Citizens Protective League of Lexington, 70
Colored Cumberland Presbyterian Church, 118
Colored Orphan Industrial Home of Lexington, 56
Columbia, Ky., 199, 201-202
Columbia, South Carolina, 208
Columbia University, 166
Colvin, George, 104
Combs, Bert T., 219

Commission on Interracial Cooperation (CIC): investigates black schools, 106, 122; mentioned, 37, 62, 92, 155, 191-92
Congress of Racial Equality (CORE), 213-16, 218
Consolidated Coal Company of Eastern Kentucky, 25
Corbin, Ky., 14
CORE. *See* Congress of Racial Equality
Corinthian Baptist Church, Frankfort, 67
County School Act of 1908, 114-15
Covington, Ky.: black high school in, 110; NAACP in, 153-55; mentioned, 11, 26, 81
Crime and vice, 37-42
Crisis, 31, 59, 101
Crumlin, James A., 199-200, 202, 216
Crutcher and Starks Men's Clothing Store, 62
Cunningham, James, 3-4
Current, Gloster, 198

Dabney, Thomas L., 16
Dabney, Wendell, 122
Danville, Ky.: has black on city council, 99; condition of black school in, 121-22; mentioned, 2
Daviess County, Ky., 2, 4
Davis, Hardin, 78
Davistown (Lexington, Ky.), 59
Day, Carl, 144, 148
Day Law: debated and enacted, 144-48, 181; NAACP calls for repeal of, 184-85, 191-92, 195; mentioned, 43, 122, 136, 138, 141
Delmar Institute, New York City, 166
Democratic party (Democrats): ignores black vote, 90; attempts to attract blacks, 92-94, 96-99, 101; mentioned, 37, 50, 52, 69, 159
DePriest, Oscar, 32
Detroit, Michigan, 26
Dickerson, Dennis, 160
Dickey, Frank, 216
Dinning, George, 51
Dixon, Thomas, 51
Dixon, Ky., 91
Dix River, 14-15
Domestic Economy Club of Frankfort, 35
Domestic Life Insurance Company, 21, 23
Donegy, James L., 99
Donovan, Herman L., 173, 175, 178-83
Douglass, Frederick, 115

DuBois, W.E.B., 31, 101, 108
Dudley, W.R., 99
Dunbar High School, Lexington, 205
Dunbar High School, Sturgis, 203
Dunham, Ky., 64
Dunne Press, 197
Dunnigan, Alice A., 148
Dyer bill, 94

Earlington, Ky., 25, 86, 152
Eastern State Hospital, 56
Eckstein Norton Institute, 112-13
Eddyville, Ky., 156
Elizabethtown, Ky., 158
Eller, Ronald, 64
Ellington, Duke, 63
Elliott County, Ky., 1-2, 107
Emancipation Day, 29-30, 33, 49
Emancipation Proclamation, 29, 30
Emmerson, Ohio, 66
Empire Cab Company, 23
Equalization of teachers' salaries, 150, 162-68
Ethridge, Mark, 167
Eubanks, Charles Lamont, 175, 176
Evans, Alvin E., 174
Evansville, Indiana, 71, 72
Ex-Slave Pension and Bounty Association of Kentucky, 93

Fairchild, Edward H., 142
Falone, Charles, 87
Fayette County, Ky.: circuit court in, 175; mentioned, 2, 32, 97
Feeble Minded Institute, 57
Female High School, Louisville, 106, 111
Fields, William J., 98
First African Baptist Church (First Baptist), Lexington, 36, 38
First Standard Bank, 23
Fisk University, 184
Fite's Studio, 17
Fitzbutler, Henry, 19
Flatt Creek (Bath County), Ky., 122
Fleming, Ky., 25
Fletcher, Gabe, 85
Ford, H. Church, 180
Ford Motor Company, 197, 211
Fort Spring (Lexington, Ky.), 59
Fourteenth Amendment, 72, 90, 147, 156, 166, 179
Fouse, Lizzie B., 29, 173
Fouse, William H., 173
Frankfort, Ky.: blacks in hired as postmen, 11; Jim Crow treatment

of blacks in, 54, 61, 67, 69-71; blacks in celebrate victory in railroad segregation case, 72-73, 90, 96; black high school in, 110, 116, 151, 178; segregation in government buildings in, 195; NAACP in, 67, 153; mentioned, 2, 18, 57, 98, 108, 129, 151, 178-79
Frankfort *Bluegrass Bugle*, 67
Franklin, John Hope, 179-80
Franklin, Ky., 88
Franklin County, Ky., 2
Frederick Douglass High School, Henderson, 115
Frederick Douglass Park, 58
Freedmen's Bureau, 5
Free Masons, 67
Frost, William G., 136, 138, 142, 143, 144, 145, 147, 148
Fulton, Ky., 4, 80, 200

Gallatin County, Ky., 109
Galloway, Oscar F., 133
Gardner, Ora, 46, 47
Garrison, William Lloyd, 147
Gary, Indiana, 26
General Association of Negro Baptists, 36, 132
General Electric Company, 196, 211
General Refractories Company, 14
Georgetown, Ky.: blacks in defend themselves against lynch mobs, 84; a black serves on city council in, 99; mentioned, 27, 31, 56
Georgia, 154
Georgia A. Nugent Improvement Club of Louisville, 35
Givens, James, 129
Glasgow, Ky.: school desegregation in, 205; mentioned 7, 52-53, 58-59
Glass, Edward W., 99
Goebel, William, 92-94
Goggins, Reuben, 93
Good Citizen's League, 38
Grace Community Center, 57
Grand United Order of Odd Fellows, 67
Graves, Cox and Company, 11-12
Graves County, Ky., 80, 205
Great Depression, 10, 14, 16-17, 23, 25-26, 31, 132, 141, 153, 168
Greyhound Bus Company, 196
Griffle, Della, 37

Hale, Jim, 86
Hale, Joe, 89, 186

Hale v. Kentucky, 43, 89-90, 187
Hampton Institute, 113
Hardin County, Ky., 29
Harlan, John Marshall, 77-78, 146
Harlan County, Ky., 186
Harris, Lawrence, 19
Harrodsburg, Ky., 14, 118
Hart, William, 52
Hart County, Ky., 107
Hatch, John Wesley, 178
Hathaway, James S., 129, 142-44
Hathaway, John, 12
Hazard, Ky., 200-201
Henderson, L.D., 10
Henderson, Ky.: successful black businesses in, 17, 19; Emancipation Day celebration in, 30; blacks excluded from library in, 54; park segregation in, 56, 58; deed restrictions in, 59; black high school in, 111, 115; school desegregation in, 199-200; mentioned, 44, 72, 88, 223
Henderson County, Ky., 2, 107-8
Henry Clay High School, Lexington, 205
Henry County, Ky., 5, 107
Hiley, Judge, 38
Hisle, James N., 100-101
Holt, Len, 216
Hopkins County, Ky., 2, 25
Hopkinsville, Ky.: Emancipation Day celebration in, 30; park segregation in, 58, 75; lawyers in challenge railroad segregation, 78-79; Democrats in warn white voters about blacks, 97; blacks elected to office in, 99; black high school in, 110-11; school desegregation in, 200; mentioned, 2, 29, 60
Housing Information Service, 221
Houston, Charles H., 156, 159-61, 168
Howard University, 94, 112, 156, 170, 176, 179

Illinois Central Railroad, 78
Independent party, 159
Indiana, 67
Indianapolis, Indiana, 26
Indianapolis *Freeman*, 31
Infantile Paralysis Fund, 35
Intelligence Publishing Company, 32
International Harvester Company, 196, 197
Interracial marriage, 45-47, 88
Irvington (Breckinridge County), Ky., 46, 199

J. Boyd Colored School (Henderson County), 107-8
J.I. Burge Company, 48
Jackson, John C., 19
Jackson, John H., 123, 128-29
Jackson, Jordan C., 70
Jackson, Ky., 197
Jackson, Mississippi, 208
Jackson County, Ky., 107
Jackson Junior High School, Louisville, 166
Jackson Purchase, 80
Jacksonville, Florida, 208
Jefferson City, Missouri, 128
Jefferson County, Ky., 2, 137, 208, 210
Jenkins, Ky., 25, 64
Jessamine County, Ky., 107
Johnson, George M., 179
Johnson, Jack, 32
Johnson, Keen, 175, 190, 192
Johnson, Lyman T., 156, 158, 177-82, 184, 188, 194-95, 207, 218
Johnson, W.D., 24
Johnson, Will R., 88
Johnson County, Ky., 1-2, 107
Jones, Donald, 199-201
Jones, Harry H., 156
Jones, Robert, 4
Jones, Thomas, 4
Jones, Thomas Jesse, 104, 116
Jones, Virgil, 4
Jordan, David M., 154

Kansas, 19, 88
Kaufman Clothing Company, 11-12
Kelly, Tom, 37
Kenton County, Ky., 155
Kentucky Association of Colored Women's Clubs, 33-36
Kentucky Board of Education, 108
Kentucky Commission on Human Rights, 207-8, 210, 213, 222-23
Kentucky Commission on Negro Affairs, 191-92
Kentucky Common School Law of 1908, 161
Kentucky Constitution, 160
Kentucky County School Law of 1908, 114
Kentucky Court of Appeals: rules on railroad segregation, 75-76, 89; upholds Day Law, 145-46; mentioned, 3, 74
Kentucky Department of Education, 158, 197-98

Kentucky Derby, 13, 63, 221
Kentucky Fair Housing Law of 1968, 221
Kentucky General Assembly: enacts railroad segregation law, 70, 79; passes Antilynching Law of 1897, 82; passes Antilynching Law of 1920, 83; Republican governor calls upon for repeal of railroad segregation law, 90-91; declares William Goebel winner of 1899 governor's race, 93-94; enacts Day Law, 144-45, 185; passes anti-discrimination law, 219; mentioned, 43, 114, 184
Kentucky Irish American, 85
Kentucky National Guard, 15, 203
Kentucky Negro Education Association (KNEA), 149-51, 172, 206
Kentucky Normal and Theological Institute, 112, 132-33
Kentucky Public Hanging Law, 159
Kentucky River, 6
Kentucky Senate, 212
Kentucky State Conferences of Branches of the NAACP, 189-90; warned about elimination of black teachers, 205-6
Kentucky State University (Kentucky State Normal and Industrial Institute for Colored Persons; Kentucky State College): founded, 123-26; problems of, 127-30, 132, 142, 150-51, 158; involved in desegregation issue, 170-71, 176-79, 190-91, 215; mentioned, 35, 67, 73, 112, 139, 144, 156, 169, 175, 181-82, 185, 224-25
Kimbler, N.O., 108
King, Martin Luther, Jr., 36, 221
Kipling, Rudyard, 7
Klotter, James C., 51, 52
Knight, David L., 21, 24
Knight, John W., 99
Knights of Pythias, 67
Knoxville, Tennessee, 14, 64
Krock, Arthur: stereotypical view of blacks, 44; as benign racist, 52-53; on black neighborhood in Glasgow, 58-59; mentioned, 6-7
Ku Klux Klan, 85-86, 98

L.E. Meyers Company, 15
Laffoon, Ruby, 158
Lander, Fannie, 75
Lander, Robert, 75
Lane, Ed, 96
League of Women Voters, 98
Lebanon, Ky., 4, 96

"Legal lynchings," 86-90, 101
Letcher, James H., 44
Letcher County, Ky., 107
Lewis, Cary B., 21
Lewis, Ronald L., 25, 64
Lexington, Ky.: black population in, 2; black employment in, 8, 10-13; black businesses in, 19, 24; migration from to Cincinnati, 27; Emancipation Day celebration in, 29, 33; blacks in protest railroad segregation, 36; crime and vice in, 37-41; white man in rapes two black girls, 51-52; racial segregation in, 56, 58-60, 62, 64, 66, 72; police brutality in, 84-85, 87, 91; blacks in refuse to endorse Democrats, 93-94, 96, 98-99; black illiteracy in, 107; black high school in, 110, 113, 116; favorable assessment of Chandler Normal School in, 119; black leaders in call for better schools, 119, 121, 134; as possible site for Lincoln Institute, 137; school desegregation in, 201, 209; school busing in, 210; demonstrations in by CORE, 213-15, 218; mentioned, 2, 28, 30, 32-33, 45, 63, 70-71, 73, 80, 97, 114, 127-29, 139, 151, 162, 178, 180, 183, 196, 205, 219
Lexington Agricultural and Mechanical Association, 31
Lexington Board of Education: pays lower salaries to black teachers, 162-63, and school desegregation, 205; mentioned 114, 119, 121
Lexington Colored Fair, 30-33, 45
Lexington *Herald*, 31, 50-52, 215
Lexington *Kentucky Standard*, 139
Lexington *Leader*, 183, 215
Lexington *Standard*, 24, 32
Lexington Vice Commission, 38
Life (magazine), 217
Lincoln, Abraham, 137
Lincoln Institute, 128, 134, 136-41, 147, 160
Lincoln Log, 139
Little Georgetown (Lexington, Ky.), 59
Little Rock, Arkansas, 208
Livermore, Ky., 82-83
Livingston County, Ky., 187
Logan County, Ky., 3-4
London, England, 47
Louisiana, 76
Louisville, Ky.: black population in, 2; black employment in, 8, 10-13, 15; black businesses in, 19-24; migration from to Cincinnati, 27; Emancipation Day celebration in, 29-30; blacks in protest railroad segregation, 36; crime and vice in, 37, 39-43, 46; racial segregation in, 54-60, 62-63, 67-69, 72; police brutality in, 84-85; city employees in join the KKK, 85, 87, 92; blacks in refuse to endorse Democrats, 93-94, 96, 98-100; black schools in lack desirable buildings, 106; black illiteracy in, 107-8; black leaders in advocate industrial training, 111-13; favorable assessment of black high school in, 116; as possible site for Lincoln Institute, 137; whites cite as a "progressive city," 195-97; suspension of black students in desegregated schools in, 210; school busing in, 210-11; civil rights demonstrations in, 218-19; opening housing controversy in, 220-22; mentioned, 16, 32, 78-80, 95, 101, 104, 110, 117, 121, 123-24, 130, 132, 138, 149, 152, 154, 156, 158-59, 163-68, 170, 177, 185, 187-89, 191, 202-8, 216-17
Louisville Association of Colored Teachers, 163
Louisville Board of Education: pays lower salaries to black teachers, 164-65, 167-68; school desegregation in, 203-4; phasing out of black teachers, 206-8
Louisville Board of Realtors, 221
Louisville Board of Trade, 137
Louisville *Commercial*, 50
Louisville *Courier-Journal*: denounces Winchester whites, 100-101; denounces "mixed" schools, 142; supports salary equalization, 163-64, 166-67; praises improvements for blacks in Louisville, 194-97; praises Adair County whites, 202; blames the Bradens for violence, 220; mentioned 5, 40, 47-49, 96, 104, 179, 190, 216
Louisville *Defender*, 158, 196, 207
Louisville Industrial Foundation, 13
Louisville *Leader*: discusses "unequal" justice, 88-89, 94, 99; condemns president of Kentucky State, 172; mentioned 49, 63
Louisville Municipal College for Negroes: closing of, 185, 190, 196;

mentioned, 132-33, 171
Louisville NAACP: agitates for equal salaries for black teachers, 162-68; works to desegregate the University of Kentucky, 168-84; civil rights activities of during the late 1940s, 188-89; denounces delay in desegregation efforts of school board, 203-4; files suit against Louisville and Jefferson County schools, 210-11; conflict of with CORE, 216, 218; mentioned, 152
Louisville and Nashville Railroad (L&N), 14, 72-74, 78-79
Louisville *Ohio Falls Express*, 19-20
Louisville *Times*, 49, 195
Lynch, Ky., 153, 186
Lynchings, 3-4, 46, 79-84, 89-90, 101
Lyon County, Ky., 5

McLean County, Ky., 83
McLeod, John C., 26
McPerkins, Anderson, 154-55
McPherson, James, 142, 148
McRoberts, Ky., 25, 64
McVey, Frank L., 173-74
Madison County, Ky.: circuit court of, 145; mentioned, 2
Madison University, 112
Madisonville, Ky.: residential segregation ordinance in, 59, 85-86; black high school in, 117; school desegregation in, 200-201; mentioned, 72
Male High School, Louisville, 106, 111, 116, 204
Mallon, Guy Ward, 146
Mammoth Life and Accident Insurance Company, 21-23
Manual High School, Louisville, 106, 111, 116
Marion County, Ky., 107
Married Ladies Industrial Club of Owensboro, 35
Marshall, Thurgood, 163-68, 174-76, 181
Martin, Arlene S., 7-8
Martin County, Ky., 107
Maryland, 160, 163-64, 169
Maxwell, John M., 123
Mayfield, Ky.: blacks defend themselves against lynch mobs in, 84; Democrats in urge white women to vote, 97-98; mentioned, 56, 75
Mayfield *Monitor*, 48-49
Mays, Benjamin, 170

Maysville, Ky.: black institutions in, 28-29, 53; lynching in, 81; mentioned, 10, 27
Meharry Medical College, 184
Meier, August, 216
Memphis, Tennessee, 30, 85
Menifee County, Ky., 107
Mercer County, Ky., 15
Merchant, Charles, 87
Merchant, W.T., 22, 55
Merrill, C.E., 97
Messick, Hank, 216
Meyzeek, Albert Ernest: opposes segregation in railroads, 69; mentioned, 67-68, 70, 129, 172
Michigan State University, 166
Middlesboro, Ky., 64-65, 186
Miles, Will, 23
Miller, C.J., 80
Miller, John A., 166
Miller, Shackleford, 168
Mississippi, 90
Missouri, 150, 158, 160, 169
Montgomery, Alabama, 78
Montgomery County, Ky., 205
Moore, J.W., 17
Morehead State University (Morehead Normal School), 127
Morgan County, Ky., 107
Morrill Act of 1890, 127
Morrow, Edwin P., 44, 83, 91-92
Morton, Lena Beatrice, 122
Mosler, Huston, 155-56
Mount Pleasant, Ohio, 66
Mt. Sterling, Ky., 99, 205
Muhlenberg County, Ky., 29, 109-10
Murphy, Isaac, 13
Murray, Ky., 94
Myers, Minnie, 73

Nashville, Tennessee, 78, 79, 184
Nation, 141
National Association for the Advancement of Colored People (NAACP): agitates for antilynching laws, 82-83; protests Klan parades, 85; and Hale case in Paducah, 89-90; praises governor for antilynching stance, 91, 101; forms branches after WWI, 102; works to equalize salaries of black teachers in Louisville, 163-69, 192; calls for immediate school desegregation, 198; surveys school desegregation, 199-202, 209; mentioned, 10, 27, 30, 37, 63-67, 84,

107, 147, 152-62, 175-77, 179-81, 184-90, 194, 203-5, 210, 212-13, 216, 218
National Association of Colored Women, 33, 173
National Bank of Kentucky, 23
National Negro Business League, 24, 60, 62
National Urban League, 15-16, 37, 67-68, 141, 191
Newport, Ky., 153
New South, 143
New York, 101, 155, 161, 164
New York *Freeman*, 142
New York *Times*, 45, 82-83, 93, 206
Night Riders, 5, 91
Ninth Street Methodist Episcopal Church, Covington, 154
Non-Partisan League, 213
Norfolk, Virginia, 216
Nugent, Alice E., 33

Oberlin College, 141-43
Ohio, 5, 122, 176
Ohio River, 6
Ohio Sunday School Institute, 66
Ohio Valley Railroad, 75
Oklahoma, 90
Oldham County, Ky., 211
Olive Hill, Ky., 14
Ottenheim, Mrs. Herbert, 98
Owensboro, Ky.: blacks sue over common school fund, 105; black schools in, 110; school desegregation in, 199; mentioned, 17, 35-36, 72

Paducah, Ky.: Emancipation Day celebration in, 30; crime and vice in, 37; rigid segregation in, 53, 78; blacks in defend themselves against lynch mobs, 84-86, 92, 94, 103; black high school in, 110; site of Western Kentucky Industrial College, 133; school desegregation in, 200-201; NAACP in, 186-88; mentioned, 2, 14, 17, 89
Paducah Junior College, 187
Paducah *News-Democrat*: highlights vice in black neighborhoods, 37; condemns interracial marriage, 47; ridicules blacks, 49, 88
Palmer, Hugh D., 6
Paris, Ky., 56, 110, 142
Paris (France) *La Petit Journal*, 83
Parrish, Charles H., Jr., 22, 111-13, 123,

138, 196
Paul Lawrence Dunbar High School, Lexington, 121, 205
Pendley, J.W., 85
People's Drug Store, 20
Perkins, William "Soup," 12-13
Perry, DuRand, 63
Perry, Ed, 63
Perry, Victor K., 163
Perry, William H., 124
Phelps, Herman, 215
Pineville, Ky., 64-65
Planter's Protective Association, 5
Pleasant Green Baptist Church, Lexington, 36
Plessy v. Ferguson, 76
Plymouth Congregational Church, Louisville, 36
Police brutality, 84-85
Populist party, 96
Porter, Will, 82
Powers, Georgia M. Davis, 212
Pricetown (Lexington, Ky.), 59
Princeton, Ky., 17, 200

Railroad segregation, 69-79, 101-2
Ravenna, Ky., 14
Ray, R. Everett, 194-95
Reconstruction Era, 80
Red Cross Hospital, Louisville, 54-55
Reed, Ky., 107
Reichert, William O., 213-16
Republican party (Republicans): supports black rights, 90-93; reluctantly endorses black candidates, 98-99, 101, 159; denounces open housing legislation, 221; mentioned, 32, 37, 44, 50, 66-67, 77, 94, 96-97
Richings, G.F., 17, 20
Richmond, Ky., 2, 127, 153
Richmond *Planet*, 72
Ridgway, John M., 201
Riley, Joseph, 4
Robard's Station, Ky., 72
Robinson, Jackie, 169
Robinson, Walter, 99
Rochester, Ky., 85
Rone, James, 220
Roosevelt, Franklin D., 16
Roosevelt, Theodore, 44
Rosenwald School, Breathitt County, 197
Rudwick, Elliott, 216
Russell, Green P., 70, 113, 129-30, 170
Russell, Harvey C., 150

Russell High School, Lexington, 121
Russellville, Ky., 153

S.S. Kresge's Store, 8, 63
Sackett, Frederic M., 94
St. Bernard Coal Company, 118, 152
St. John's Sunday School, Cleveland, Ohio, 66
St. Louis, Missouri, 30
Sampson, Flem D., 155
Scholtz, Joseph D., 164-65
Schorman, William R., 185
Separate Coach Law, 70-77, 91, 93
Shelby County, Ky., 137, 205
Shelbyville, Ky.: city council men of as Klan members, 85-86, 99; school desegregation in, 199, 201; mentioned, 2, 7, 138
Shively, Ky., 220
Simmons, William J., 111-13, 123
Simmons University, 132, 133
Simpson County, Ky., 51, 107
Simpsonville, Ky., 137-38
Singleton, Orillia, 88
Slaughter, Miss E.B., 20
Smith, Milton H., 78
Smith, Samuel, 153
Smithland, Ky., 187
Somerset, Ky., 93
South Carolina, 90
Southern Regional Council, 195
Southern Women for the Prevention of Lynchings, 30
Spencer, Benjamin F., 18
Spencer, Sue, 18
Springfield, Ohio, 91
Stanley, Augustus O., 92, 94, 133
Stanley, Frank, 226
State National Bank, 10
Steward, William Henry: employed as a messenger, 10; as newspaper editor, 20, 68-69; opposes railroad segregation, 70-71; praises Justice John Marshall Harlan, 77-78; mentioned, 9
Stoll, Richard C., 181
Sturgis, Ky., 202-203
Sweeney, P.O., 168
Swinford, Mac, 202

Talbert, Charles G., 180
Tandy, H.A., 19, 24
Taylor, William S., 93
Taylor County, Ky., 74
Tennessee, 177

Tennessee Central Railroad, 78
Texas, 122
Thomas, Prentice, 167-68, 175
Thomson, A.E., 138-39
Timberlake, Clarence L., 129
Tolley, Sam L., 11
Tolliver, "Gold Tooth Annie," 37
Transylvania University, 213
Trigg County, Ky., 5-6
Trotter, Monroe, 50
Trout, Allan M., 194-95
Tucker, C. Eubank, 156, 158-59, 216
Tuskegee Institute, 111, 113-14, 136-37, 145

Underwood, Edward E.: opposes railroad segregation, 71; is appointed to Kentucky State's board, 129, 153; mentioned, 66-67
United Brothers of Friendship, 67
United States Bureau of Education, 132
United States Congress (House or Senate), 32, 94
United States Constitution, 70, 75, 147, 166, 172
United States Department of the Interior, 132
United States District Court: rules on railroad segregation, 72; rules on school taxation, 105; rules on teachers' salaries, 168; rules in Lyman Johnson suit, 180, 184; mentioned, 211
United States House of Representatives, 145
United States Office of Education, 205
United States Post Office, 10-11
United States Senate, 169, 203
United States Supreme Court: rules on residential segregation ordinance, 60; upholds railroad segregation, 76-77; rules on the Joe Hale case, 89-90, 186-87; upholds the Day Law, 146-47, 160, 176; mentioned, 43, 59, 136, 150, 172, 180, 193, 198, 201, 221
University of Chicago, 196, 213
University of Iowa, 170
University of Kentucky: and desegregation, 170-84, 190-91; is urged to silence a professor, 215-16; mentioned, 127, 133, 158, 160, 185, 189, 213
University of Kentucky Bureau of School Service, 162
University of Louisville, 132, 133, 158, 185, 196

Index / 277

University of Michigan, 166, 177
University of Minnesota, 214
University of Nebraska, 216
University of Wisconsin, 177
Uttingertown (Lexington, Ky.), 59

Versailles, Ky., 17, 83
Villard, Oswald Garrison, 147
Virginia, 163, 206
Virginia Union University, 177

W.H. Lancaster Pharmacy, 17
Wade, Andrew, 220-21
Wade, C.H., 8, 10
Walker, Mr. and Mrs. Charles, 29
Walker, William, 12
Ward, William, 96
Warley, William, 156, 158
Warsaw, Ky., 4
Washington, Booker T.: complains about discrimination on the L&N Railroad, 78; criticizes president of Berea College, 143; urges Berea officials to challenge the Day Law, 145; mentioned, 20, 23-24, 60, 62, 69, 111, 113, 129, 136, 148
Washington County, Ky., 107
Watterson, Henry, 47, 142
Wayman, A.W., 118
Wayman Institute, 118
Wells, Ida B., 71
Wentworth, _____, 39-40
Western Kentucky Industrial College (WKIC), 133-34
Western Kentucky University, 127
Western Kentucky Vocational Training School for Negroes, 134
Western Reserve Medical College, Cleveland, Ohio, 67
West Virginia, 158
Wetherby, Lawrence W., 195, 197-98
Wheeling, West Virginia, 156
Wheelwright, Ky., 64
White, Albert S., 93, 95
White, Charles, 153
White, Lula, 74-75
White, Thomas, 74-75
White, Walter, 152, 160, 176
Wiegandt, George, 63
Wilberforce University, 156, 170, 174-75
Wilkins, Roy, 198
Williams, Frank L., 147
Williams, John Taylor, 127
Willis, Simeon, 191
Willson, Augustus E., 3, 15, 46, 77, 83, 91, 129
Wilson, Woodrow, 11, 50
Winchester, Ky., 2, 100-101, 110, 120, 122
Winchester *Sun*, 100
Winkfield, Jimmie, 12
Winnie A. Scott Memorial Hospital, 35
Woman's Improvement Club of Lexington, 34
Woodson, Carter G., 148
Woofter, Thomas Jackson, 40, 59, 62
Wooldridge, Noah, 11
World War I, 6, 13, 15, 62, 67, 92, 152
World War II, 16, 151, 186, 188-89, 220
Wright, R.R., Jr., 149

Yancy, Bell, 29
Young, Julia Sohmers, 139
Young, Whitney M., Jr., 141
Young, Whitney M., Sr., 140-41
Young Men's Christian Association (YMCA), 27-28, 68, 142
Young People's Socialist League, 185

www.ingramcontent.com/pod-product-compliance
Lightning Source LLC
Chambersburg PA
CBHW022053160426
43198CB00008B/217